# POLICE, ARRESTS & SUSPECTS

About the Author:

John Donoghue never set out to be a writer... he wanted to be a sailor... and a soldier... and a policeman.

He has been all of the above and has written four books covering his escapades so far...

He is still a serving police officer.
Other books by John Donoghue

**Police Books**
(*The True Story of a Front Line Officer series*)

Police, Crime & 999

Police, Lies & Alibis

**Humour / Travel**

Shakespeare My Butt!
'*Marsupial Elvis*' to '*No Place*'... *ramblings, meanderings, digressions... and a dog*

# POLICE, ARRESTS & SUSPECTS

*The True Story of a Front Line Officer*

John Donoghue

Matador
9 Priory Business Park,
Wistow Road, Kibworth Beauchamp,
Leicestershire. LE8 0RX
Tel: 0116 279 2299
Email: books@troubador.co.uk
Web: www.troubador.co.uk/matador
Twitter: @matadorbooks


ISBN 978 1785890 079

British Library Cataloguing in Publication Data.
A catalogue record for this book is available from the British Library.


Printed and bound in the UK by TJ International, Padstow, Cornwall
Typeset in StempelGaramond Roman by Troubador Publishing Ltd

**Matador** is an imprint of Troubador Publishing Ltd

*For Bethan*

# CONTENTS

# ACKNOWLEDGEMENTS

When I first set out to write this book, I bought myself a new thesaurus. However, it was poor. Very poor. Very, very poor. In fact, I have no words to describe how disappointed I was!

So, it will come as no surprise that I've had invaluable help from a select band of talented people that I should acknowledge here otherwise they may be after me for money.

A special thanks to:

Sharon: Walking Thesaurus & Singing Dictionary.
Your help and assistance in this project has been invaluable and is greatly appreciated.
Honourable mentions go to:
Rich: Director of First Impressions.
Jane: Ambassador of Buzz.
Margot: Cowboy Junkie.
Nancy: Tea & Biscuits.
I could go on, so I will.

As always, I wouldn't be able to write about my escapades in the police without my colleagues on E shift. Thanks to them and all who serve the noble cause on The Thin Blue Line.

I also need to add that the views expressed herein are my own and not endorsed by any constabulary. As ever, names and places have been changed to protect the guilty, but if you do think you recognise yourself and you're not happy with your portrayal, then you're probably wrong, and I'm not the John Donoghue that you actually think I am. In fact, if you are offended by anything in the book, then I'm offended at how easily offended you are, and, for your information, from now on I will only accept criticism in the form of song. If, however, you like the book then, yes, it really is me!

These are my own tales from the sharp end of the fuzz, but every police officer has a wealth of stories to tell, so buy them a pint or a cup of tea and I'm sure they'll happily share them with you.

Finally, thanks to you, dear reader, for taking the time to pick up this book/kindle (delete as applicable). It's no use being a Writer of Wrongs unless someone actually reads about it.

I hope you enjoy.

John Donoghue

# CHAPTER 1

# Drive Time

"January the first already," commented Gwen, momentarily glancing towards me as she held onto the steering wheel. "And so begins another year of policing for the men and women of E shift."

It was dusk and we were navigating our way around the town centre ring road. Gwen was driving and I was looking out at the shoppers, wrapped up against the cold, scurrying from shop to shop, their bags laden with bargains. Occasionally, one would dart across the zebra crossing to get to another sale on the other side of the road, causing the cars in front to brake hard. I pondered over why so many pedestrians seem to confuse *right of way* with *immortality*.

All the cars, meanwhile, were driving very carefully, rigidly adhering to the speed limit. It could only mean one of two things: perhaps all of the driver's good underwear was in the wash or everyone becomes a model driver when there is a police car right behind them. Mind you, I'm the same; even when I'm *in* a police car if there's a traffic cop behind me I drive like I'm back in training school.

Some are more careful than others though, and the elderly couple we had let out at a junction a while back were hesitantly crawling up Central Avenue in their Rover Connoisseur; driving so slowly that a man walking in front of their car waving a red flag wouldn't have

1

looked out of place. We were directly behind and were randomly illuminated by their brake lights as they tabbed on them every so often for no particular reason. A long tailback of traffic was growing in our wake.

"What the…" exclaimed Gwen suddenly, glancing in the rear-view mirror. "Some maniac's overtaking all the cars behind and speeding towards us on the wrong side of the carriageway."

I pushed myself up in my seat to catch a glimpse of what she was looking at, but I needn't have bothered as the offending vehicle sped past us, coughing up road debris.

"Worth a pull!" we both remarked at the same time and, as Gwen pulled out around the car in front, I hit the lights and siren. The shortest ever police car chase then ensued as the vehicle immediately pulled over, mounting the kerb in the process. Gwen pulled up behind and I got out to speak with the driver.

With blue strobes slicing through the air, I approached the sporty BMW and knocked on the driver's window. The woman inside looked over at me and I did a winding motion with my hand, requesting her to lower the glass so I could speak to her. A button was pressed and, with a gentle purr, the window was lowered releasing warmth from the vehicle, as well as the unmistakable strains of *Cameo* blasting from the stereo. I nearly enquired if you could still wave your hands in the air if you *did* care, but thought better of it.

"Could you turn the ignition and the radio off, please?" I shouted over the noise. She partially complied with my request by turning the engine off and lowering the volume.

"And how can I help you today, Officer?"

"Do you know why I pulled you over?"

"Well, I'm a 36DD, so I think so," she answered confidently.

I was immediately taken aback. I'd never encountered

a response like that before. Usually, people either sheepishly admit their offence and hope they'll get away with a warning, or categorically deny that they've ever done anything wrong in their entire lives. I chose to ignore her comment and continued with my line of questioning.

"Madam, do you know how fast you were driving?"

"To be honest with you, Officer, I'm more concerned with whether *you* know how fast I was going."

Touché. I hadn't had time to check our own speed let alone hers. I decided to proceed to safer ground: Gwen had seen her suddenly pull out, and I'd seen her driving on the wrong side of the road and speeding past the other motorists.

"You were also driving erratically, madam."

"Don't you mean *erotically*, darling?"

I felt like I had suddenly been transported to the set of a *Carry On* film.

"No, madam, I don't mean erotically. And, to compound matters, you're not even wearing a seat belt."

"Well, Officer, how are you supposed to see my boobs if I do?"

There she goes again!

"I'm going to have to check your documents."

"And by 'documents', I presume you mean these titaaaays…" She accompanied her statement with a thrust of her chest in my general direction – the contents of her low-cut dress wobbling like jellies on a plate as she did so. I stood in silence at the door of her car, whilst looking desperately over at Gwen for moral support. My colleague, however, simply smiled back at me through the windscreen of the panda car, completely oblivious to my plight.

"Madam, can you take a seat in the back of my car, please?"

"Oooh, you are forward, you naughty boy!"

If this had been anywhere else, I would have given as

good as I got, but I was on duty, in uniform, at the side of a road, talking to someone about possible driving offences. I surreptitiously glanced around to check that I wasn't on some kind of hidden camera show. I tried my best to maintain my professionalism but, despite the cold, I could feel my face flushing.

The woman slowly got out of her vehicle; an expensive looking high-heeled shoe emerged first, followed by a shapely leg. As she extracted herself from the confines of her BMW, her short dress rode up, revealing a fleeting sight of a lacy black stocking top. I turned away to give her some privacy, but I was certain that she must have done it on purpose as she giggled when she asked me if I had caught a snatch of a glimpse.

"It wasn't that short!" I replied defensively, before realising I had got the words of her question in the wrong order. When I turned around again, she was stood before me in a short black cocktail dress, her long red hair tumbling over her shoulders like a communist falling down a hill. I motioned towards the police vehicle and indicated for her to get in.

"You're staggering," I informed her.

"Well, you're not so bad yourself, Officer," she replied, winking at me.

"No, I mean you're not walking in a straight line."

I accompanied her, holding onto her arm to ensure that she didn't fall into the road, before opening the back door of the police car for her. As she sidled past me, I caught a whiff of alcohol.

"Aren't you going to get in the back with me?" she pouted. I explained that it was probably best for all concerned if I sat in the front. I gave Gwen an eye roll as I got in the passenger seat, which she returned with a wry smile.

"Can I have your name please?" I asked, getting my notebook out.

"Astrid," she replied.

"Surname?"

"Stevens…with a V," she added, leaning through the gap between the seats and tapping the top of my book. She then sprawled back in the seat, which is something I wouldn't normally advise considering some of the customers that we transport in the back of our cars. A variety of offenders and victims have all sat back there, leaving behind their own particular form of DNA; some have thrown up; others have spat everywhere; a few have bled on the upholstery and more than a handful have wet themselves. We try to keep them tidy, but police cars are the workhorses of the constabulary; as soon as one shift finishes and gets out, another shift starts and gets in, not even giving the engine time to cool. It's rare that pandas are taken off the road long enough to go in for a deep clean, so the back seat is not the sort of place I'd choose to lounge around in.

"It used to be White!" she exclaimed, sitting back bolt upright.

"What did?" I queried, hoping she hadn't sat in something left by one of our previous guests.

"My name, silly! Before I was married."

I added 'White' in brackets and then told her that, although I knew it was rude to ask, I would need to have her date of birth. She informed me that she was a Capricorn, which didn't really narrow things down that much. Eventually, after a frustrating guessing game that she obviously enjoyed more than me, I was rewarded with the relevant information.

"Comms, can I have a person check with the following details…?"

"You're doing a check on *me*?" she suddenly squealed. "Just like a common criminal?"

I informed her that that was exactly what I was doing.

"Ah, I see," she purred conspiratorially, tapping the side of her nose and glancing in the direction of my colleague. "You've got to pretend to do it because *she's* here." She sat back and proceeded to pick some lint off the shoulder strap of her dress.

"From your manner of driving and your demeanour, I've reason to believe that you might have been driving whilst over the prescribed limit."

The check had come back negative; she had no previous convictions on record. I therefore began with the next part of the procedure. "Have you been drinking, Mrs Stevens?"

She gave me a coquettish look. "Call me Astrid."

"So, how many have you had, Astrid?"

"I say, Officer! How rude! You're not shy, are you sweetie? A lady never reveals the number of past lovers."

"Astrid, answer the question, please. How many drinks have you had?" I half expected Barbara Windsor and Kenneth Williams to appear at any moment.

She held up two fingers in a V shape.

"Two?" I enquired.

"Five," she clarified, "glasses of Prosecco, darling. When in Rome and all that..."

"Five glasses of Prosecco," I repeated as I wrote it in my book.

"And an eggnog. Well, it is still Christmas; technically."

"And a glass of pancake batter," I added, noting that down too, and affording myself a little smile. It was just as well I did, as nobody else seemed to share my humour.

"And some margaritas, sweetheart."

"Well, they're not going to regret themselves, are they?" I commented as I added those to my list. I began to get the feeling that my funnies were landing on stony ground. I pressed on regardless. "It's hardly necessary, considering what you've just told me, but I'm going to conduct what we call a roadside breath test to ascertain if you're over the legal limit to drive."

Usually, it's at this point that the subject starts to filibuster, telling you that they only have one lung and

6

it's made of cardboard, or that the doctor has advised them not to exhale; however, Astrid immediately pursed her lips and leant forward into the gap between the front seats. After I had explained what she needed to do, she made a perfect seal with her lips around the tube and blew, all the while maintaining direct eye contact with me before leaving behind a perfect ring of bright red lipstick on the white plastic.

"You can keep that as a souvenir," she purred. Normally, that was my line! We all sat in silence, waiting for the result to show up on the display. Eventually, it bleeped, announcing that it had a decision for us. I had a quick look and informed her of the outcome.

"I'm afraid you've failed the test. Therefore, I'm arresting you for drink-driving. You do not have to say anything. But it may harm your defence…"

"You're not *actually* arresting me?" she interrupted, sounding genuinely surprised.

"Yes, I'm doing just that."

"Oh, I think there's been some sort of misunderstanding here. I'm not some sort of miscreant. Don't you know that my husband is a leading businessman in the town?"

I continued with the police caution, continuing on from where I had left off.

"I think you'll find that I know quite a few of the members of the Chamber of Commerce here. You don't incarcerate people like me in a squalid jailhouse." She then tried in vain to open the doors, but found she was thwarted by the child locks that are used in the back of every police car to foil such an escape attempt.

"Look, Astrid," said Gwen, twisting round in her seat to address our charge, "if the sample from the roadside apparatus is above…" but before she could finish she was cut off mid-sentence.

"Oh, shut your cake-hole!"

"Cake-hole?" repeated Gwen – more to herself than

anyone else – and turned and sat back in her seat. It was a rebuke of sorts, but, as rebukes go, it was considerably gentler than those usually expressed by our customers.

"I'm sorry, Officer." Her comments were directed at me rather than my colleague.

It'll come as no surprise that most people say they are sorry when they're arrested, although I think it's more regret at having been caught than having actually committed the crime. "Is there anything I can do to extricate myself from this silly situation?" she continued, lowering her head and suggestively looking up at me. "Is there anything else I can... *blow*?"

She accompanied her question by making a jerking motion with her hand, whilst simultaneously pushing the inside of her cheek out with her tongue. I politely declined and she then changed tactics.

"Come on, Officer. Nobody's been harmed. Can't we just put this down to experience and you can take me home?"

True; no one had been harmed, but when nearly one in six of all deaths on the road involves drivers who are over the legal alcohol limit, someone might easily have been. It wasn't something that could just be glossed over.

"You're treating me like a common criminal," she pouted as she sat back in the seat and crossed her arms.

"That's because you are," remarked Gwen. She may not have read the latest edition of *How to Win Friends and Influence People,* but she was perfectly right. Whenever I'm asked by drink-drivers why we are harassing motorists instead of catching killers, the answer is because often they're one and the same. While I explained to my prisoner what would happen next, Gwen went and secured Astrid's BMW.

"Well, as they say," replied Astrid with a wink, "when life gives you melons... wear a low-cut top." Something in her demeanour told me that she felt sure that she could still get away with the offence through the deployment of her charms when we got to custody.

When Gwen returned a few moments later, I had changed places and was sat in the driver's seat.

"Rosa Parks!" I announced. I was here now and there was no way I was going to move and sit in the back with Nell Gywnn. Gwen didn't seem to relish the prospect either and I instantly knew that she didn't find it even remotely funny when she began her sentence with, "I just find it funny how... "

After she reluctantly climbed into the back with Mrs Stevens, we made our way to the police station in silence. Five minutes later and we were stood in front of the desk in the custody suite. As an aside, my advice to anyone who finds themselves in custody is to preferably avoid any of the following, as they generally do not endear you to the sergeant booking you in.

1. Do not interrupt the arresting officer by constantly shouting 'allegedly' whilst he or she is explaining the circumstances of the arrest.
2. Refrain from embarking on a long diatribe about what is wrong with 'the law' in this country and using air quotes each time you repeat the aforementioned term (which was approximately fifteen times if we're counting – which I was) when asked by the sergeant if you have understood what the officer has said.

"I admire your conviction," Sergeant Ingarfield informed her when she had finished. "I mean, you're wrong and possibly a little deranged in maintaining that you should be exempt from being arrested because you have a lot of money, but you do stick to your guns."

"So this is really going ahead?"

As the sergeant explained once more to a genuinely surprised Astrid Stevens why she had been arrested, she offered another unabridged rebuttal. Personally, I didn't follow much of her rationale, but I was left pondering over why people always say 'I'm not arguing with you' when they clearly are, and that the origin of the phrase 'you're shitting me' must be one hell of a story.

"It's a black and white offence, madam." I could sense that the sergeant was becoming exasperated, but trying to tell a drunken woman to calm down works about as well as baptising a cat. "You are either over the legal limit whilst driving a car on the road or you are not."

"Yes," she replied, "but you'll agree with me that there is a fine line between two things separated by a fine line?"

He chose to ignore her conundrum, and instead continued to book her into custody, although he did have to apologise to her on several occasions as it appeared that the middle of his questions were constantly interrupting the start of her answers.

"Just admit it: you're obsessed with me!"

"Madam, I can assure you that I'm not, but there are some risk assessment questions that I need to ask you that I would be delighted if you could answer for me. So, if we can please continue. Have you any medical conditions?"

"I'm bi."

"Polar?" queried the sergeant, his fingers hovering above the keyboard.

"Sexual."

Ingarfield shook his head and then asked her how she was currently feeling.

"Is *apocalyptic* an emotion?" she replied; although from the defeated look on his face, I think that it was more applicable to the sarge. He let out an audible sigh and asked her if there were any other factors that should be taken into consideration during her stay with us.

"Well, I have suffered from low self-esteem ever since Lou Bega didn't mention me in his 'Mambo Number 5'."

"Really?" he asked, sounding irritated.

"No! Of course not!" Then began her impassioned monologue to the assembled crowd: "Look, I'm a rich, bored, attractive housewife with an incredible bust. I'm a wanton woman in her prime with time on her hands. That's the real crime here. I should be wined and dined and made love to like I'm still under warranty! I'm a cougar! I should be lured into a heavenly trap with a bottle of Pinot Grigio and a copy of *Journey's* greatest hits rather than caged in, caught by a random policeman," she lowered her voice and turned to face me, "regardless of how cute he is."

I've been called a number of names by the people I've arrested, but I'd never been described as 'cute' before. I made a mental note to ask Barry to put it into my annual appraisal. Sergeant Ingarfield, however, was not so impressed with her comment, and called for the new probationer on secondment to come through.

"James!" he roared. A young, fresh-faced looking officer emerged from the back office and led our charge through to the room that housed the station breathalyser.

"Well, if anything convinced me she was drunk, it was that last comment," added Gwen, rather unkindly, in my opinion. Personally, the moment that had convinced me that she was intoxicated was her hysterical reaction while walking past the dog-section vehicle that was parked in the backyard when we had been making our way into custody; the rear doors of the van had been opened to give the animal some fresh air, and a large German Shepherd had been sitting in the cage, attentively noting everything that was going on; Astrid had suddenly become distraught, demanding to know why the dog had been arrested and what he had done wrong.

"Well, the CAMIC machine will confirm it either way," commented Ingarfield, bringing me back to the present. To drive legally in England and Wales you must have under 35 microgrammes of alcohol per 100 millilitres of breath in your body and the CAMIC is the name of the calibrated apparatus that gives us that reading. Two specimens of breath are analysed by the machine printing out the result, but even then drivers are given the benefit of the doubt, as it's only the lower reading that is used for evidential purposes. As we waited for our prisoner to return, conjecture set in as we started to ruminate over what the result might be.

"I wonder what she blows?" commented Gwen quietly to herself before suddenly jumping to her feet. "Oh dear God, we'd better check on James!"

We both sprang into action as a wave of realisation swept over us. We raced through to the side room to find a very flushed young probationer fending off the advances of Mrs Stevens.

"She asked me if I had a giant peach," he stuttered as I led him out to safety, "and she told me she had two superpowers and that they both had nipples." The poor guy seemed shell-shocked. I took him through to the back office to make him a cup of tea, while he continued with his babbling. "She told me that she would turn me from a boy to a man in six weekly instalments if I blew into the machine instead of her."

Clearly, he had valiantly held out against her overtures. Gwen now led Astrid back to the custody counter, announcing that she had blown over 100 and proving that despite her contacts in high places, she was indeed as guilty as any other drink-driver. The sergeant informed her of the result, and told her that she would now be processed.

"I am NOT a cheese! I will NOT be processed," was her indignant reply.

"I'm sure the officers will do it *Caerphilly*," he replied, winking at Gwen.

I desperately racked my brain to think of another cheese pun, but all I could manage at the time was that the only cheese to greet itself in the third person is *Halloumi* but it didn't really seem appropriate. Whilst I was wasting time, the sergeant explained to Astrid that it just meant that we needed to take her DNA, fingerprints and photograph. They say it takes seventeen muscles to smile and forty-two to frown – Astrid must have used about fifty-five by including a jerk-off motion and an eye roll to accompany her scowl.

Despite her finely manicured nails, the prints were taken easily enough. Since scans replaced the old-fashioned ink block, the reduced level of mess has been matched with a reduced level of resistance to the whole procedure; even taking the DNA sample went smoothly enough, but, when it came to having her photograph taken, things came to a grinding halt. They say that procrastination is a dish best served eventually, and Astrid now used every trick in the book to buy some time as she preened herself; ready for her close-up.

"It's just a head shot," explained Gwen, as our prisoner straightened her dress. Astrid's eyes lit up and she beckoned me over, doing the whole tongue in cheek thing again – it would seem that a 'head shot' can mean different things to different people. Astrid was eventually persuaded to calm down before being instructed to sit in the photo booth – only for her to start a commotion again a few moments later. Apparently, a guaranteed way of driving a woman mad is to take a photo of her and not show it to her within three seconds so she can vet it. Once the process had been finally completed, Astrid was led to the cells.

"Oh, one last thing," interrupted Sergeant Ingarfield, "when you were with the officer taking the CAMIC procedure, you indicated that you had drugs on your person that you were willing to share if he let you off. We're going to have to strip-search you now."

"I just said I had some crack he might be interested in!" she protested. "It was just some unsubtle flirting! I also told him I had an opening that needed filling, but I wasn't offering him a job!" But it was too late: the words had been said and the consequences were upon her. "Oh well," sighed Astrid, resigning herself to her fate, "I should have suspected something was up when my gynaecologist gave me a safe word last week."

I thought it would have been funnier if he had said 'At your cervix, madam' but I decided to keep that gem to myself.

As she was led into the cell, I couldn't quite work out who was more horrified by the thought of the procedure: Astrid or Gwen. The idea of the strip-search is to ascertain if the individual has anything hidden on their person that wasn't found on the usual 'pat down'. I wasn't sure why Gwen was so worried: she should be pleased that our subject was so presentable. She was certainly far cleaner and more fragrant that any of the males I've had to deal with! As for Astrid, the whole process was nowhere near as invasive as she had feared. Nevertheless, within minutes of Jessica arriving to assist and the search commencing, I heard the first anguished protests emanating from within.

"Please stop cupping your breasts, Mrs Stevens. I believe that they're natural, but I'd rather not feel them, if it's all the same to you."

It seems that Astrid had found her inner exhibitionist and had turned the tables on my colleagues; relishing the opportunity to flaunt herself in front of her captive audience as she sashayed around the room. Meanwhile, Gwen and Jess tried desperately to complete the job in hand, whilst also fending off their charge's questions.

"No, madam, I've never heard of a vajazzle, but it sounds like something my nana might like for her birthday as she is a big Acker Bilk fan... oh, it's nothing to do with jazz music... it's WHAT? Oh, dear God!"

"No, Astrid, I don't select my attire based on ease of removal – that must just be you."

"No, I don't actually know what a MILF is so I couldn't possibly comment on whether you are one or not, Mrs Stevens."

"There were a couple of eyebrows raised when I had my first facelift," Astrid remarked, striking a pose, and then resuming her catwalk. "You need to check my underwear? I was waxed at the spa yesterday, darling – so they'll slide down easily."

"If you can take your underwear off yourself, Mrs Stevens, I'd greatly appreciate it."

"No, madam, I don't want to try your underwear on, I just need to smooth them down to make sure that there's nothing hidden in them... no, I can't do that whilst you're still wearing them."

"Agent Provocateur, sweetheart," I could hear Astrid telling Jess. "You can keep them as a memento."

"It's not really appropriate," came the response. "If you could please put them back on now and get dressed."

"You can get my number off the sergeant. Sext me! ... Oh dear! That was a Droidian slip!" giggled our prisoner. "I mean *text* me!"

"I don't think that will be happening," replied my colleague over her shoulder as both she and Gwen quickly exited the cell and closed the door behind them. They came over and leant on the custody desk, shaking their heads just as the cell buzzer went off, indicating that Astrid wanted something else. To save them from any further embarrassment, I went to see what her latest request was.

"I could really do with a frappuccino, honey."

"We don't really have those sorts of things here, Mrs Stevens. I can offer you a tea-flavoured drink or a coffee-flavoured drink. At a push, you can have a warm cocoa-based beverage. What will it be?"

"Send that gorgeous young James out to Starbucks!"

"Astrid, no one is going to Starbucks. I can get you a coffee, accompanied by one of our range of microwave meals if you're hungry. You have a choice of: all-day breakfast, beans and sausage or mince and dumplings."

"I'd rather starve!"

Ten minutes later, I was called back and Astrid quietly and demurely informed me that she'd have a tea and an all-day breakfast. I went and prepared the food. Two minutes later and a 'ping' announced that the magnificent feast was ready. I duly delivered it through the hatch, along with a plastic fork and a large plastic mug that wouldn't look out of place in a nursery. The reason for the plastic accoutrements became clear when, a few minutes later, I heard the sound of them smashing against the wall, followed by a shout claiming that even Bear Grylls wouldn't eat that (expletive deleted)!

"As much as I don't really want to deal with a drunken, violent male," remarked James, as we sat in the back room of the custody suite completing our paperwork, "I think I'd rather do that than face Mrs Stevens again." A general murmur went around the room; as much as drunken, violent males can be dangerous and unpleasant, they are no match for an intoxicated, predatory female.

Then, as though prearranged, the buzzer went off again in Astrid's cell. We all looked at one another and, after an embarrassingly long pause, Sergeant Ingarfield volunteered the young lad to go and see what she wanted.

"You do know what a cougar is?" I queried. Ingarfield replied by shaking his head and offering a shrug of the shoulders. "Jess will explain," I told him, "but I think it's probably best if I go."

It turned out that Astrid wanted to know if I would smuggle a file hidden in a cake into her cell. I informed her that that wouldn't be possible, and that sawing through the bars was a bit old-fashioned, especially since there weren't actually any bars in her cell. In a desperate bid to sway me, she then lowered her voice and in a conspiratorial whisper, informed me that when she was released, that thing that Meatloaf *'wouldn't do for love'* – well, she would... I told her it was an intriguing offer but that my shift was almost over and I'd be gone when the morning comes.

# CHAPTER 2

# "Here's Johnny!"

"Urgent: RTC reported on Dominion Road. All available units to attend. Casualties reported."

As the radio call broke the silence, I instantly sat up straight in my seat. At eight o'clock on a Tuesday morning the rush hour would be well underway with traffic and pedestrians all going about the business of commuting to work, doing the school run or making their way to the shops. It would be manic.

As I lit up the roof with blue flashing lights and edged into the traffic, I could hear sirens in the distance as a series of other units announced they were on their way. I informed Comms that I was also en route and added my own two-tones to the mix. Soon a cacophony of sound reverberated through the town as units raced through the rush-hour traffic. Comms came back quickly with an update and, even before the dispatcher spoke, I sensed the urgency in the call. "We now have reports of children running amongst the traffic."

Children? Had I heard that right?

"Units attending the RTC, please be aware that we now have sightings of at least one, maybe two toddlers on the road. Additionally, we have several other reports coming in of a further accident at the same location."

Where could the children have come from? Had they been in one of the cars, or had they been on their way to school on foot? Had their mother been hit as she crossed the road? There were so many unanswered questions and more clarity was required. I wanted to know who precisely was involved, what the extent of the injuries were and where exactly I needed to be, but I knew how difficult it was to get a clear picture of events; sometimes, the only thing worse than not getting enough information is getting too much. At this moment the control room would, no doubt, be inundated with calls and would be struggling to distinguish which were duplicates and which were new incidents. Some callers would expect the police operator to have precise local knowledge, too, unaware that the person to whom they were speaking was sat in a control room thirty miles away, taking calls from across the entire county, while others, although well intentioned, would be giving the wrong location or incorrect information, or exaggerating or underplaying the crisis. Striving to establish a clear, logical picture for the attending units speeding to the scene from the plethora of confusing and often conflicting reports can sometimes be a real art form in itself.

I knew it was no good conjecturing on what might have happened – the only definitive way to find out was to just get there. I shifted gear as I weaved through the traffic, my progress hampered by drivers either hogging the road or not paying attention: "Not today and not on a call like this. GET OUT OF MY WAY! MOVE!"

Dominion Road is one of the main arteries through the town. It is over a mile long and at this time of the morning it would be jammed with traffic. As I put my foot down, Comms announced that traffic cars, fire and paramedics were also en route. We now also had a precise location: the junction with Loganberry Way. I was less than a minute away now. Drawing nearer, I could see that traffic was at a standstill on the approach into the town. I drove the last thirty yards on the opposite side of the carriageway before reaching the scene. Andy got there seconds before me and positioned his car to block the road. In the distance, I could see Geezer next to two vehicles that had collided; he was already on the airwaves giving an initial on-the-hoof update as he raced from car to car.

My main priority was to find the children. I got out of my vehicle and ran to the nearest car to ask if they had seen the kids. They had – they had swerved to avoid a toddler who had run out in front of them, causing them to plough into a road sign, and had then looked up just in time to see another vehicle narrowly miss another child. They hadn't witnessed anything else, but had heard the commotion; the squeal of brakes and the blaring of horns further down the road. As for the children, they had no idea where they had come from or where they had gone.

I scanned the area but couldn't see them anywhere. A sickening thought then dawned on me. With my heart racing, I quickly dropped to my knees to check under the vehicle to see if anyone had been caught under the chassis. Mercifully, there was nothing.

As Geezer shouted over to me that he couldn't see the children either, I noticed a young woman desperately waving at me from a house on the other side of the road. I ran over and she quickly ushered me inside. In the lounge, sitting on the sofa watching television, were two toddlers.

"Are these your children?" I queried. "The ones that have been in the road?"

"Well, yes, and no," she replied.

"Which is it?" I asked tersely. I was in no mood for semantics. It appeared that the collisions were all down to drivers swerving to avoid the kids. Moreover, who would put their children in danger like that?

"These are the kids that were on the road, but they aren't mine. They belong next door."

I got on the radio and informed Comms that the children had been located and were safe, before asking the woman to give me her version of events. It turned out that I had been curt with the wrong person: the woman stood before me, dressed in a smart business suit, was actually the Good Samaritan in all of this. She had been getting ready for work when she had heard the horns and furore outside, and had looked out of the bedroom window to see her neighbours' children running amok in the road. She had dropped everything and raced outside, managing to gather them together before taking them into her house for safety. She had already tried to contact their parents but had got no response. Taking me into the hallway, she then confided to me the numerous issues that she had with her neighbours.

"It's not the children's fault," she added, "but what sort of start in life have they got there?"

We went back into the lounge and I knelt down beside the children.

"Hello, what are you watching?" I asked softly.

"*Peppa Pig*," one of them replied, her speech difficult to understand.

"I like cartoons, too. *Scooby Doo* is my favourite. My name's John. What's your name?"

"Demi. And her name is called Maddison." She pointed to her little sister. The younger child momentarily looked up before becoming distracted by the cartoon pig dancing across the TV screen.

The girls looked to be aged about two and three years old. Both were slight and had pale, almost translucent complexions, with dark shadows under their eyes. Their long blonde hair was thin and wispy, and looked in need of a wash. As the younger one rubbed her nose, spreading mucus across her cheek in the process, I could see the ingrained dirt under her tiny fingernails.

Demi had a dirty, stained vest on that was clearly too small for her, whilst Maddison wore a grubby, pink Hello Kitty T-shirt that was on back to front. Each wore stained light-blue leggings and whilst the older child had filthy, damp ankle socks, her baby sister was barefoot; neither had shoes nor coat despite the bitter January temperature.

I thanked the neighbour for her help, and asked if she could look after the children for just a bit longer while I sorted things out. I stepped back into the street – into the hustle and bustle of colleagues rushing back and forth, dealing with the aftermath of the collisions. *My* mind, however, was elsewhere.

I marched straight next door, but as soon as I started to walk up the short path, I could see immediate differences in comparison to the house I'd just left: here the formal borders of the Good Samaritan's garden were replaced by something that resembled a corner of a field from the Somme. The churned-up mud was littered with empty lager cans, rubbish and cigarette butts – the majority of the latter looked to have been stubbed out on the front door as the white PVC was dotted with numerous burn marks, while in the centre someone had spray-painted: 'If your from social services then Fuck Off'. I made a mental note to remind them of the difference between *your* and *you're*, once my other concerns had been addressed.

I went to knock, but the door was already ajar. I stepped inside shouting 'police' loudly, but there was no response. I had no idea what to expect or how long I'd be there, so did an about turn and went to see who else was available. Lloyd and Andy seemed surplus to requirements so I called them over. After quickly briefing them on what the neighbour had told me, Lloyd accompanied me back to the property, whilst Andy went next door to see the children.

I shouted again as we entered the house, announcing our presence loudly, but to no avail. Instead, we stood in the hall and surveyed our surroundings. The layout of the house seemed identical to the one next door, but instead of pristine carpets and painted walls, I was standing on a sticky floor and looking at torn and dubiously stained wallpaper. Walking into the kitchen, every surface was covered with unwashed dishes and dirty pans – the grease inside them solidified into a white goo. The floor was filthy; strewn with discarded packets, used tea bags, half-crushed cans and plastic cider bottles. The only surface that was clear of any clutter was the one that should have been covered with paper but, instead of a colourful collection of children's drawings, the fridge door was bare, save for a multitude of grimy fingermarks. The stench of the room was so overpowering that we were forced to beat a hasty retreat and explore elsewhere.

My boots made suckering noises on the lino as I ventured into the dining room. The curtains were closed; the room in darkness. I flicked on the main light but the bulb was out. I went over and opened the curtains to let some light in, but it didn't help much; the walls stained sepia by the effects of years of second-hand smoke seemed only to add to the dingy feel of the place. The room itself was relatively spartan except for an old table covered with numerous copies of the free local newspaper and several cardboard cases that had once contained bottles of lager. A stained and crumpled duvet was stuffed underneath the table alongside a muddy pair of children's shoes.

"There's something moving there," remarked Lloyd, pointing to the pile. Up until this point, we had been looking in stunned silence at the state of this so-called home. The fact that children were expected to live in this squalor made everything seem much worse. I bent down beside the table and saw a small head. I gently shook the shoulders and a young boy – aged about eight or nine – looked up at me, his eyes thick with sleep.

"It's ok," I reassured him. "I'm a policeman. Where are your mum and dad?"

He stared at me wide-eyed and wary. "Upstairs," he eventually mumbled.

I looked at Lloyd and we started up the stairs, but not

before glancing into the lounge. I had to do a double take: the room ran the whole width of the house and was dominated by a massive 52" flat-screen TV. A large leather sofa ran along one wall, whilst in the middle of the room a state-of-the-art gaming chair sat on a plush red carpet. It just seemed so at odds with the state of the rest of the place... As we made our way up, I made the mistake of holding onto the handrail; discovering that it was sticky to the touch. I swiftly let go – I'd rather risk falling.

We looked in the children's bedrooms first: no beds, no wardrobes, no pictures, no shelves, no chest of drawers, not a single toy, book or teddy bear – just piles of crumpled clothes and a mattress on the floor for the kids to sleep on.

Since joining the police, I'd seen some filthy homes, but even my usually cast-iron stomach heaved when I entered the bathroom. The toilet was particularly disgusting; faeces caked around the bowl, rusty-coloured water lying stagnant at the bottom. Soiled, threadbare towels lay on the floor. Various substances stained the sides of the once white enamel sink, while a kind of gelatinous mush floated around the top where a bar of soap might once have been. Dusty and half-empty shampoo bottles lay in the bath, while numerous other containers littered an even dustier shelf. The floor beneath my feet was damp, my boot leaving a visible print in the swampy carpet around the bowl. The acrid smell of stale urine permeated throughout – someone in the household obviously liked asparagus.

I wasn't in the best frame of mind when, finally, I entered the main bedroom and my mood wasn't helped when I saw that the adults had a bed – a huge, king-size wooden bed. They certainly didn't appear to have skimped on furniture and accessories for themselves either, as a flat-screen television played mutely from the wall opposite the bed. One of the chests of drawers was adorned with different bottles of designer perfume; the other had a collection of empty glasses and half-drunk bottles of wine. An expensive laptop lay on the floor next to a couple of iPods and the latest mobile phone. The place had an unpleasantly warm and stifling odour, and I didn't want to linger any longer than was absolutely necessary. I banged loudly on the door until I got a reaction from one of the sleeping figures. A hairy leg poked out from beneath the covers and a deep voice demanded to know who was disturbing their slumber: "Who the fuck's that?"

"It's the police," replied Lloyd. "There's been an incident with your children. I need to see you downstairs now."

"Well fuck off, then, and let me get dressed."

"We'll need to see your husband, too," I added.

Leaving them to dress, we made our way back to the lounge. I called our sergeant to update him, and asked if anyone else could come out to join us. He told me that Jess was the only other officer available. She was currently on her CID attachment, but this situation took priority and I was informed that she was already on her way. Just as I terminated the call, Bed Woman slumped into the lounge, yawning as she tightened the waistband of a towelling dressing gown around her ample form. Her look was somewhere between being pulled backwards through a hedge and recently surviving a flood. She still looked drunk. Who would have thought that sugar and spice and all things nice could end up like this when mixed with alcohol?

"Well," she slurred, "what the fuck are you doing in my house?"

"There's been an incident," I started to explain.

"There's been an incident?"

"Your children have been in the road," I continued.

"My children have been in the road?"

"Listen!" interrupted an exasperated Lloyd. "Your

kids have almost been killed in a multiple pile-up. They're lucky to be alive. Now, how did they get into the street?"

Before she could answer, Jess knocked at the front door and I shouted for her to come through.

"And who the fuck is this coming into my house now?" the woman exclaimed, hands on hips.

"She's a plain-clothes officer," I explained.

"Very plain clothes from the look of it," she sneered, looking my colleague up and down.

Jess glanced over at me and then down at her own navy tailored skirt and jacket, as if I had lured her into some sort of fashionista trap. I think she felt even more slighted since the remark had come from someone who was clearly trying to bring Rubenesque back into style.

In order to spare Jess any further unpleasant and unwarranted criticism, and to expedite matters, I quickly explained the circumstances – as far as I understood them, and how they had led to us all standing here.

"I bet that fucking bitch next door has had a hand in this!" the woman jeered.

"The lady next door has probably saved your children's lives, by the sound of it," I told her.

"I'll ask again," persevered Lloyd. "Who was looking after your children? And how did they get out of the house?"

The woman turned and shouted through to the dining room. "Get in here you little bastard! Have you fucking well let them get out again? I've fucking told you about that before, you little shit!"

Before we could stop her, she had marched into the dining room, grabbed the young boy by his arm, yanking him from his sanctuary under the table, and flung him into the lounge, sending him sprawling to the floor. He got up quickly and sat on his haunches with his head bowed, cowering in his dirty grey boxer shorts. Unnervingly, the child didn't call out in pain, but instead quickly shuffled backwards across the floor and away from his mother.

"There's your fucking suspect!" she declared, standing back and folding her arms. Lloyd stepped forward and put a protective arm around her son, looking back at the mother in utter disgust. Any other child would surely have cried, but he seemed to know better than to do so in his mother's presence.

What I had just witnessed sickened me to my core. Aren't these meant to be a child's golden years, the ones that shape their future? They should be full of happy memories, of joy and delight – not fear and neglect.

It seems that every parent thinks they're a terrible parent, except those parents who *are* actually terrible; to them, it's always someone else's fault. This job can sometimes make you hardened to life's inhumanity, but I know that I'll never get used to this sort of wickedness.

"Right, that's it!" I announced. "I'm arresting you for assault on the boy, I'm taking your three children into police protection and you're also being locked up for child neglect."

"And that goes for you, too," I said, pointing towards the woman's partner who had just appeared. "You're under arrest for child neglect too."

There followed a tense moment when he stared directly at me, his tattooed face contorted with rage; nor was his inking restricted to a solitary home-drawn teardrop, which, I presumed, was meant to suggest: 'Yes, I may have been in prison, but I also have an undiscovered sensitive side'; no, this was an elaborate piece of 'art' that covered the entire length of one side of his face – a real Mike Tyson tribal affair. And neither was his rage that mildly indignant feeling you experience when you see two bus drivers who pass one another on the road yet fail to wave to each other: this was the sort of fury that looked like it may soon be accompanied by extreme violence. I instinctively placed my hand on my pepper spray; however, instead of leaping ten feet and grabbing me by the windpipe, he disappeared from view.

"He's run out the back door," confirmed Lloyd, before going after him.

"Don't worry about that," I countered, breathing a sigh of relief. "It's an enclosed yard. He's not going anywhere."

"He's raking around the place," added Jess, looking out of the window. "It looks like he's trying to find some sort of weapon."

I peered out to see him picking up lengths of wood and then discarding them. He then grabbed a set of training weights, but they, too, were cast aside. It was as if he was looking to arm himself with the ideal weapon for his planned revenge attack.

"Just lock the back door for now," I suggested. "We'll deal with him when we have a few more people here."

The boy ran and locked it himself, and then asked if we could leave. He seemed petrified. As Jess led the woman out in handcuffs, her prisoner began to laugh, telling us we should leave now if we had any sense. As she finished speaking, the whole of the back door shook violently as something from outside smashed against it. Jess shot me a questioning look.

"Don't worry," I informed her. "Those PVC doors are as hard as *Sophie's Choice*. He'll never get through it."

She raised her eyebrows quizzically and then carried on her way, taking the child with her.

"But if you are going out to the car, can you see if anyone else is free?" I tried my best to make it sound like a nonchalant comment, but I wasn't fooling anyone. "Well, look at him," I whispered, turning to Lloyd, "he's bloody potty!"

The banging at the back door stopped.

"Maybe he's worn himself out?" remarked my colleague hopefully.

BOOM! A contorted face slammed against the living-room window. His shirt was off and he clearly meant business. Sometimes, bodybuilders look like they have a

27

tiny head because their bodies are so big and muscular; this guy's head appeared to be normal size – it was his body that looked *extra*-massive. His skinhead haircut and snarling face merely served to reinforce the menacing picture in front of us. After stepping back a few yards, he then picked up a barbell and hurled it through the window, sending glass flying in every direction. He pressed his face through the gap, the jagged edges puncturing his cheeks.

"Here's Johnny!" I quipped feebly.

"Neither the time nor the place," rebuked my colleague sternly.

All of a sudden and quite unexpectedly, Ron marched into the room, pulled out his irritant spray and directed a stream of pepper into Johnny's eyes, sending him reeling backwards. He turned to us in triumph and blew on the top of the canister like a Wild West gunslinger. "I think my job here is done," he said and then began making his way back out the door.

Just then, there was an almighty crash. We all turned and looked back in time to see a shovel being smashed into the window and raked around the four edges to clear the glass from the pane. Johnny then started climbing through the gap like a rampaging silverback, seemingly oblivious that he was getting cut and bloodied in the process.

"You've gone and poked the wasps' nest now," I announced, my voice rising by a few octaves. "He's bloody crazy!"

"I'll radio for backup," added Lloyd.

"Don't worry," said Ron calmly. "We can take him." And with that he racked his baton. Lloyd and I followed suit. Seconds later we were forced to jump back as Johnny swung his spade in an arc in front of him – missing us, but managing to embed it in his 52" plasma. As he struggled to wrench it free, I grabbed hold of the end to try and wrestle it from him but he managed to pull it out, propelling me into Lloyd in the process. Ron used the opportunity to deliver a leg strike with his baton in the hope of getting our man to the ground.

Our attacker let go of the spade, sending Lloyd and I staggering backwards. He now turned his attention to Ron, giving him a right hook which sent him sprawling to the floor. I dived at his legs to try and topple him – if we could get him to the floor, we had a better chance of controlling him – but he just bent down and punched me between the shoulder blades, causing me to splay my arms out and release him. It was Lloyd's turn now and he grabbed him from behind, but the guy just ran backwards into the wall, crushing our colleague and forcing him to release his hold. Ron and I were back on our feet, raining blows upon him, but they didn't seem to make one iota of difference. Lloyd began delivering knee strikes, but they also seemed ineffectual. We now kept contact close as we continued to battle with him; none of us wanting to give him enough reach to punch out, but I was already becoming exhausted. It doesn't take much fighting to tire you out. As I was hurled to the floor yet again I heard a warble, signalling that someone had finally pushed their emergency button. I got back up and dived in again, praying that the cavalry would arrive soon.

In a fight like this nothing is choreographed. If everyone was coordinated, we'd get a better result, but, in the melee, as one person is trying to get the suspect over in one direction, someone else is trying to get him down the other way; someone is pushing him to the right, someone else pushing him to the left, cancelling it out. Invariably, it becomes a free-for-all, and the structured tactics in training school simply go out the window.

Andy and Geezer burst through the door and immediately tried to assist, but it's difficult to distinguish who is who in the heat of battle, and there isn't always room to get in and grab the assailant, and with everyone spinning around... I felt a blow to my face and could taste the blood in my mouth. In a bizarre way, I hoped it was from our suspect and not a stray elbow from one of my colleagues.

It was Charles Harper Webb, the American professor, psychotherapist and poet who once said: *'There is no "nice way" to arrest a potentially dangerous, combative suspect. The police are our bodyguards; our hired fists, batons and guns. We pay them to do the dirty work of protecting us. The work we're too afraid, too unskilled, or too civilised to do ourselves. We expect them to keep the bad guys out of our businesses, out of our cars, out of our houses, and out of our faces. We just don't want to see how it's done'.*

It was just as well that there wasn't anyone to see how it was being done now because it wasn't a pretty sight, and by no means civilised. One minute the maniac had been on the floor with five officers on top of him, the next he had thrown us all off and was punching the hell out of us. Eventually, however, slowly but surely and little by little, we gained control and our prisoner was finally handcuffed and bound with leg restraints around his ankles and his thighs. Still snarling, and continuing to stare menacingly at each officer in turn, he was then unceremoniously carried out to a waiting van. Puzzlingly, he hadn't uttered a single word throughout, which somehow only served to make things seem worse. Barry was stood holding the door open as we placed him in. The rest of us, meanwhile, were either stood leaning against the sides of the vehicle or were bent double with our hands on our knees, our breathing laboured and blood smeared all over our hands, faces and uniforms, with aching joints and bruises to every part of our bodies.

"At least everyone still has their teeth, and there're no broken bones," observed our leader. He had a point: no major injuries and we were all still alive – always a bonus!

"Donoghue, what are you up to? Why are you

grinning like a psychopath?" Barry had seen me out of the corner of his eye, leaning against the van, beaming broadly.

"Smiling, Sarge – not grinning. I read about it. It says you should smile after something stressful. It lowers your heart rate." Apparently, it's got to be a genuine smile – engaging both your eyes and mouth. Laughing also has a myriad of benefits such as lowering stress, easing pain and boosting the immune system. I had toyed with the idea of chuckling away, but I wasn't sure if the general public was quite ready to witness a bunch of police officers carrying a violent thug out to a van and then standing around laughing like drains.

"You never cease to amaze me." Barry shook his head before clarifying his position. "And by *amaze*, I mean *deeply concern.*"

Note to self: don't do the smiling thing when Barry's about.

Our sergeant then rallied the troops. "Now, the exciting part of the day: get back to the office and start writing up your statements. And you", he added, addressing the monster in the back of the van, "are further arrested for resisting arrest."

Our prisoner was driven to custody with a guard of honour in case he kicked off again when we tried to get him out of the cage at the other end. Those of us remaining finally headed back to the parade room.

"Apparently," Jess informed us as we all sat typing up our statements, "the guy you arrested has got that *Congenital Analgesia* thing." She folded up the piece of paper that she had written the term down on and put it back in her pocket. "His wife told me."

She was greeted by a series of shrugs from the rest of us.

"It's a disorder that means he can't feel any pain," she clarified.

Pain signals run through neural pathways to the brain,

and pain levels themselves are graded 1-10 by the medical profession. Grazes are ranked at number 2, a broken nose at 4, while childbirth and migraines register 8. At the highest level scoring 10, are dental pain and renal colic or kidney stones, although I would personally add toilet splashback and eating a Toblerone straight from the fridge to the list.

"That explains a few things," muttered Lloyd, holding a wad of damp paper towels to his forehead. "There had to be something super-human about him."

A general murmur of agreement spread around the room. A further murmur of approval followed when Barry came in and announced that traffic was taking on the collision investigation. The child neglect case, however, would remain our responsibility. In fact, in a room just along the corridor, the children were already being looked after by Chad until social services came to collect them. It's a sad state of affairs, but today more children than ever before are looked after by the State due to abuse or neglect at home.

Social services are hard to second guess, and I had no idea whether the children would be taken into long-term care or quickly returned to the family home. However, even when local authorities do remove children from immediate danger things often don't get much better despite multi-agency involvement. Statistics show that 50% of girls who leave the care system become single mothers within two years; half of all inmates in young offender institutions are, or have been, looked-after children, and a massive 80% are unemployed after two years of leaving the care system. Yet, even with those depressing figures, I felt certain that the children we had rescued this morning would have a better start in life in care than if they remained in such an abusive household.

An hour later, I was waiting in Barry's office to discuss the case when he returned in the company of a young woman. "Social services!" he announced as he ushered her into the room, before disappearing off down the corridor. Her phone rang almost immediately, and I could hear her talking about the children to whoever was on the other end of the line, explaining that she had just arrived at the police station.

As she stood chatting away, I noticed that she looked very prim and proper: an ankle-length, navy linen dress; hair scraped back in a bun and not a scrap of make-up. Large, horn-rimmed glasses, perched near the edge of her Roman nose, gave her the appearance of an old-fashioned school ma'am. What was most evident about her, though, was that she was clearly heavily pregnant.

Being a gentleman, I caught her eye and, not wanting to disturb her call, quietly offered her my seat. It was only when I saw the look of abject horror on her face that I began to appreciate that something was drastically wrong. I mentally replayed my actions and after a few seconds and to my own intense dismay, I realised that to all intents and purposes I had made direct eye contact with this expectant mother while pointing enthusiastically at my crotch and mouthing, 'Do you want to sit here?'

I immediately felt that familiar warm glow of embarrassment rushing to every part of my body. Thankfully, at that very moment, Barry re-entered the room carrying a chair for her. Why hadn't I thought of that?

"It's me," she announced as she put her phone away and sat down. Well, maybe I had misjudged her – she seemed to have a sense of humour after all.

"Hello you. It's me, too!" I proclaimed happily in response.

"No, that's my name," she replied frostily. "My name is Esme."

Barry looked over at me and shook his head before formally introducing us both. She wrote down our names but seemed to be pressing just a little bit harder with her pen when she wrote mine.

The rest of the meeting was a sober affair. I reported on the state of the house, the condition of the children, the attitude of the parents and so on, whilst Esme took notes. I felt like I was being cross-examined and after an hour of questioning I was beginning to feel as if I was the guilty party. It was like the Spanish Inquisition... and nobody expects the Spanish Inquisition! On a couple of occasions, when my answers clearly weren't as detailed as she wanted, I was tempted to suggest that she might want to visit the property herself, but the occasional withering glance from my sergeant suggested to me that this wouldn't be a good career move. It was nearly an hour later that she finally declared that she had heard enough and would be temporarily taking the children into care pending a full case conference. She then proceeded to get up and thank Barry for his support, completely ignoring me.

Barry once again disappeared off down the corridor, this time to find Chad and the children, leaving me standing in an awkward silence with my interrogator. Eventually, I felt I had to clear the air and offered my hand and apologised for the lap-pointing debacle.

"Sorry about the misunderstanding... about the lap-pointing thing."

And that's where I should have left it, but instead I decided to try and make light of the whole sorry episode. "I guess that's how you got into that predicament in the first place," I joked, pointing to her bump. As she glanced up and met my gaze, I could tell that I had misjudged the situation entirely.

I'd often heard that if you lose one sense your other senses become enhanced. That might also explain why people with no sense of humour have an increased sense of self-importance. As Esme began her retort in a calm and measured tone, I realised that this was definitely the case here.

"Are you suggesting that I am with child because I sit

on random strangers' laps when I attend meetings?"

It sounded like a question, but it was more of an accusation.

"No..." I replied hesitantly, making it sound like it should have had a question mark at the end. I shook my head and looked down at my boots. I tried a nervous laugh but it clearly wasn't cutting any ice. She was deadly serious. I started to edge out of the room, trying to extricate myself from this uncomfortable situation as quickly as possible. However, she wasn't finished with me yet.

"And *predicament*?" she hissed, as she repeated my ill-chosen words back to me. I sensed the scale of indignation in her voice. "My *predicament*? I most certainly do not call bringing life into this world a predicament!"

She turned abruptly on her heel to face Barry, who had just returned in time to catch the tail end of my ritual humiliation. As she informed him where the children would be taken to, I felt my stress levels rising and went to combat it with a broad smile... just at the very second Esme chose to turn around. She shot me one of her school-ma'am glares.

"Oh, so you think it's all a big joke, do you?" She sounded angry – very angry.

"No, no, he's not happy about whatever has happened; he's just read somewhere that..." Barry tried in vain to explain but it was too late: our guest was already storming off down the corridor.

Note to self: start reading notes written to self.

Meanwhile, Barry just looked at me, shaking his head in exasperation and pointing towards the door. As I sidled past him, I could hear him muttering those familiar words, "Donoghue, Donoghue, Donoghue."

# CHAPTER 3

# Hitler in Tights

"I hope you have a lovely day at the spa, sir," beamed the receptionist as she handed over the small, foil-covered chocolate heart. "And enjoy the Valentine's Day treat, with compliments of the hotel."

The smartly dressed male thanked her before making his way towards the changing rooms. He was still sat there twenty minutes later when Peter Erskine arrived and began to get changed. The two men exchanged pleasantries – the seated male revealing that his wife had arranged the visit to the spa as a Valentine's Day present, whilst Erskine divulged that he was a regular visitor to the facilities, and that today he was booked in for a massage. When he had finished changing, Erskine donned a towelling robe, bid his new friend goodbye and then made his way through to the treatment rooms to await his pampering.

As soon as he was out of sight, the other male retrieved his bag from underneath the bench, removed a crowbar and proceeded to jemmy open Erskine's locker. Once inside, he helped himself to the Rolex he had seen Erskine wearing, and then patted down the pockets of the suit jacket. Finding his wallet, he quickly glanced inside to see a number of cards and some cash. After helping himself, and then carefully closing the locker, he put his stash in his bag and then hastily sent a pre-worded text from his phone. Within seconds, a car could be heard pulling up outside the rear of the spa. Exiting through a fire door, the male got in the back of the vehicle and was quickly driven away.

Half an hour later, a call came through to the hotel that sent the young receptionist scurrying down the corridors to the spa. Soon a flustered Peter Erskine, wrapped in a white towelling robe, was taking a call that had been redirected from the main switchboard.

"Is that Mr Erskine?"

"Yes, speaking."

"Hello, Mr Erskine, this is Colleen from the bank. I just need to carry out a few security questions before we can continue, if that's ok?"

When requested, his full name, date of birth, mother's maiden name, first line of his address and details of his last purchase were duly given. Once the woman at the other end of the phone was satisfied that she was speaking to the account holder, she continued.

"We've been contacted by the police, Mr Erskine, to inform us that they have apprehended a man who has your wallet and a Rolex watch in his possession."

"That's mine!" exclaimed Erskine. "Whilst we've been talking, the spa manager went to check and he confirms that my locker has been broken into!"

"Well, the good news is that the police have recovered your property, and that the male responsible is now in custody."

"Excellent!" replied Erskine. "I hope they throw away the key!"

"Pleased to be of service," continued the woman. "Just to confirm: the police have your watch and the two credit cards, and we will arrange to have them all returned to you as soon as possible."

"Hang on, did you say two cards? There were three in my wallet."

"Actually, the police did say that a second male ran off," conceded the woman. "He may well have the third card. I'll arrange to have it cancelled straight away."

"Thank you."

"I'll just need a further security check before I can continue."

"Fine. Go ahead."

"I'll need the last three numbers of the security code on the back of the card."

"I'm afraid I don't know it. It's not something that you really remember."

"No problem, Mr Erskine. I can still cancel it with your PIN number."

"Now, that I can tell you; it's the year that Tchaikovsky's opera *Jevgeni Onegin* was premiered in Moscow."

"I beg your pardon?"

"1879."

"That's excellent, Mr Erskine," she laughed. "That checks out. Your card has now been cancelled. We'll have another one sent out to you. It usually takes up to five working days to arrive. In the meantime, if you could wait at the hotel, I've arranged for the police to come out to see you within the hour. Is there anything else I can help you with today?"

"No, you've been more than helpful. Thank you very much."

Peter Erskine put the phone down, and took a seat in the garden room. The spa manager, who had been hovering nearby, approached his guest to apologise profusely for the unfortunate set of events that had occurred, whilst the receptionist brought him a brandy to calm his nerves.

Meanwhile, on the other side of Sandford...

"You do not have to say anything. But it may harm your defence if you do not mention when questioned, how nice you think my new hairstyle is." Jess had wandered into the briefing room and was now doing a twirl, showing off her new look.

"So what's this in aid of?" asked Chad.

"It's a dual celebration," declared Jess. "Not only is it Valentine's Day, but it's also my birthday, and yours truly is getting an early finish this evening as I have a hot date tonight!"

"Ooh, how romantic," cooed Gwen. "You'll have to tell us all about it tomorrow."

"But if it starts with: 'He was the perfect gentleman', then I'm not interested," muttered George.

"Oh, just ignore the statue from Easter Island," voiced Gwen, slapping George's knee. "He's just jealous because his hidden admirers take their job very seriously over Valentine's."

"You what?" said George, looking up with a perplexed expression on his face.

"She means they stay well hidden, and that you didn't get any cards," laughed Ron.

"I did!" remarked an indignant George, producing a dog-eared card from inside his stab vest with a flourish, only for it to be immediately whipped out of his hand by Geezer.

"Roses are grey, violets are grey..." he read aloud, whilst holding it out of George's reach. "Hang on – it's from his colour-blind dog!"

"It doesn't say that!" objected our Lothario, as he made attempts to snatch it back, but it was too late as Ben now had it in his clutches and was studying the message with interest.

"Isn't it strange how your mum, Santa and your secret Valentine all have the same handwriting?"

"You bunch of..." His comments were drowned out by the laughter of his colleagues as he snatched his battered card back off Ben before it could do a full round of the station. I was chuckling along with the rest of the shift when Jess came and stood in front of me.

"Well, John, what do you think of my hairdo?"

I must admit, I preferred the old ponytail to her new bob style, but I couldn't tell her that.

"It's fantastic! Best thing I've seen all day!"

"Oh, you could have at least *pretended* to like it!" she pouted. I guess my face must have given it away.

"I *was* pretending!" I protested. From the look she gave me, I hadn't made things any better. I really must work on my *Oh, my gosh! You've got a wonderful new hairstyle* expression.

"Hey, Jess," I began, in a bid to divert attention from my unintentional slight, "remember when that woman rang in to report a bad haircut? Just how bad does your hair have to be to warrant a 999 call, eh?" My efforts were met with a stony glare.

"I don't think you're helping there," whispered Gwen.

"No, no. Not that I'm saying *yours* is bad..." I was starting to turn red. As I looked over I could see Andy and Lloyd grinning at me and back-pedalling an imaginary bicycle from their seats on the other side of the room, whilst Ron and Chad were standing behind Jess, pretending to dig a giant hole with an invisible spade. Over in the corner, Andy was miming trying to fit his foot in his mouth, whereas Gwen just stood shaking her head.

Before I had time to redeem myself, Barry strode in to start the briefing, clutching the handover log. "Before we begin, who's supposed to be over at the Sandford Manor Hotel?"

My colleagues and I exchanged blank looks.

"I've had a call from the hotel saying someone was supposed to be there over an hour ago. Did the last shift say anything before they went off?"

The blank looks were now accompanied by head shakes and Gallic shrugs.

"I'll take that as a no. Any volunteers, then?"

My hand immediately shot up. Not only would it be a chance to extricate myself from an awkward situation, but I also hoped that a cup of tea and a nice biscuit might be on offer at the hotel.

"Thanks, John. No idea what it's about, but they sounded quite curt on the phone. If you could get over there sharpish…"

"No problem, Sarge," I replied, springing from my seat and making my escape; but not before pointing at Jess's hair and giving her two thumbs up. She responded with a solitary finger.

Five minutes later and I was on my way to the hotel, enjoying the peace and quiet of the country roads after my earlier embarrassing faux pas.

Sandford Manor, with its distinctive honey-coloured stone and set against a backdrop of beautiful landscaped gardens and enchanted woodlands, dominated the landscape. Built as a celebration of wealth, it was the archetypal Jacobean country house with its sophisticated symmetry, grand entrance hall, elaborate carvings and Renaissance-inspired decoration. Nowadays, it was the haunt of the rich and well-heeled who wished to relax in luxury, surrounded by attentive staff.

I always enjoy my trips to the Manor as it's always a welcome change to be surrounded by opulence. In turn, the hotel staff are always delighted to see the police; our presence providing that extra element of reassurance for their guests. They encourage us to drop by, and we are often rewarded for our diligence with a hot beverage and, if we happen to time it just right, a sample from the chef's home-made biscuit platter. A trip to Sandford Manor is always a pleasure and I smiled to myself as I drove up the long, sweeping, tree-lined drive.

However, before I had even slowed to a halt, my smile evaporated. The sound of my engine appeared to have attracted a group of angry-looking individuals outside onto the gravelled entrance to the hotel. As soon as I opened my door the shouts and questions began in earnest.

"You said you'd be here hours ago!"

"Have you got my watch with you? It's a Rolex!"

"Are they in custody?"

"Where are my credit cards? I need them back!"

"What's kept you?"

"Did you catch the crook that ran off?"

Walking toward the impressive main doors with my head swimming, my tormentors followed me on either side, firing questions as they went. I was encircled as soon as I got to the reception. I felt like General Custer at the Battle of the Little Bighorn.

"Can you all please stop!" I shouted above the melee. "Can someone just tell me what all this is about?"

"No, Officer," came the angry response from a rather irate-looking businessman. "YOU can tell us what it's all about!"

My bemused expression seemed to have wound my besuited inquisitor into some sort of apoplectic frenzy. I half expected to see steam shooting out of his ears at any second.

"Well, let's start with you taking over an hour and a half to get here, shall we?" he challenged. Now, I'm no Hercule Poirot, but I could detect a distinctly sarcastic tone to his question.

"Who told you I'd be here by then?" I asked him, lowering my voice in the hope that he would do the same.

"THE BANK! THE BLOODY BANK!" Judging by the sheer volume of his response, my tactic had clearly failed.

"The bank?" Before I had time to seek further clarification, the duty manager had stepped forward to intervene.

"Look, Officer, you can understand why Mr Erskine is a tad vexed?"

It sounded like a bit of an understatement to me. At the risk of incurring the wrath of the entire maddening crowd, I explained that I had no idea what he was talking about, but that if he started from the beginning, then I might be able to assist. My response was met by a loud chorus of exasperated sighs and mutterings. Several in the crowd wandered off, complaining that they had far better things to do than to listen to the whole story again. Soon the only people left were me, the duty manager, the spa manager, a still angry Mr Esrkine and the young receptionist.

"Would you like a cup of…" Before she could finish her question, the manager shot her a withering look as if to indicate that I hadn't yet earned any privileges. I suspected that a biscuit would definitely be off the cards.

"You have to see it from our member's perspective." He indicated towards the seething mass of rage perched on the edge of a chaise longue who was currently staring intently at me. "Mr Erskine has come to use the facilities at the spa and, regrettably, his locker has been broken into. Whilst it appears that the police have promptly arrested those responsible, it's actually been left to the bank to contact our guest and to arrange for you to come out and see him. In fact, there has been a distinct lack of communication from the constabulary in relation to this."

"You incompetent flatfoots!" Erskine added, pressing home the point. "It's just as well you lot aren't in charge of communications at *my* company!"

"The bank?" I repeated. I registered his barbed comment, but it was the manager's revelations about the bank that I was most intrigued about.

"Yes, lucky for me that someone *there* bothers about customer service!" Erskine sneered. I was then, in a less than polite manner, taken through the whole scenario again. "Don't you follow any procedures in Sandford Police?" he jibed, leaning back into his seat, satisfied that he had made his point.

I excused myself, and retreated to a distance that was out of earshot of both men before I made a quick call to my colleague, Gary, who was based over in the next town. After a brief conversation, I was back and ready to face Peter Erskine. Admittedly, I had been more than a little frustrated by his accusations and put-downs.

"We do have procedures, sir," I countered, picking up on his last point. "And could I suggest that you give your bank a ring and check theirs?"

"Your superintendent will hear about this!"

"First of all though, sir, I would urge you to give your bank a ring and cancel your cards."

"Have you not been listening?" Erskine started to shake uncontrollably. "THE BANK HAS ALREADY DONE IT!"

"Sir, if you could just keep your voice down and make the call, I'll explain." I then proceeded to inform him why I had contacted my colleague earlier. Last year, Gary had dealt with an almost identical crime involving what I suspected was a very similar modus operandi:

First of all, the alleged 'wife' arrives at the hotel and explains that she has forgotten all about a special celebration and books a last-minute spa day for her 'husband'. She pays in cash, thereby avoiding any credit card trail.

The following day, the 'husband' comes in and, as he is here for a spa day, no one bats an eyelid when he carries a bag into the changing room where he sits waiting for a suitable target to arrive. When one is identified, he makes small talk while noting which locker his victim has used. When the coast is clear, the target's locker is forced open and the valuables are stolen. A quick text to an accomplice ensures the getaway car is waiting outside the fire exit to whisk him away.

The operation is then stepped up a notch, whereby the next stage escalates the whole incident from a simple theft to a clever fraud by someone making a call to the hotel pretending to be from the bank.

My audience had been nodding sagely as I had gone through the opening stages of the crime, but the last revelation generated a series of bemused looks.

"Well, how could your bank possibly know that you were here today?" I asked.

"I hadn't thought of that," Erskine replied quietly. It seemed like the wind was slowly being taken out of his sails.

"And the story that the police had stopped two men, and that one had run off was a fabrication," I added. "At this stage, we were unaware that anything had occurred."

"But why would they say that they had recovered two of the cards?" interjected the manager.

"To make Mr Erskine think that the game was almost up – to make him think that we had foiled the criminals before they'd had a chance to close the deal. As a result, he let his guard down, making it easier to get the card details from him."

"But the woman at the bank confirmed all my security questions," protested Erskine, still desperately holding onto the faintest glimmer of hope that he hadn't been scammed.

"You could have said anything," I told him. "They had no idea what the answers were – what your mother's maiden name is, what your last transaction was – they just agreed to whatever you said."

"I suppose you never ask the bank for any passwords to confirm that *they* are who they say they are," added the spa manager.

"Exactly! And, finally, they weren't interested in the three-digit security number on the back of the card. That was just a bluff. They probably assumed you wouldn't remember it anyway – who does? It was just a clever way of manoeuvring the conversation around to getting you to reveal your PIN number."

Erskine now sat in silence, trying to reconcile how he, a leading captain of industry, had allowed himself to become a victim.

"I believe that you probably also told the man that you chatted to in the changing room that you were having a massage. That gave the thieves a window of opportunity to work within. They wanted to drive as far away from the scene of the crime as they possibly could, but they still needed to call the hotel and get your card details *before* you returned to your locker. If *you* had discovered the theft first, you would have called us and the bank straight away and blown their plan straight out of the water. This way, they still had control of the situation. They were able to con the card details out of you, and then by pretending that they had called us on your behalf they bought themselves an extra hour with which to make good their escape."

Erskine looked like he had heard enough, but, regardless, I continued with my tale as the two managers and the receptionist clearly hadn't, and were sitting on the edge of their seats, listening intently.

"Draw a radius of thirty minutes' travelling time from here and that's where they probably made their initial call from, and where they then used the stolen bank card once they had the PIN number." My audience was enthralled. "Add on another hour's drive from there, and that's where our crooks probably are now; well out of our area, and into another county."

"Get that man a biscuit!" declared the manager triumphantly when I finished my account. As the receptionist hurried off, I radioed to request CSI to attend, and then asked to view the hotel's CCTV.

The gang had been meticulous in the execution of the whole operation. The getaway car had been captured driving off on the CCTV, but the crooks had covered the possibility that the vehicle might be checked by using false plates that would almost certainly have been ditched by now. There was no way that the male and female could have avoided being caught on camera, but I didn't recognise either of them. They were most likely travelling criminals, executing their scam all over the country.

By the time I had finished reviewing the camera

footage and returned to the seating area, Mr Erskine had departed; the spa manager had now resumed his duties, the receptionist was back at her desk, and so I was left with just the hotel manager. As I sat down, one of the serving staff came over with my coffee, and I was also presented with a couple of the Valentine chocolates.

"It's the least I can do to make amends for my reaction earlier," apologised the manager. "It's the chef's special creation," he explained, pointing to the hearts, "One milk chocolate and one dark."

I thanked him and gave my drink a stir. "Oh, and before I go," I enquired, "would it be possible to have a look at the massage rooms?"

"Very good!" he replied excitedly. "I'd never have thought of that!"

Never have thought of what? Then it dawned on me: following my explanation of the villain's MO, he obviously now regarded me as some sort of master detective – an Inspector Morse figure, seeking inspiration and clues from the places our victim had visited.

"I'll get it sorted ASAP," and with a click of his fingers he summoned the receptionist and instructed her to fetch the masseuse, suggesting that I was about to open a new line of enquiry. The girl gave me an admiring look before returning to her desk to telephone the treatment room. I was loath to burst his bubble and tell him that I was just curious to see what it looked like – and check the prices out – as I was planning a treat for my friend, Miss Jones.

"Whilst we're waiting for the head masseuse," he added, "please help yourself to the chocolates. What do you think of them?" He was clearly keen to get my opinion.

I unwrapped the dark chocolate heart, took a bite and adopted an expression of extreme concentration as I savoured the taste. Now that he obviously regarded me as a man capable of complex thought, I felt I had to offer him the in-depth analysis that he was clearly anticipating.

The chocolate had that sharp tang that you'd expect with such a high concentration of cocoa. It wasn't unpleasant; it was a sophisticated flavour – almost classy. There was something else, too: it was rich with a pleasantly sour aftertaste. I had no idea what it had been mixed with, but I was impressed.

"Well?" He was sitting on the edge of his seat awaiting the verdict.

"Bitter... tart..."

"I beg your pardon!" My considered response was interrupted by the arrival of the masseuse who now stood above me with an outraged expression on her face.

"No! No, I wasn't insinuating *you* were a..." Before I could protest my innocence, she indicated for me to follow and I hurried after her, but not before the receptionist had caught my eye, winked and mouthed: 'Hitler in tights.'

Once within the confines of the treatment room, Hitler gestured for me to sit down and then asked how she could assist with my investigation. I realised I was going to have to keep up the pretence of looking for clues – at least for now – and asked if today she had noted anything different about Mr Erskine's appointment.

"Can I be blunt?" she began. Normally, I might have replied with a quip that she could so long as I could be Philby, but she didn't look like the sort to appreciate a little Cold War humour; instead I just nodded.

"To be frank with you, I'm actually surprised he's come back after his behaviour with Natasha."

I opened my notebook to indicate my interest, and Natasha was duly summoned. I don't know what it is, but I find there is something incredibly sexy about a woman speaking in broken English – though slightly less so when English is actually her first language... I tried not to look too disappointed when I realised that I had let my imagination run away with me and that Natasha wasn't a mysterious Russian émigré after all. She was actually from Birmingham.

The girl explained that she hadn't long been working at the hotel when Mr Erskine had come for his usual massage. After twenty minutes of massaging his back, he had turned over and it became obvious that he was, in Natasha's words, 'quite excited'. She had then asked him if he wanted 'hand relief', to which he had replied enthusiastically in the affirmative, whilst licking his lips and muttering something along the lines of: 'wait until I tell them about this down at the golf club'. Natasha explained she had then slipped out of the room, only to pop her head back around the door five minutes later to enquire if he had finished yet.

"I don't know what sort of establishment he thinks we run here," added Hitler, "but, after that, I decided it was better if I dealt with Mr Erskine in future."

I had no doubt in my mind that she would deal with things with a firm hand. Aside from a randy customer, I had gleaned nothing new to add to my investigation, and I still hadn't managed to find out the spa prices. Finally, I came clean and explained that I was looking to treat a friend and asked if they had any ideas.

"Would she like a facial?"

I told them that it was a nice thought but that she really wanted a spa treatment.

Half an hour later and I was back at the police station. The bank had already phoned to confirm my initial theory that the card had been used in a small town a thirty-minute drive from Sandford. CSI also contacted me to tell me that they had managed to get a decent fingerprint-lift from the locker. I was in the middle of updating my notes when Gwen and Jess walked into the room.

"I thought you were supposed to be leaving early for your hot date?" I asked.

"So did I," she replied, "but we got tied up with a job, so I had to cancel."

Sadly, that is the reality of policing: you can never guarantee that you'll be off duty on time. Often, even if you plan something on your rest day, you can find that your plans are cancelled by the constabulary if a big case comes along, or you're unexpectedly called to attend court.

I made a suitably sad face, and then, after letting a few seconds of silence elapse to illustrate how sincere I was, I launched into the tale of my hotel scammers. Gwen and Jess seemed suitably impressed at the level of thought that had gone into pulling off the stunt, and made all the right noises at the salient points of my story.

When I had finished my tale, they began relating the adventures of their own arrest caper. Where mine was a planned and well-executed operation, it appears that in their escapade 'thought' had taken a back seat. Gwen explained that on the Black Estate, two twenty-two-year-old female chavs were hungry...

The story begins with the local pizza shop taking a phone order for two twelve-inch pizzas and two large drinks. When the delivery driver had pulled up outside the address twenty minutes later, two masked girls had run out of a side alley brandishing a knife and demanded the food. The driver had duly handed over the goods, and the girls had then lifted the lids to examine their booty. "Mine's the pepperoni – yours is the meat feast," one was heard to comment as they swapped the boxes over before disappearing into the night.

The driver clearly wasn't too traumatised by his ordeal as he finished the rest of his deliveries before driving to the police station to report the robbery. When they were given the job, Jess and Gwen's first port of call was to the house the food should have been delivered to. As they stood chatting to the two girls who answered the door, Gwen asked Comms to ring the phone number that had called the order in to the pizza shop. From one of the girls' pockets came the unmistakable sound of a mobile phone ringing. Automatically, she answered it only to discover that it was actually the police on the other end of the line. When Gwen and Jess escorted the pair through the house and into the kitchen, they found the crusts from the pizzas plus the boxes in the bin. To cap it all, when they were interviewed, one replied with indignation: "How could the driver have possibly known it was me – I was wearing a mask!"

The mention of mobile phones had reminded me that I needed to ring Mr Erskine to let him know that we'd had a forensic hit on the locker. I dialled the number and prepared to give him the good news.

"Good evening, Mr Erskine. Just to let you know that we've got an excellent fingerprint off the locker, which is a great start in helping us to identify and, ultimately, track down the thieves. They may still have your watch in their possession, and, if we pick them up, hopefully, there's a good chance that we might get your Rolex back for you. I know you didn't have a good massage today but it seems you might get a happy ending after all…"

Click. Brrrrrr.

I looked back at Gwen and Jess with surprise. "I don't believe it – he's put the phone down on me!"

## CHAPTER 4

# The Queen of
# False Alarms

Jessica came racing down the stairs from the canteen, slinging on her body armour. The sergeant and I were stood chatting in the corridor and we both looked up at her expectantly.

"Domestic in the old part of town," she informed us as she sped past. "Eileen and Geoffrey Crawford. Ring any bells?"

Barry and I gave each other a little nod of recognition. I dashed out to the panda car after her and jumped into the passenger seat.

"Fire up the Quattro!" I instructed.

"You what?"

"Just start the car," I muttered.

A minute later and we were nosing out of the station yard, ready to merge into the busy traffic, announcing our intentions with blue lights flashing and a series of whoops from our siren.

"I can't believe you've never heard of Eileen Crawford," I remarked to Jess as she began manoeuvring through the gaps in the traffic. "She's a bit of a legend. She thinks she knows the law back to front, and will try and bamboozle you with ambiguous legal parlance and quote subsections of obscure legislation at you, although most of the time it's wrong. The truth of it is that she thinks she's better than anyone else and can be very condescending if you dare to disagree with her. I would be surprised if she didn't record everything, too. She's always looking for an opportunity to put a complaint in if she doesn't get her way."

My colleague glanced over at me, her face betraying her concern. I also thought it best to prepare Jess for the type of 'heinous' crime that we could expect to encounter when we eventually arrived at chez Crawford.

"The last time she called us was because her husband's snoring was keeping her awake. She had woken him, and when she had told him the reason why, he had sworn at her, turned over and immediately gone back to sleep. She then rang 999 to demand that her husband be removed forthwith and arrested. When they asked her where he now was, she replied that he was lying next to her. "

Seeing a look of disbelief cross Jessica's face, I continued.

"The time before that, she had rung in claiming that her husband was wrecking the house. When we got there it transpired that after getting up off the sofa he hadn't straightened the throw properly."

Eileen and her husband, Geoffrey, were actually highly educated people. They had both held good jobs at the local university, but their big downfall was alcohol. 'We work hard and we play hard' was their mantra. In reality, 'play hard' should be substituted for 'we drink every opportunity we get'. As a result, they no longer had good jobs at the university. In fact, neither one had a job at all now nor a driving licence. Consequently, they had been forced to move out of their large five-bedroom house in one of the neighbouring villages and into rented accommodation in the town.

"I came here expecting a dump," remarked Jess as we pulled up outside the house.

"I'm sure they'd let you use their facilities if you ask nicely," I reassured her.

"You're terrible! No, I meant because you said they'd spent all their money," giggled Jess.

It was a modest house in the old part of Sandford, but the Crawfords were a testament to the power of an overdraft and maxed-out credit cards. Keeping up appearances was important to both of them but particularly to Mrs Crawford. Mr Crawford was normally an amiable enough chap, whereas his wife was a different kettle of fish altogether. We leapt out of the vehicle and raced up the short path past the neatly arrayed pots of winter clematis and ornamental berry bushes.

"Afternoon, Geoffrey," I announced as the door was opened by a male in his mid-fifties, gin and tonic in hand. He was impeccably dressed in a maroon cashmere V-neck jumper, tie and dark green corduroy trousers but, somewhat incongruously, was also sporting an enormous pair of red fluffy slippers. I involuntarily raised my eyebrows.

"They were a present." He obviously felt the need to apologise for his footwear as he let us in. "I don't really care for them much to be honest with you, but 'she who must be obeyed' bought them for me for Christmas so I feel like I've got to wear them now." He then raised each foot in turn to show me the full technicolour glory of his massive furry boots. "You should get yourself a pair."

"I could say exactly the same thing," I grinned.

"So why have we been called today, sir?" enquired Jess.

"Lumpy mashed potato," came the reply.

Jess and I exchanged glances, whilst Geoffrey rolled his eyes heavenwards.

"You had best see 'the Queen of False Alarms', who will no doubt explain all in her own inimitable style." He then disappeared off into the lounge with his G&T, waving liberally with his free arm in the general direction of the stairs.

We ascended and began peering around each of the

doors in turn, searching for his wife. We eventually found her in the master bedroom, where she had apparently taken to her bed following the trauma of the vegetable-related incident. She was sat, propped up by several pillows, with the heavy, pure white duvet pulled up to her middle. From the waist up she appeared to be immaculately dressed in a lilac silk dressing gown, a single string of pearls adorning her neck, whilst a pristine black bob perfectly framed her slightly elongated face. Unfortunately, the portrait was somewhat spoilt by her purple teeth – a product of years of drinking too much red wine.

"How can we help you today, Mrs Crawford?" I queried as I stood in the doorway.

"Oh, it's you!" she replied tersely as she looked up from her reading. "You're a bastard!"

Eileen and I weren't on the best of terms since I had refused to ring the *actual* Queen on her behalf and inform her that one of her loyal subjects was being restrained against her will by a uniformed oaf. The reason why I had refused to carry out her request was that I doubted Her Majesty would have particularly thanked me for disturbing her Sunday tea to tell her that I was actually preventing an extremely drunken Eileen Crawford from running barefoot into the traffic on the nearby motorway during one of her drinking bouts. Relations between us had been a little strained ever since.

"Why have they sent *you*? I told you I didn't want to see you again." I was finding it hard to decide whether she was speaking in italics or just slurring her words.

"Well, to be frank with you, I'm not exactly delighted to be here," I replied, "but I don't have the luxury of saying which homes I will or won't go to – it's my job. You rang 999 and told the operator it was an emergency. We've come to see if we can help."

"I don't want you in my house." Eileen pointedly turned away, put on her reading glasses and continued reading her newspaper.

An awkward silence descended, disturbed only by the gentle snoring emanating from a rotund-looking dog lying fast asleep at the foot of the bed. If I wasn't mistaken, it was a corgi – bred originally, I am led to believe, to register gas fitters.

"So what's happened?" asked Jess in an attempt to break the impasse.

"Ah, at last a sensible voice in the proceedings!" The glasses and paper went down, and Eileen was ready to engage. "I want that man downstairs arrested."

"Your husband?"

"Yes, young lady, my 'so-called' husband. He may come over as a mild-mannered gentleman, but he can be a monster!"

I had a bizarre image in my head of a cross between David Niven and Frankenstein. Maybe those were his actual feet and not comedy slippers after all…

"And can I ask why I'm locking him up?"

"*Mise en place!*" she declared emphatically, "*Mise en place!*"

Three words that meant nothing to either me or my colleague. I thought it might be something to do with cutting sandwiches into triangles, but that was just a guess. They always seem to taste nicer that way.

"I think you're going to have to help us out here," Jessica prompted.

"*Mise en place*, my dear," she repeated. "It's from the French – MISE. EN. PLACE." She repeated each syllable in turn, slowly and loudly, assuming that would explain all.

Our facial expressions must have given away the fact that we were no closer to understanding why her husband ought to be in custody. "Nope. Still nothing," declared a confused Jessica.

"Don't they teach French nowadays?" Eileen gave an exasperated sigh.

Before she had a chance to reply, I subtly tried to

nudge my colleague's arm as I knew that no matter what Jess said, it would only serve to play right into Eileen's hands; but it was too late: Crawford must have seen the tiniest of movements and the advantage was hers.

"Really, did they teach Modern Foreign Languages at the establishment you went to?" pressed Eileen, relishing the opportunity to display her assumed superior education and standing in society.

"So, I'll ask again," my colleague valiantly persevered. "What has happened today that has necessitated in you calling the police?"

Yet another exasperated sigh came from our bedridden victim. Clearly, she wanted us to know how much effort she was putting herself to by having to explain everything to us. For my part, I made a mental note to enrol both Jess and myself on the mind-reading course when we got back to the station.

"I am a practitioner of the *mise en place* school of cookery." Eileen addressed us akin to a Victorian school ma'am summarising a lesson. "To wit: I have a professional, organised kitchen and preheat my oven and arrange my ingredients and cooking implements prior to the event, as this is the most efficacious modus operandi in recipes with specific time constraints. *Mise en place* – the literal translation means 'putting in place'." Eileen left a pause, inviting Jess to fill the void.

"You mean you get the stuff out ready. Yes, carry on."

"I was preparing Sunday luncheon in the kitchen area when I asked my husband for his assistance in preparing the meal; namely I required him to cream the potatoes."

"Mash the spuds. Yes, I've got that."

"Well, my husband entered the arena as requested, and, apparently, looked for the required implement within the confines of the drawer. Quite obviously, he didn't find it there. He then slammed the drawer shut and bellowed: 'Where's the fucking masher!'"

Cue dramatic pause.

"Well," she continued after she was satisfied that there was enough tension hanging in the air, "he knows very well that I'm an advocate of *mise en place.*"

Eileen was sitting up in bed now. "He should know where the 'fucking masher' is! It's on the 'fucking surface' laid out alongside all the other 'fucking utensils'!" Her face contorted, turning as purple as her teeth, as she venomously spat out the words.

She fell back against the pillows, exhausted after her outburst. The flowery prose had wilted under her onslaught. It was hardly an image of *mise en place* bliss.

"What happened then?" Jessica appeared eager for Eileen to continue. Even the dog had roused and cocked its head expectantly.

"Well, the mashed potato was bloody ruined!"

"And?" We braced ourselves for the dramatic finale.

"And I rang you and then took myself off to bed."

Jess and I looked at each other – just to make sure we hadn't missed the point. We had received an urgent call for assistance: Where were the threats? The smashed furniture? The broken crockery? The violent assault?

"I was distraught!" she added, as if to add credence to her story of suffering and deprivation. And here was I thinking that only an onion could bring tears to your eyes – or a turnip if it hits you hard enough in the face.

"And then what did Mr Crawford do?"

"Well, he simply sloped off like he usually does." Her story concluded, she picked up her paper and replaced her glasses.

"So let me get this straight," clarified Jess. "He's shouted because he couldn't find the potato masher, he's then gone into the lounge and you've taken yourself to bed? And that's it – nothing else?"

"Does there need to be?" asked Eileen.

"Well, when you call 999 there usually is," I answered.

As Eileen continued to feign deafness to anything I said it was left to Jessica again.

"So, what do you want us to do now?" asked my colleague, with mounting incredulity.

Another elaborate sigh followed. First of all, off came the spectacles, slowly and deliberately, before being carefully placed on the bedside cabinet. Next the paper was ceremoniously folded and set alongside them. Finally, Eileen Crawford turned her full attention to us.

"Do I have to repeat myself again? I want him taken away and locked in one of your prisons."

"For not mashing the potatoes? I'm afraid that's not going to happen," replied Jessica.

Eileen picked up the phone and started dialling. I took the opportunity to turn to Jess, needing to verify that we had both actually heard the same thing. Granted, Mr Crawford might have been a bit rude, but he had committed no offence. There was nothing to arrest him for. I could see that my fellow officer was finding it desperately hard to believe that Eileen had called us out for no other reason than some spoilt potatoes.

Our ruminations were interrupted by Eileen jerking the phone in our direction. "They want to speak to you."

"Who does?" I queried.

"The police," she replied.

I tentatively took the receiver. It *was* the police. I couldn't quite believe it: Eileen had called the police on the police! An awkward conversation ensued. Eileen had rung, demanding different officers be sent to the address to do what those already present were refusing to do. This was a first for me. The call handler at the other end was also just as confused as I was, and it was agreed that it was best for all concerned if we just carried on with the task at hand ourselves.

"Have you been drinking, Eileen?" I enquired as I handed back the phone.

"It's *Mrs Crawford* to you, and, yes, of course, you

know I have! One has had a bottle and a half of Cabernet Sauvignon. One is allowed to drink in one's own residence. We've both been drinking. We work hard and we play hard."

"I thought you weren't actually working at the moment," I added, seeking clarification.

"We just play hard then," she corrected herself. "And dispense with the semantics!" She was out of bed now and steadying herself. "Look, she's clearly incompetent," asserted Eileen, waving towards Jess, "but I know you. I've dealt with you before. You're a sensible officer. You'll lock him up, won't you?"

Ten minutes ago I was being marginalised; now I was being buttered up.

"Well, are you going to arrest the old fool or not?" she asked expectantly.

"I agree with my colleague. Lumpy mashed potato doesn't warrant me arresting him, Mrs Crawford. I don't take depriving someone of their liberty lightly."

It had been my intention to try and bring some perspective to the whole affair; maybe agree that whilst the altercation with her husband might not have been very pleasant, it wasn't exactly a matter of life or death. At this very moment, somewhere in the world there could be a turtle on its back that couldn't flip itself upright again, not to mention that it's thought that an octopus eats itself when it's stressed… so best not to get too wound up over a few King Edwards, although I personally would have recommended the red-skinned Desiree for mashing. However, before I could deliver my sermon, Eileen came and stood directly in front of me, hands on hips. I couldn't help thinking that somewhere, perhaps on the other side of Sandford, there were people who might actually need our assistance yet here we were wasting our time on some spuds. I wanted to tell Eileen Crawford that enough was enough and then leave, but I suspected that she would have anticipated this and would have something up her sleeve to detain us.

"So you're taking his side!" It wasn't a question: it was an accusation.

Before I could explain that I wasn't taking anyone's side, Eileen barged past us both and strode out onto the landing. "Now I know how Blanche felt about Baby Jane," she muttered.

Jess and I once again exchanged confused looks. We were doing it far too often today.

"Well, if you're not going to do anything..." Eileen shouted before bounding down the stairs. We were both startled by the sudden turn of events, but quickly rallied ourselves and darted after her, suspecting that she was off to confront the mild-mannered Geoffrey. To our surprise – and his, she ran through the lounge, straight past her startled spouse and into the dining room. As we reached the doorway, we were just in time to see her kneel down next to the sideboard. Both Jess and I stood looking down at her, wondering what had possessed the woman.

"What the bally hell?" Geoffrey added his own contribution to the proceedings.

"Oh, shut up, you old halfwit!" Eileen shouted through to her confused spouse. "You sound more like some confused old major every day. All you're missing is a toy dog on wheels to push around!"

"'Til death do us part," mused Geoffrey. "Does that mean in heaven I'm single?" he enquired of no one in particular.

"This isn't getting us anywhere," I interjected, trying to bring some sanity back to the proceedings.

"So," Eileen continued, turning her attention back to Jess and me. "For one last time, are you going to lock the old duffer up?"

"For one last time: NO!" I replied emphatically.

Suddenly, Eileen swung open the cabinet door and pulled out a large carving knife from within. In one swift, fluid movement, she raised it above her head, holding the handle with both hands. "THEN I'LL KILL MYSELF!" she shrieked, bringing the knife down in a dramatic arc towards her stomach.

The next couple of seconds were a blur as Jess instinctively turned and pushed Geoffrey away from the danger, whilst I dived towards our she-devil. There wasn't time to draw my spray or press the emergency button or to even think – I just had to get the weapon out of her grasp. My outstretched hands grabbed her wrists, the momentum sending us both crashing into the sideboard. I heard the knife clatter as it fell to the floor. In an instant Jess was by my side, kicking it out of harm's way.

It had all happened so fast. In a matter of minutes events had escalated from a conversation in bed to an attempted suicide – and all because of a few potatoes. I could barely believe what had occurred.

As I lay across Eileen, sweat forming on my brow and with my mouth dry from the exertion, she broke the silence. "Oh, you silly man! I wasn't really going to kill myself. That was a John Lewis own brand carving knife. If I was going to kill myself I would have used my classic Henckels gourmet knife. I do have standards, you know."

"Never knowingly undersold," was all I could think of to say.

"As for you," she hissed over my shoulder at a bewildered Geoffrey, "this is all your doing, you old buffoon."

"Charming!" he muttered back.

"And you can let go of my wrists now," she snapped, turning to me. "This is police brutality, you utter moron!"

I extracted myself from my prone position and pushed myself up, not sure whether I had actually witnessed a genuine suicide attempt or if I was just part of some elaborate play-acting.

"Come on, Eileen," said Jess, reaching out her hand. "I'll help you up."

Eileen grasped my colleague's hand and pulled her floorwards towards her before delivering a stinging slap across Jess' face with her free hand. "It's Mrs Crawford to you!"

Jessica reeled from the blow. "Well, Mrs Crawford, you are now under arrest for assault on a police constable," my colleague curtly informed her as I grabbed her wrists again and started to apply the handcuffs. "You do not have to say anything but..." The rest of her words were lost in the commotion as the situation descended into a frenzied tangle of arms and legs. Trying to cuff a drunken woman is like trying to cuff an octopus.

Finally, when Eileen had exhausted herself and the cuffs had been applied, she realised the game was up and her demeanour changed as she slumped to the ground.

Appeals to our better nature then began: pleas for sympathy and general begging not to be taken away were interspersed with requests for Geoffrey to intercede on her behalf. Eventually, her husband came over and knelt down beside her. Everything went quiet for about thirty seconds before the silence gave way to a series of noises not dissimilar to the sound of whales communicating with one another in the depths of the ocean. Jess and I exchanged bewildered looks on realising that the noises were coming from both Mr and Mrs Crawford. Slowly, Geoffrey raised his right hand and offered it to his wife. In response, Eileen raised her cuffed left hand and slowly stretched it towards her husband. The little fingers on each of their hands were then extended until they were touching... and then entwined.

"Pinkie promise?" beseeched Geoffrey in a hushed tone.

"Pinkie promise," came the barely audible reply from Eileen.

With the bizarre ritual now complete and the solemn

oath undertaken, Geoffrey rose to his feet, cleared his throat and informed us that he had reached an agreement with his wife. Apparently, there would be no further need for any police involvement and, if we could just release her from her manacles, from this point on he would take full responsibility for her welfare.

"I think it's a bit late for that now," I remarked to Geoffrey, and told him that his wife would be coming with us, pinkie promise or no pinkie promise. "She's just assaulted my colleague."

"Please. I'll be good now," intoned our sorrowful prisoner, adopting a childlike voice for best effect. "It's the drink that does it," she conceded.

"Maybe alcohol doesn't love you back," I suggested to her. I decided to leave out the bit about going to Alchitraz.

"But we've got the vicar coming over for tea," voiced Geoffrey, as though willing me to provide him with a solution to his afternoon dilemma.

"Well, I hardly think Mrs Crawford is in a very Jesus-y mood," I concluded. I toyed with suggesting that he inform the vicar that the Karma had just run over the Dogma, but decided to save it for another day.

As we brought her to her feet, Eileen decided to summarise what she thought of us. "Oh, you bunch of cu…"

"Can we stop that, please?" Jess interjected just in time. "If you can't be nice, at least have the decency to be vague."

The Queen of False Alarms was then led out into the police car and conveyed the short journey back to custody. En route we had to explain over and over again to our charge why she'd been arrested as clearly, in her mind, she'd done nothing wrong. When we reached the station she asserted this belief again, in no uncertain terms, to the custody sergeant, before informing him that she had a doctorate in Fine Arts and that there was no way on earth that she was going into a cell like a common criminal. Demands were also made to see someone with 'real' authority who would sort this issue out once and for all; and once she had spoken to her friends in high places heads would roll, and they would have her out of this place 'in a flash'. Indeed, according to Eileen Crawford, hell would freeze over before she was incarcerated in Sandford Police Station.

Five minutes later, I opened the viewing flap to the cell.

"Hello, Mrs Crawford."

"And why are you here again?" she replied contemptuously.

"Because apparently stone smashes scissors." It was true – I had lost out to Jess in the deciding game. I was going to choose paper, but had changed my mind on the second shake. I can appreciate the animosity between scissors and paper, but rock? Clearly, he was just coming over for a fight!

"I've come to ask if you'd like a cup of tea or coffee?"

"Why don't you go fuck yourself!" was her reply.

I took that as a no.

# CHAPTER 5

# Indecent Proposal

"Report of a male sitting in a car outside Sugar Rush Primary School *'furiously masturbating'* according to the headmistress."

As soon as I heard the call, I tipped my cup of tea into the sink and raced into the parade room to see if any vehicle keys were hanging up on the board. Gwen had obviously had the same idea and was already reaching for a set. We had arrived for the late shift and had been making a brew in preparation for the briefing when the message had halted us in our tracks. The school day was nearly at an end and the area would soon be awash with children. The last thing we needed was a paedophile in their midst. The police station was just around the corner from the school and in all probability we would get there before any of the day shift could respond. Within seconds, we were in the car and pulling out of the yard, lights on but no sirens; we didn't want to spook our predator. Ideally, if we could catch him in the act, we would have a decent, albeit indecent, case with which to bring him before the courts.

I radioed Comms, telling them that we were on our way, but had to cut the dispatcher off mid-sentence as only moments later we were at the school. There was a long line of cars outside as parents waited patiently for their children to finish class. A quick glance at the entrance to the building revealed the head and her receptionist peeking out through the blinds and feverishly pointing over towards the car in question. I switched on the body-mounted camcorder that we had all now been issued with; although I didn't relish the prospect of having footage of a male pleasuring himself, this would provide irrefutable evidence. I checked my watch: it was almost half past three; the place would soon be swarming with small children and I didn't want them seeing this. I jumped out of the car and ran, crouching along the line of parked cars so as not to alert our quarry. Gwen, meanwhile, accelerated our vehicle, driving alongside the suspect's car in order to block any potential escape route. Just as the panda braked into position, I reached the target vehicle and whipped open the driver's door before he had time to react. The suspect was so engrossed in his occupation that his hand was still a virtual blur. I quickly took the keys out of the ignition to further ensure that he couldn't get away and then stood back to get a clearer view of him…

"Oh, I am sorry, sir." The man stared up at me in shock. I quickly waved over at Gwen, indicating that she should stay in the car, but it was already too late; before I had a chance to stop her, Gwen had thrown open his passenger door, and triumphantly shouted: "You filthy beast!"

As the male turned towards her, a bewildered expression on his face, all my colleague could do was mumble, "Oh, dear!" as the horrible realisation swept over her. She slowly withdrew, closed the door gently and went and sat back in the car. I curtly waved her off, signalling for her to park elsewhere, and then carefully reinserted the gentleman's keys back in his ignition. I apologised once more, explaining that there had been a terrible mistake, before slowly clicking his door shut and going in search of the caller.

As I made my way up the path to the school, I glanced over at our police car and saw Gwen inside, attempting to make herself look as inconspicuous as possible. But I wasn't going to let her get away with it that easily! I gave her a shout over the radio, insistent that she should come and join me. She reluctantly got out of the car and slowly walked over to the school entrance, her hands in her pockets, trying to look as nonchalant as possible. We were buzzed in and made our way to the head's office where the reception committee was eagerly waiting for us.

"Did you catch the pervert?" they queried in unison. "Can I let the children out now? Is it safe?"

"I think you can let the kids out now," I ventured. "And I think it best that we don't refer to him as a pervert any more either."

From their expressions, I could see some further explanation was required.

"He wasn't masturbating – furiously or otherwise," I told them. "He was actually rubbing away at a lottery scratch card. There was a small pile of them on the passenger seat next to him. He was just filling in time until his son came out of school. We surprised him mid-scratch."

"Oh, dear God!" spluttered the head. "He must have been mortified when you accused him?"

"Thankfully, I managed to avoid that particular embarrassment," I informed her. "I diverted the conversation by pretending that I was just really keen to see if he'd had any winners."

It had been obvious to me that the poor man was still in shock when he had spoken to me; after all, it's not every day that you are sitting in your car, minding your own business, when two police officers violently yank open the door – one of whom accuses you of being a filthy beast, while the other politely enquires if you've had any luck on the instant wins! I stared hard at Gwen, but she would do anything but meet my gaze.

"And did he have any luck?" enquired the receptionist hesitantly, keen to salvage some sort of positive ending to this sorry incident.

"He did, actually," I clarified, "which probably accounts for the reason he kept looking up with a smug grin on his face every now and again between rubbings."

"Well, *that's* what made me think he was doing a *selfie*," asserted the head.

"A SELFIE!" declared the receptionist, clearly confused. "Just to clarify here, Alison, what exactly do you think a selfie is?"

"Well, it's Australian slang for touching yourself, self-abuse... for masturbating," came the reply from the head, as though she were reading from a thesaurus.

"Oh, my Lord!" sighed her colleague. "So what on earth did you think I was referring to when I came back from my holidays and told you I did a selfie on top of the Eiffel Tower?"

"Well, I did wonder why you were being so candid with me," confessed her boss. "And so proud of the fact, too," she added in an embarrassed whisper.

"Good grief!" cried the exasperated receptionist. "A selfie is a photograph that you take of yourself!"

"And when you told me you had a selfie stick..."

"Oh, please!" exclaimed the indignant receptionist. "Is that why your husband always gives me such an odd look when he picks you up?"

The head chose to ignore the last comment, and instead tried to change the subject by saying that they really should press on with sending the letters out to parents about the next school trip.

"Would you mind giving me a hand with these?" she asked her assistant.

"Sure," came the muted response.

"C'mon. Sound a little more enthusiastic!" her boss encouraged, trying to sound upbeat as she grabbed a handful of notices.

"YEAH, DON'T I JUST LOVE STUFFING ENVELOPES!" declared her assistant sarcastically.

"Rachel, a word please – in private."

As a distinctly frosty atmosphere descended, Gwen and I took the opportunity to quietly slip out of the office, hoping that our own faux pas would soon be forgotten now that the head and her secretary appeared to be reviewing the very foundations of their working relationship.

We travelled back into town in silence: today hadn't been one of our finest moments. We were just heading back past Tesco when Gwen spoke again, informing me that she needed the loo. She drove into the car park, pulled up abruptly and, just as quickly, was off. I sat aimlessly in the car for a few minutes until I realised that she hadn't even left a gap in the window for me. Admittedly, I'm not a dog and it wasn't hot, but that's beside the point! Just as I was bemoaning Gwen's inconsideration, I saw a girl I recognised, and jumped out to have a quick chat with her. A minute later, Gwen reappeared, so I said my goodbyes and got back in the vehicle.

"Did something weird just happen when I went to the toilet?" my colleague queried.

"Quite possibly," I replied. "You told me you had three bowls of All-Bran this morning."

"No," she continued, ignoring my quip. "Did I really hear you say to that girl: 'even Hitler had a girlfriend'?"

"I was trying to make her feel better," I explained.

"Feel better?" asked Gwen quizzically. "Please enlighten me as to how on earth telling someone about the relationship status of the most evil dictator in history could possibly make them feel better?"

"I don't think you understand the idiom," I protested.

"I think you'll find it's pronounced 'idiot', actually."

I gave a heavy sigh. "Well, my doubting Thomas, I shall tell you, and then you shall duly understand and following on from that, I shall then accept your humble apology."

"Go on, then," she challenged. "Try me."

"It all started a week ago," I began. "It was a day shift. I was patrolling past the posh apartments on Shakespeare Road, when a clearly flustered young woman almost jumped out in front of me as she tried to stop the car."

I explained to Gwen that after managing to calm her down, the female in question had informed me of her dilemma. It seems that the previous evening, whilst she had been out drinking with her friends, she had been chatted up by a handsome man. One thing had led to another: his cheesy chat-up lines had resulted in a few more drinks, and, eventually, she had ended up at his place where, she told me, they had shared an intimate night together. When she had woken up the next morning her new lover had already gone to work and she was left alone in his flat. Walking around dressed in one of his oversized white work shirts – just like they do in the movies – she had perused his book and music collections, admiring his taste and in awe of his style. She even recalled wondering to herself how lucky she had been that fate had brought them together in that anonymous bar in Sandford.

Making her way into the kitchen, she had then seen that he had thoughtfully left a mug out for her next to the percolator which had filled the air with that wonderful, rich roast coffee aroma; alongside it on a scrap of paper he had sketched a cherub holding a bow and arrow. She poured herself a cup, smiling inwardly and knowing in her heart of hearts that she had finally found 'the one'.

After getting ready, and just before leaving, she had popped to the loo, but, unfortunately, the toilet wouldn't flush. The last thing she wanted her ideal man to see when he returned home from work was her faeces lying at the bottom of the bowl! Undaunted, she found a plastic bag in one of the cupboards under the sink and returned to the bathroom to scoop out the offending motion to dispose of later in a bin outside. She was just about to leave the flat when she realised that she hadn't given the new love of her life her contact details and so quickly ran back into the kitchen where she added a heart under the picture of the cherub, along with her name and number. She left the note in the exact same place on the bench, complete with a lipstick kiss.

She then finally departed with an enormous smile on her face and feeling as if she was floating on air until, however, she clicked the door closed behind her and the horrible realisation suddenly swept over her that she was no longer in possession of the bag of poop! Her blood ran cold and a horrified expression crossed her face, as it dawned on her that she had left the fresh turd in a clear plastic bag next to the note on the bench. There was nothing she could do except have a panic attack, which finally culminated in her running out into the street and flagging me down.

"She wanted me to break into apartment number three so she could retrieve her number two," I explained, "but, alas, I had to inform her that we are here to stop people doing that sort of thing." There's a reason why cupid rhymes with stupid…

As Gwen sat, open-mouthed, I explained that I had just seen the girl in question, and had asked if she had heard from the guy. She said she hadn't, and told me she despaired of ever finding a boyfriend.

"That's when I told her that even Hitler had a girlfriend – to give her hope."

"Heavens above!" declared Gwen. "Remind me to never ask you for relationship advice!"

I told my crewmate that it couldn't actually have been *that* much of a traumatic event for the girl as she had disclosed to me that she had written to a magazine problem page about her plight and had even had her letter published.

"Which magazine?" Gwen asked, clearly intending to look it up.

"Well, that's the bizarre thing," I told her. "I think it was a French magazine about cats."

"*Chat*?" sighed Gwen, shaking her head. "I dread to imagine what you think the *TV Times* is about."

Before I had time to offer my thoughts on the matter a call came through on the police car radio. A woman was kicking off in a chemist shop in the town centre. The blues and the sirens were switched on, and we were off.

"Apparently," Comms added, "she's got a priest with her."

We exchanged glances. "Good God!" I exclaimed. "You'd think that he would be calming her down!"

A minute later, we were parked up and running to the shop. Entering, we stepped over several shelving displays that had been knocked over, their contents scattered over the floor. Behind the counter we could see the staff, huddled together. In the opposite corner a woman was sat on the floor snoring, with her legs splayed out in front of her and a half empty bottle of wine lying between them. The smell of drink emanating from her was almost overpowering. She looked dishevelled and unkempt, but what was most striking about her were her hands and face – they were bright yellow.

"What's been going on here?" I asked, keeping a wary eye on our suspect as I glanced around for her accomplice.

It transpired that the woman had entered the pharmacy and informed staff that although she didn't have a prescription, she wondered if it would still be possible to have a bag of cocaine. When the staff had politely declined, she had gone berserk; screaming and shouting, pulling over displays and kicking at anything and everything in sight.

"The priest smashed the cough sweets," the pharmacist added, pointing to a pile of broken packets littering the counter. Well, at least he hadn't been as violent as our snorer, although it did seem a bit out of character for a man of the cloth. Perhaps someone had told the old joke about sucking a Fisherman's Friend one too many times and he had lost it. We all have our breaking point.

"And where is he now?" I queried.

"Where's who?" she replied.

"The priest," I stressed. It seemed like an obvious question to me. "Is he still here?"

"There's the priest!" she answered, looking at me as if I was completely stupid, whilst pointing to the floor.

I looked down but could only see a small wooden baton. I looked back up at her, still none the wiser.

"The priest," she repeated. "The priest!" She was beginning to sound like that annoying person in every game of Pictionary whose drawing is indecipherable, yet they just keep circling it over and over until we all die. I shrugged my shoulders again, adding a raise of the eyebrows for good measure. As she repeated herself again, I had flashbacks of Tattoo in *Fantasy Island* telling his boss that the plane had arrived.

"I guess you're not a fisherman." There was more than a hint of exasperation in her voice.

"No, and I'm not a fisherman's friend either before you ask," I stated, covering all bases just in case that was her next question.

"Well, my husband is," she explained. "A fisherman," she clarified with a sigh before I could say anything else. "And that's what they call one of those batons. A *priest* is a tool for quickly killing fish after you catch them. Apparently, it comes from the notion of administering the 'last rites' to them."

"Thanks for the history lesson," I told her, "but if you had just said she had a stick that would have been fine." She shrugged and mouthed a 'whatever'.

Meanwhile, Gwen was with the sleeping woman, kneeling down beside her and examining her hands. "So what's this?" she asked, glancing over at the pharmacist.

"Lemsip," came the response. "She started to open packets and packets of Lemsip, and was snorting it and rubbing it all over her face. I don't know, maybe she thought it was lemon-flavoured cocaine?"

Indeed, amongst all the other debris, there were dozens of opened cold-remedy packets littering the floor. I wondered if such a thing as flavoured cocaine actually existed. I also hoped that it wouldn't give the drug dealers any new marketing ideas.

"Has she taken anything else?"

"She seemed to be necking anything she could get her hands on," she replied; "tearing packets open and washing it all down with her wine."

I called for an ambulance before crouching down next to Gwen.

"Isn't that Iona Rocket?" she whispered to me. I stared at the face in front of me and imagined it without the yellow dusting. It was. Iona had her problems, but she wasn't usually violent. I wondered what had tipped her over the edge.

"C'mon, wake up, Iona," I coaxed her, shaking her by the shoulders. "She's well known to us," I commented, turning to the pharmacist. "She's a local alcoholic."

"I'm NOT an alcoholic," declared Iona indignantly, momentarily waking from her slumber. "An alcoholic *needs* a drink. I already *have* a drink," she mumbled, fumbling for her bottle. "So I'm good, and you can fuck off now!" With that, her chin dropped onto her chest once more and within a few seconds the snoring had recommenced. Gwen moved the bottle out of her reach, and we both stood up, awaiting the arrival of the paramedics. It wasn't long until our friends, Lysa and Steve, came climbing over the detritus towards us with their big green bag of medical kit. I showed them the wine bottle and then explained what we believed Iona had taken. Soon Lysa was kneeling next to her, trying to rouse her and establish exactly what she had consumed. Iona coughed and spluttered, and then was sick on the floor.

"Wine into vomit," commented Lysa, dryly; "your move, Jesus!"

Usually, at this point I might have made a priest joke but I didn't particularly want to give the chemist any credit after her attitude towards me regarding my lack of knowledge of fishing protocol.

"She can clean that up, too!" declared the pharmacist.

"Calm your tits, love!" slurred an inebriated Iona in a defiant response.

"Calm my tits!" the chemist responded, clearly incensed. "They're an A cup! How much calmer do you think they're going to get?"

We decided that now was the time to beat a hasty retreat, before it all descended into a full-scale tit-for-tat argument. Ten minutes later and we were following the paramedics down to the hospital. Iona had lashed out just as we had put her in the vehicle and we wanted to make sure she behaved herself for the rest of the journey. On arrival, we provided the welcoming committee as she alighted from the ambulance.

"I've come to trade a kidney for vodka!" she shouted as we wheeled her into A&E.

"She hasn't really," I explained to a foreign-looking couple, who were clearly wondering what the NHS had been reduced to since the funding cuts.

Once Iona had been safely delivered into the care of the nursing staff, I carefully cleaned my hands with some hand-sanitiser which, I've discovered, always acts as a helpful reminder if you've forgotten that you've got a paper cut. We bid our goodbyes to Ms Rocket and were just about to leave when a ward Sister came running over to us.

"Thank God you got here so quickly!"

I didn't think we had driven particularly fast, but I am always happy to receive a little praise and recognition – it makes a pleasant change! I smiled, and thanked her before continuing towards the exit.

"You are here for the patient who has barricaded himself in the toilet, aren't you?" she queried, taking hold of my arm.

"Not as such," Gwen responded. "We've just escorted a woman with a possible overdose to A&E, but since we're here we'll see what we can do."

This wasn't even our patch. The hospital we were at belonged to the next policing area, Delta Section, but it looked like Gwen had just volunteered us for the job and so we followed the Sister along the corridor while she explained the situation. We soon discovered that a young cancer patient – with drip in tow – had made his way to the toilets where he had then proceeded to barricade himself in. Simon had recently undergone surgery to have a testicle removed and was now convinced that he had contracted HIV from a blood transfusion. Believing that no one was taking his concerns seriously, he had blockaded himself in the bathroom. He claimed he had a knife, and had threatened to harm himself or anyone who tried to get him out. The Sister further explained that they had tried to reason with him but had failed, hence the call to the police. She ended by emphasising the need for him to be back on the ward as soon as possible.

As we climbed the stairs, I instinctively shook my pepper spray in case it was needed. Gwen, on the other hand, had different ideas. She prided herself on her communication skills; on her ability to diffuse a potentially volatile situation by reasoning with the subject rather than resorting to physical force. There was no denying it: she had a knack of connecting with people and resolving issues using brain rather than brawn. She placed a hand on my shoulder and said that she would talk to Simon.

"I'll get him to come just by using my mouth," she announced to the small crowd of medical staff gathered outside. As soon as she saw the horrified look on the Sister's face, and heard the stifled sniggers from the other nurses, she realised what she had just said and immediately clasped both hands over her mouth, as if she wanted to stuff the words back in; but it was too late.

Shooting Gwen a disapproving glare, the Sister instead ushered me towards the toilet door. I cleared my throat, and then told the spectators to move back, all the while desperately trying to think of an opening line. However, even before I could introduce myself, the door opened and a hand beckoned me inside. I bent down to waist-level and tentatively peered around the opening. If anyone was waiting to thrust a knife in my eye, I'd at least be at the wrong height. The patient in question, though, had retreated to the back of the washroom and was now leaning against his drip, his gown hanging open. Registering what was now in my direct line of sight, I instantly regretted my decision to crouch down.

"I think you've got it on back to front," I told him.

He grunted and pulled the two sides together. "Promise you won't rush at me?" he pleaded.

"I promise," I replied, edging into the room. Well, not while the front of his gown was hanging open anyway! Gwen, meanwhile, took up position on the other side of the door.

"I'll kill myself if you do," he threatened, showing me a blunt butter knife. "I really mean it!"

"I believe you, Simon," I reassured him. "I believe you've got the ball to do it."

"I just need someone to talk to," he confessed, his voice wavering.

"I'm not really the right person... I don't know anything about medicine, but..."

"No, that's not the point!" he interrupted. "Look, I know they'll check to see if I've got HIV. I just needed to talk to a man about... other things." He seemed to be embarrassed, looking down at his bare feet to avoid eye contact.

"I'll help if I can," I responded, hoping that there

weren't any questions about Pre-Raphaelite poetry... or penguins.

"I want to talk about women," he began. "You look like a man of the world."

I could hear my colleague sniggering on the other side of the door. I chose to ignore her, instead inviting Simon to continue. It appeared that his main concern wasn't about the operation or the blood transfusion – that was merely a smokescreen. What he really wanted to know was if women would still be attracted to him now that he was, in his words, only 'half a man'.

"You know, statistically," I told him, "everyone in the world only has one testicle." For some reason he didn't find that very reassuring. I decided to take another tack and advised that what most women were really interested in was what was on the inside, rather than physical appearance. I tried to sound convincing, but, in the back of my mind, I kept hearing Gwen's voice telling me that: 'You can tell a lot about a man by the type of shoes he wears,' and then Jess when she informed me that she found 'men with a sense of humour really attractive... well, except for the ugly ones'.

Simon questioned me further on how a female would be able to tell what he was really like as a person when she first met him. To be honest, I had no idea. All I knew from bitter experience is that you never ask a woman if she's pregnant unless you can see an actual baby being born, and even then you should always act surprised. However, I didn't think this pearl of wisdom would be of any help in this particular instance. Instead, I decided to bluff it out.

"A woman just knows," I responded confidently.

"Which woman?"

I wasn't prepared for that! Simon went on to tell me that he was a virgin; how he had been saving himself for the right lady, but thought that now it was probably too late. Due to his operation, he felt that he would probably never have sex with a woman. In the circumstances, it was just as well he hadn't heard Gwen's earlier offer! He told me that he thought he looked like a freak. I tried to tell him that he was wrong, and that no doubt he'd go on to have a very fulfilling life, but I was floundering and running out of examples to use to convince him.

"HITLER!" I could hear my colleague hissing through the door. "Tell him about Hitler! He only had one…" I quickly pushed the door shut, and then asked Simon what he knew about the Weimar Republic.

Twenty minutes later, I was helping my new friend push his drip back to his ward. He was a brave young man and, with the right treatment, I was certain he'd recover quickly. As the nurses helped him into bed, the Sister came and thanked me for all my help. I must admit, I was feeling pretty proud of myself. I must have said something right as Simon seemed to be looking a lot happier. As I prepared to leave, I shook his hand and wished him all the best, telling him to keep me updated on his progress.

"Remember what I told you about women," I quipped with a wink. "And as for the HIV thing, just stay positive!"

As I walked out, Gwen, the Sister and the couple of nurses standing nearby shot me a horrified look … and I thought they hadn't heard the dating advice!

"You're unbelievable!" Gwen informed me as we got back into our police car. I thanked her, but she just gave me a strange look and shook her head.

She then dropped me off back at the station, while she continued on to the chemist to get a statement and collect the CCTV in relation to Iona Rocket's rampage. I sauntered happily into the parade room to see Lloyd looking at a map on the computer showing the town's crime hotspots.

"What's occurring?"

"Inspector Soaper has set up a mini operation," he

replied, looking up from the screen. "He wants a couple of us to take a plain car out at the end of the shift. I've volunteered, but he still needs another body. Go next door and see him now. It should be interesting!"

It sounded like it might be fun. There had been a spate of thefts from vehicles, and the chance to catch the culprits red-handed was just too good to miss. I marched next door to where the inspector was chatting to our sergeant.

"Good evening, Inspector," I announced as I poked my head around the door. "Good evening to you too, Sergeant."

My offer was readily accepted by the inspector, and a few hours later Lloyd and I were scouring the streets in an unmarked CID car looking for the thieves. Eventually, at around midnight, we parked up in a back lane and were keeping obs on a couple of vehicles that seemed to be getting an undue amount of attention from the occupants of a small hatchback that had driven by several times already. So far, our operation hadn't yielded any results but this could be our big opportunity. We sat in the dark in silence, staying low in our seats, engine off, just waiting for them to make their move. It was only a matter of time.

The display on my radio suddenly lit up indicating a private call was about to come through. I quickly covered it up with my hand so as to not give away our presence.

"John, we've got a job for you." It was Nancy in Comms. She sounded apologetic before she had even passed out the details.

"We're on an operation," I whispered back. "And we're off in an hour. Can't any of the night shift do it?"

"They're all committed. You're the only unit available, and the sergeant has specifically asked for you."

I looked at Lloyd. We were tantalisingly close to catching our car thieves, but ours is not to question why.

"What's the job?"

"I'm sorry about this," she continued, "but we need

you to check on a boy who has inserted his finger in a potato."

"You are joking, aren't you?"

"Sadly, no. His father rang the NHS helpline at about seven o'clock this evening saying his four-year-old son had put his finger in some hot mash, and was crying. He was advised to bring him into accident and emergency, but he didn't turn up. Apparently, they've reviewed their calls and now they want someone to go out and check if the child's ok."

"I'm confused," I replied. "We're the police."

"Don't make it any more awkward for me," pleaded Nancy. "I'm just the messenger. The NHS has contacted us with the request, and now the sergeant wants you to check on him."

"The guy's wife will have been out when it happened," I ventured, "and when she's returned, he'll have told her about the potato incident, and said that he's rung the medical helpline. I bet she'll have told him not to have been so silly, and that he should just have run the boy's finger under a cold tap. That's why he won't have turned up!"

"Probably," came the weary response. "But, be that as it may, can I put you down as attending?"

"Go on, then. Seeing as it's you."

We left our position, but not before driving to the target cars and getting out so the passing hatchback could clearly see that we were police before it sped off into the night. We then drove to our destination in one of the small villages on the outskirts of town, scarcely believing that our operation had been called off for this.

The house was in darkness as we pulled up onto the long, gravel drive. The sound of chimes echoed down the hallway when we rang the bell. We paced up and down outside in the cold air in an effort to try and keep ourselves warm. After a couple more rings a light appeared in an upstairs' bedroom followed by the hall and then an outside light came on, illuminating us before the front door was finally opened. A startled-looking woman in a black silk nightie rubbed her sleepy eyes and pulled a thick dressing gown around her as she asked what was wrong.

Embarrassed, I stated the reason why we had arrived at her door in the early hours of the morning. Visibly relieved, she took it in good humour, telling us that she had gone out for the day and that when she had returned her husband had explained about the potato incident.

"I told him he was silly for ringing the hospital, and to just put Elliot's finger under the cold tap!"

"I thought as much," I replied, exchanging a knowing glance with Lloyd. The woman's husband had now also come to the door to find out what had necessitated two police officers calling at their home at such an unearthly hour.

"While I explain things to your husband, is it ok if my partner goes and sees your son?" asked my colleague. The woman nodded, and I followed her into the house. Lloyd and I would only be questioned by our superiors if we didn't actually physically check on the child. I apologised for the disturbance as I accompanied her through the house.

"So, you're partners?" she queried as we made our way up the stairs, "and they let you work together? That's very open-minded of the police."

"No, not partners like that," I corrected her. "Not that there's anything wrong with that, but we're not *together,* if you know what I mean." For emphasis, I used air quotes as I uttered the word 'together'.

"Oh, I see," she replied as we reached the bedroom, but she appeared to be only half listening. Opening the door, she peered into the gloom, her voice dropping to a whisper as she pointed out her son. The room was pitch black except for a dim night light glowing from a plug socket. I got out my torch and shone it near the bed to illuminate the scene, careful not to wake the child with the main beam. I could see him, stretched out, sound asleep under his Gruffalo duvet. To my untrained medical eye, he appeared to be fit and well. We crept out and back to the front room where Lloyd and the husband were still chatting. We apologised once again for disturbing them before starting to make our way back to our vehicle.

"So, are you on all night?" asked the wife, snuggling up to her husband for warmth.

"Nope," replied Lloyd, smiling. "Shift is just about over. We're both off to bed now."

As the woman smirked and gave me a knowing wink, I quickly got into the passenger seat.

"What was all that about?" asked my colleague starting the engine.

"Don't ask!" I hissed. "Just drive!"

CHAPTER 6

# The Ginger Bread Man

"I have a particular set of skills; skills that I have acquired over a very long career. Skills that make me a nightmare for people like you. I will look for you, I will find you, and I will kill you." I even put on my best Liam Neeson accent as I misquoted his line from the film *Taken*. Unfortunately, my sister didn't seem to appreciate me adding this hint of realism to the proceedings and, as a result, I've been banned from ever again playing hide-and-seek with my ten-year-old niece.

The point I'm making is that not all threats to kill are meant to be taken seriously. However, whenever someone reports such a threat to the police and, believe me, with the advent of Facebook and social media they do report them on an ever-increasing basis, we have to investigate each and every incident.

It was a quiet Saturday afternoon and I was currently sitting on a sofa in a house on the Red Estate, with my pocket notebook open and resting on my knee, listening to one such report. Helen, the female sitting opposite me, was in her early forties, slightly orange in hue and was sporting a revealingly short dress. As yet, I wasn't sure if she was planning a night on the town, or had just returned from one.

She explained that she had separated from her husband, Tom, last November and that he had moved out of the family home and into rented accommodation whilst they talked things through. At first, relations between them had been fairly amicable but, a few months later, he had found out that she had been seeing someone else or, as he had apparently described him, 'a fucking toy boy'.

The woman's young boyfriend, Ryan, the aforementioned toy boy, was sitting next to her on the sofa, ignoring everything that was being said. He looked to be about nineteen; baseball cap on back to front, baggy tracksuit and bright white trainers.

It soon became apparent that Ryan wasn't just her friend with benefits – he was her friend *on* benefits, too. With his pasty skin and hatred of manual labour, he would have been a big hit in Georgian society. Apparently, according to Helen, when they met it was love at first sight. Despite the fact she wasn't even divorced yet, he had already proposed and Helen proudly showed me her engagement ring. Personally, I can't understand why they aren't called a 'Kneel Diamond'.

Her fiancé hadn't looked up from the moment I'd arrived, and continued to be completely engrossed in rubbing his finger back and forth across his lap. I had assumed it was his phone nestled in his crotch, although I suppose a hamster could have been getting the stroking of its life. I thought it best not to dwell on what the third option might be...

"And that's when he said that he would kill me." Helen's words derailed my unpleasant train of thought; thankfully, there were no survivors. I scribbled the statement down in my notebook and glanced back up at her.

She appeared quite shocked as she uttered those chilling words, although I wasn't sure if this was due to genuine consternation or because she appeared to have shaved off her actual eyebrows and pencilled in a new set slightly too high on her forehead.

"And how serious do you take this threat?" I asked. The sixty-four thousand dollar question.

There was a short pause whilst she looked down at

her boyfriend's crotch, either to see what game he was playing or to check on the well-being of the small mammal. "I dunno," she replied, not even bothering to look up. "But when he says he'll do summat, he always does it! He's said he'd kill me before."

"So he doesn't *always* do it, then?" I didn't want to appear pedantic, but it was quite an important point. "I mean, you're still alive now."

"Yeah, but he meant it *this* time." She looked up and we had eye contact again. She then began to describe how unhappy her relationship with her husband had been; how he hadn't supported her when she had needed him most and that meant that he had now forfeited his chance to have her back.

"I told him," she informed me, "if you can't handle me at my Lindsay Lohan, you don't deserve me at my Beyoncé." She explained that her husband hadn't been there for her when she had been feeling down. Clearly, Ryan was here now to feel her up.

I asked Comms to check the police systems for information on her husband, but he wasn't recorded as having any previous offences. I told Helen as much – not to contradict her assertion, but rather in a bid to allay her fears; instead, it had the opposite effect as Helen and her new partner now seemed at pains to tell me what a nasty piece of work her husband, Thomas Gwain, really was.

"Tell the copper how jealous he is," the boy suggested, swiping his finger vigorously across his lap – that poor hamster!

"Oh yeah," the female informed me. "He said if he can't have me, no one can."

"Tell him about the sex," he added.

"Oi! Cheeky!" the woman squealed, slapping his knee. "We're trying for a baby, Officer."

"No, not me! Him!" Clearly, the rodent was very demanding, as he didn't even stop the stroking for a second to look up as he served his rebuke.

"Oh yeah." She leant towards me and her expression changed as if she wanted to convey that as this involved her ex-partner, carnal dealings now had to be spoken of in hushed undertones. "I think he must be one of them sex addicts." She quickly looked over her shoulder and around the room, as though checking to see if anyone else was listening, before continuing in a conspiratorial whisper. "He always wanted it – morning, noon and night; anytime, anyplace, anywhere. I used to have to beat him off with my bare hands!" She sat back and crossed her arms, leaving me with a particularly unpleasant image in my head.

"Look, I think I've got the idea now," I informed her, symbolically closing my book. I felt we were going a little off topic, and I wasn't overly keen on hearing the ins and outs of her punishing romantic schedule; but I had thrown out a hint that they had failed to catch.

"Tell him how rough he liked it," the boyfriend droned.

"No, please don't!" But it was too late. My words appeared to have fallen on deaf ears as she seemed intent on telling me every gory detail.

"Oh yes! He was very energetic in the bedroom," she was on a roll now, leaning forward again, uncomfortably invading my personal space, "and in the kitchen and the…"

"Yes, yes, I think I've got the picture, thank you, Mrs Gwain."

"Tell him about your boobs." The boyfriend was at it again.

"Oh yes! He *loved* my boobs." She thrust them at me just so there could be no confusion over what we were talking about. "I'd be left with bruises all over! Bite marks on 'em and everything!"

I felt that out of politeness I had to glance at them and nod.

"Tell him about your ring!" he prompted.

Oh dear God, no! I winced in anticipation.

"And he threw my wedding ring into the garden and I still can't find it."

"Thank God for that!" I muttered as I breathed a sigh of relief.

She shot me a disapproving glance, and even phone-boy looked up from his stroking.

"No. Not nice at all," I clarified. Not nice, but not half as bad as the horrendous images that had flashed through my mind. I used their momentary silence to take back control of the conversation. "I think I've got the picture now. So, did he give any timescale or any more details about this threat?"

"Ask him yourself," the boyfriend urged, holding up his phone. "This is the number he's been calling from all day." He dialled it and thrust the ringing mobile into my hand. I felt pressurised to act, but I decided that I might as well see if I could head the whole incident off at the pass. After a few seconds, a woman answered.

"It's the police here. Can I speak to Mr Gwain, please?"

"There isn't anyone by that name here." She sounded quite well-spoken.

"Tom. Can I speak to Tom, please?" I wasn't sure if she was just playing for time.

"There's no one else here. There's just me."

I felt some urgent tugging on my arm, accompanied by feverish whispers. "She's lying! He's been ringing from there all day. I bet it's him putting on a voice."

"Look, stop this facade. I know he's there." I felt I had no option but to become a little more robust with her. "This is a serious matter, but hopefully it can all be sorted if I can just speak to him."

"But I don't know what you're on about, Officer." The voice was wavering now. I had her on the ropes.

"I think you should know that you could end up in trouble if you are covering for him – or is that you, Mr

Gwain, putting on a pathetic, feeble voice? Just tell me where you are and I'll come round."

A pregnant pause followed.

"Well, speak up. What's it going to be?" I gave my ultimatum in an authoritative tone.

"Please don't shout at me, Officer. I'm in the bungalow near the florists, just up from the library." Bingo! I'd cracked it. My pretend 'lady' was even pretending to cry now. Crocodile tears, no doubt!

"Where's that?" I probed.

"St Austell." The heavy-handed tactics had clearly worked! Hang on: did I just hear 'St Austell'?

I covered the handset and looked quizzically at the couple beside me. "She's said she's in St Austell."

"Where the fuck's that?" they chorused.

"Cornwall."

They exchanged blank looks. An uncomfortable silence descended. Cornwall was hundreds of miles away. Eventually, the boyfriend spoke up. "That's where my nana lives!"

I looked down at the phone. 'Nan' was written at the top of the screen. I shook my head in disbelief. He had rung his own grandmother and put me on the phone to her! I looked at him, anticipating some rational explanation for this debacle, but he just shrugged. I was pretty sure that somewhere a village was missing its idiot... but I wasn't entirely sure at this precise moment whether the idiot was him or me. I just had time to grit my teeth and shoot him my death glare, before I was back on the line. I had a terrible image in my head of an old woman, with a face like a wizened apple, sobbing fearfully as she cradled the handset.

"Yes, madam... I'm awfully sorry. I seem to have the wrong number... yes, you can have my name. It's PC Donoghue. No, I'm sure my sergeant won't be happy. No, nor my inspector. Yes, I'll tell him to expect a call from you..."

The wizened apple seemed to get a second wind when she realised I was on the back foot, and let me have it with both barrels. By the time she had finished with me, I felt physically drained. My face was beetroot and my ear was positively glowing!

I hadn't felt so stupid since the time an old girlfriend had rung me saying that she was bored and was just sat at home watching 'the fucking Olympics' on the television. I had immediately raced round to her place only to discover that it was just the regular Olympics.

I gave the phone back to Einstein and he pressed a few buttons before he handed it back to me.

"Never mind about me nan, this is the right number."

Never mind! NEVER MIND! So speaks a man who doesn't already have a complaint hanging over his head courtesy of Eileen Crawford for use of excessive force after I stopped her killing herself! However, before I could dwell any further on my predicament, the call was answered.

"Yeah?"

Why don't people answer the telephone by repeating the number you've just dialled like they used to in the old days? It would solve a lot of problems.

"Mr Gwain? This is the police."

"Fuck the police!"

His response didn't bode well.

"Look, Mr Gwain, I just need to speak to you about an allegation."

"Fuck the allegation! I know what you're on about! All I'm going to say is that today's a good day to die! It's me or her..." Then there was just silence. I strained to listen for any background noise that might give some possible clue as to where he was. "OR YOU, COPPER!" I was almost deafened as he bellowed down the line.

"Or me what?" I asked, slightly taken aback by his ominous afterthought.

"Or *you* are going to fucking die!" He sounded irate

that I hadn't immediately understood his threat. "Do I have to spell it out for you? It's either: her, me or you that is going to die tonight, hence my initial comment: *'today's a good day to die!'*"

"It's just that you seemed to add that bit about me *after* the killing bit was said," I explained, so he didn't think I was entirely stupid.

"Die. Her. Me. You. It's that simple." Click. Brrrrrrrrrrrr.

The line went dead. How very rude! I tried to ring back but his phone was now switched off.

"What did he say?" asked the couple, both now giving me their full attention.

"He's keeping his options open," I answered.

This was rapidly turning into a nightmare. There is only one thing worse than an angry male intent on killing someone, and that's an angry, *condescending* male intent on killing someone. If he was going to carry out his threat tonight he had to be found – sooner rather than later. Murder rates fluctuate from year to year, but what is fairly constant is the fact that over two-thirds of victims are killed by someone they know. This case was no different but I needed to know who we were looking for. I asked for a picture that I could circulate amongst my colleagues. Unfortunately, Helen had already destroyed all the photos of her husband, but did tell me that he had distinctive red hair and worked in the local bakery, although she had been made aware that he hadn't turned up for work over the last few days. I made a note that we were looking for the ginger bread man.

She added that he was a big guy and knew how to handle himself. I imagined that he'd have little choice if he was a sex addict and lived on his own.

"So where do you think he is now?" I asked.

"Trying to guess where Tom is, is like trying to predict the weather!" she replied cryptically.

"You know they can actually do that now?" I told her.

"Well, in that case, you could always try the house on the Black Estate," she conceded. "That's where he's renting." Once she had given me the address, I told her to stay inside, lock all doors and to telephone 999 if he showed up.

"He'll have to deal with me if he comes round here," stated Ryan defiantly as I left.

"Ignore him," called Helen. "He's a lover not a fighter!" … and besides, no one sounds tough when they have a set of braces on their teeth.

Returning to the station, I updated Barry, picked up Lloyd, and then headed straight to the suspect's address.

Ten minutes later, we were at the property: a new-build terraced house. Each home had a small garden at the front; small enough that the residents didn't think it was worth buying a mower to cut the grass, but big enough for it to look overgrown and untidy. The daylight was fading fast so we trod carefully, avoiding the ubiquitous dog turds along the path. The house itself was in darkness. The front door was locked so we went round the back where we found the door slightly ajar. I slowly pushed it open and glanced at Lloyd.

"Well, you said he told you someone was going to die," he whispered, "so we'd better make sure he's ok."

Now we had our reason to enter, I racked my baton and Lloyd got out his can of pepper spray as we tentatively stepped inside. There is something particularly disconcerting about searching a house when you don't know if anyone is at home; even more so when threats have been made and especially when those threats involve murder. You can never be sure what booby traps might have been set, or who might be hiding in the shadows.

It was freezing inside, suggesting that the heating hadn't been on for some time. The kitchen seemed unusually bare, too – just a half-eaten carton of Chinese takeaway on the work surface. I prodded it; it looked congealed. We had our first indication of the sort of person we were dealing with when I looked at the microwave: what sort of monster doesn't clear the unused time down?

I had searched a similar property on my own a few weeks ago after neighbours had reported that the patio door was open. On that occasion, I had got my baton out and started up the stairs, entering each room cautiously, checking for anyone inside. I had made particularly sure to keep a safe distance as I bent down to check under the beds, remembering a colleague in the north of the county who had been conducting a similar search when a hand had shot out and grabbed her ankle, like something straight out of a horror film. She had managed to press the panic button on the radio as she struggled against being dragged underneath, but it took an exhausting seven minutes of frenzied fighting before backup finally arrived.

At least there were two of us checking this place. Having someone with you more than doubles your confidence; even so, we still proceeded with caution. I flicked on the light switch, but it appeared that someone hadn't topped up the electricity meter. This wasn't exactly a good start: we would have to search by torchlight.

I'm never too sure whether it's best to go for the stealth approach, or take the overt route. If we announced our arrival he could prepare himself for a fight, but on the other hand, however, we were in his property uninvited, giving him every excuse to attack us by saying that he thought he was being burgled. I have never really trusted anyone called Tom anyway – they get up to far too much peeping and foolery for my liking. On that basis, we opted for loudly shouting "Police!" to announce our presence. There was no response. The house remained eerily silent. Cautiously, we started to move from room to room.

Downstairs was empty. We came across an occasional empty beer can and discarded pizza box, but otherwise nothing of any note. The whole house just looked like the sort of place where happiness comes to die.

We crept slowly up the stairs, keeping our backs to the wall, alert to any movement as the light from our torches cast awkward shadows in the gloom. Every few steps we stopped to listen out for the slightest sound. Apart from the noise of my own heart beating everything was deathly silent. It's funny what can spook you when you're least expecting it. It's been said that no one has felt true fear until they have been lying in bed in the middle of the night and a poster has slid off the wall.

At the top of the stairs was the bathroom. Entering, I could see that the bath was full to the brim with water. I dipped my finger in to check the temperature: it was freezing. I started to get goose-bumps. A shiver ran up my spine followed by a flashback to one of those films where someone struggles frantically for breath as their face is pushed under the water.

Next the back bedroom, where the space was bare except for a large wardrobe standing, oddly, in the centre of the room.

"What do you think is in there?" whispered Lloyd.

"It's Narnia business."

"What's none of my business?"

"It was just an inappropriate wardrobe joke…" My apology trailed away to nothing as he shot me a disapproving look.

"Sometimes, John, I seriously wonder how we are friends."

He was right to be unimpressed. The incident with the grabbing hand under the bed was obviously playing on his mind, too. I think we were both half expecting a homicidal maniac to leap out of the cupboard at any moment. With our hearts thumping, I slowly placed my hand on the door. Then, as Lloyd levelled his spray, I suddenly jerked the door back, pulling it off its hinges in the process. We both rushed forward to stop the whole thing collapsing. Damn flat-pack furniture!

The wardrobe itself was bare except for a couple of

blurry photographs lying discarded on the bottom. The snaps were distance shots of Helen Gwain and her toyboy. I didn't like the way this was going. Evidently, this guy hadn't seen many psychological thrillers: the photographs are always stuck on a cork board alongside a few press cuttings. I made a mental note to report him to the Deranged Stalkers' Union.

Finally, we were left with just the two remaining bedrooms; the sooner we finished this search the better. We each chose a door and kicked it open. I quickly entered and scanned the room – nothing except for a mattress on the floor with a worn duvet lumped on top of it. With only the diluted moonlight coming in through the net curtains it was difficult to make out if it was just laundry – or could that possibly be someone hiding underneath? I inched closer and used my baton to prod the pile.

BANG! Just then the door slammed behind me. I spun round to see an angry-looking male, dressed all in black, staring straight at me. He had something in his hand; it glinted as he quickly raised it menacingly above his head. He brought it down towards me at a lightning pace. Instinctively, I let out a cry and did the same. I made hard contact with my baton, vibrations shooting up my arm as it struck. I recoiled, waiting for his blow to strike me hard… but it never came.

Seconds later, there was an almighty smash and I was almost knocked over as Lloyd burst through the door.

"What's happened?" he demanded breathlessly.

"I think I've just killed myself in the mirror," I replied sheepishly, standing amongst the shattered remains. I had also just discovered that I make exactly the same noise if I think I see a violent male intent on murdering me as I do when I step on a piece of seaweed at the beach when I'm out for a paddle, but I thought I'd best keep that last bit of information to myself.

"You silly Welshman," muttered Lloyd.

I kicked over the duvet to make sure there was nobody hiding underneath, and satisfied that the house was empty, we returned to the office to report our findings to Barry.

"You two are like a well-oiled machine that someone forgot to oil," he informed us. "So we don't have the suspect, but, following your visit, we do have a house with a broken wardrobe and a smashed full-length mirror?"

"That's about it, Sarge," we replied.

"But you're saying that our potential victim takes the threat seriously, and from your phone conversation with him and the photos you've seen, it looks as if our suspect means business." Our sergeant was now fiercely scribbling notes as he spoke. "I'll get onto the inspector to instigate the full Threats to Life procedure. We won't be able to get a panic alarm in her place until tomorrow, but from what you're saying, it looks like he's intending to make his move tonight. I can get the night shift to do some patrols, but we'll need more than that. So, do both of you fancy some overtime?"

Overtime: keeping observations on a house at this time of year would mean standing in the freezing cold and drizzle for hours on end, waiting forlornly for something to happen. In this weather, even if we had an unmarked vehicle to plot up in, as the overnight temperature dropped the car would cool and it would become an ice block inside.

"Yeah, we'd love to, Sarge!"

Both Barry and Lloyd looked slightly taken aback by my enthusiastic response – more so Lloyd as he would be the one braving the sub-Arctic temperatures with me, but I had a reason to be so cheerful. As Barry picked up the phone to update our victim, I led Lloyd out of the office and informed him that I had a cunning plan.

"How does the old saying go?" I asked him. Who doesn't love a rhetorical question? Lloyd, by the look of it, as he stared silently back at me.

"*A good cop never gets cold, wet or hungry,*" I prompted, filling the awkward void that had quickly developed. "And neither shall we, my friend, neither shall we."

Anticipating that our potential murderer wouldn't be caught that easily, I had guessed that there would be some sort of mini operation put in place overnight. I had also assumed that I would somehow be involved. With that in mind, I'd done a bit of forward planning: I had seen that there were some new houses going up on Troy Street, just over the road from our potential victim, and so before going on our abortive manhunt I'd popped in and spoken to the saleswoman in the show home. As a result, I now held in my hand a shiny new key for one of those very same houses.

"Tonight," I explained, "we shall carry out our covert observations from the comfort of '*The Hampton: a beautiful three-bedroom starter home, ideal for the aspiring young family*', or, as we shall call it, 'John and Lloyd's overtime den'."

"And", continued Lloyd as we drove over to the address in an unmarked CID vehicle, "we shall dine in style." It seems that he had now bought into the whole overtime idea since discovering that we would be warm and cosy all night.

"Every move you make, every step you take, we'll be watching you! It's a Sting operation," I told him. He chose to ignore my last comment. He wasn't *that* overjoyed with the whole scenario to enable him to laugh at my rubbish jokes.

"I'm just a boy standing in front of a girl, who's standing in front of a guy, who's in front of a family of four." Lloyd had dropped me off at the supermarket, while he had begun setting up observations at the house. I had phoned to tell him that I was in the checkout queue with our midnight feast, and to ask if he wanted anything else.

"Yep. Get me some fruit – a banana or something."

I grabbed one and placed it on the conveyor belt along with our selection of pork pies, crisps and pop. As I did so, I heard a cough. Looking up, I saw Helen Gwain and her boyfriend, queuing at the next checkout, glaring over at me.

"I thought you were supposed to be guarding my house," she mouthed.

"My colleague is there already," I mouthed back defensively. "And I thought you were supposed to be staying in with all the doors locked." Touché.

I urged Helen to get back home with her bottle of vodka and twelve-pack of lager as quickly as she could and to then go into lockdown. Meanwhile, I took our rations back to our den.

As I took position at the window, Lloyd started on his banana. I looked over in confusion as he peeled the whole thing before starting to eat it. How bizarre! It was like taking all your clothes off just to use the toilet. I quickly glanced away before he saw me staring at him taking a bite of it. That would just have been *too* awkward.

An hour in, and our food supplies had already run out. I looked at my watch – it had just turned midnight. All conversation had died, and we now sat in the darkness, staring out of the bedroom window at the street below. A solitary lamp post illuminated the footpath outside the address.

00:30: I was busy doing the crossword, while Lloyd took his turn at staring out into the darkness. I read the clue out to my colleague: four-letter word ending in UNT, meaning 'undersized or weak person'. The answer he gave me was not only wrong, but was also probably the reason why he should never be invited to appear on *Wheel of Fortune*.

01:00: My faith in humanity was restored when I saw four guys pushing a broken-down car along the road.

That's a lovely thing to do I thought, until I realised that it could have been a stolen vehicle. I quickly contacted the night shift to tell them to keep an eye out.

01:30: One of the residents of the street was taking his dog out for its last pee before retiring to bed. We watched as the dog spent an eternity with his leg cocked against the pole, a little stream of steaming liquid running down into the gutter.

"How long did that go on for?" Lloyd asked in amazement.

"You'd think he was going for the Nobel Piss Prize," I replied.

02:00: Apart from occasional lovers returning from the local nightclub, everything was quiet. We watched the age-old courtship ritual as a couple made their way slowly up the street arm in arm, avoiding the pools of light that acted as makeshift chaperones.

02:30: We watched as the neighbours from three doors along returned home. After four failed attempts at parallel-parking, the male driver abandoned the vehicle half on and half off the kerb. As he and his partner got out of the car, I almost felt like shouting down at him to shave off his beard and give back his wife as he clearly hadn't earned either.

03:00: As Lloyd returned with two cups of tea, I produced a tin of luxury biscuits from my bag. Well, we were getting paid overtime for this, so I thought we may as well treat ourselves. My delight soon turned to consternation when, a few biscuits later, Lloyd lifted up the top tray to access a biscuit underneath. Frankly, I was shocked! You NEVER start the bottom tray before finishing the top tray! Learn your goddamn bisc-etiquette!

03:30: We were struggling to stay awake.

"John!" Ten minutes later Lloyd broke the silence. "How about him?" He nodded towards a figure slowly making his way up the street. "I hope he's a drunk and not a zombie," he chuckled.

He had a point. The male appeared to be dragging his left leg as well as having problems remaining vertical, let alone moving in a straight line. From my own personal observations of films of this genre, it would seem that most zombies die from some sort of foot-related injury. How on earth they ever managed to perform the *Thriller* dance is beyond me, although Michael Jackson probably looks the part by now. Following suit, our particular subject also looked very dishevelled. "Why do zombies always have such ragged clothes?" I whispered. "I mean, they've only *just* died?"

"I've heard that embalmers at the mortuary insert a butt plug into corpses to prevent leakage. That would probably explain the way they walk," added a pensive Lloyd.

"And the way they groan," I suggested back.

I'd always hoped that zombies would start killing those people that confuse *there*, *their* and *they're* in emails, but I guess funeral directors would be the first on their list judging by Lloyd's revelation. We continued our observations in case it was actually Gwain, but our subject hauled himself past and off down the street. We settled back down and continued our lonely vigil.

"John, hold the fort!" Fifteen minutes later and Lloyd broke the silence with his desperate plea.

"Now?" I queried.

"Now!" came the adamant reply as he disappeared out the door.

When nature called, it seemed to demand an immediate answer from Lloyd.

As police officers, we can never be sure how long we'll be out of the station and away from basic facilities. A quick detail can turn into a job that takes hours, and from there we can be sent to another incident and so on. It's not uncommon to leave the station at the start of the shift and not return until the end of play. Scene preservation duties bring their own set of problems too:

crime scenes need to be preserved for forensic examination whenever and wherever they may occur. The image of a police officer or community support officer standing outside a house where some horrendous murder has occurred is pretty commonplace on the news and in TV dramas – we can't just nip away to use the toilet or have a break. It's not unusual for me to become dehydrated by the end of the day as I try not to drink too much to avoid such problems.

But with Lloyd nature didn't slowly meander up the path, gently announcing its impending arrival by whistling a merry tune en route, and giving him time to think where he could do his business. No, with Lloyd, nature seemed to jump out of nowhere and hammer at the door – in his case the back door. You would think that for a man for whom poop has no concept of time, he would prepare himself for such eventualities. However, as 'Exhibit A' demonstrates, it seems this was clearly not the case. In this particular incident, Lloyd had been standing in dense woodland in the dead of night and in pitch darkness, miles from anywhere. Some sort of satanic ritual had occurred there that CID were looking into. Amongst other things, a goat's head had been discovered stuck on a pole in the middle of a clearing. The scene had needed to be guarded to prevent anyone coming and disturbing it before it was fully examined.

Four hours later and at about three in the morning, Lloyd felt those familiar rumblings. He called up on the radio asking if anyone could take his place as he had an urgent matter to attend to, but after having to endure listening to everyone respond with: 'I ain't afraid of no goats!' it seemed that all other units were tied up on other jobs. Ten minutes of pacing followed, and the rumblings still wouldn't take no for an answer. Eventually, he could take no more. Urgently waddling to the car, with legs straight and buttocks clenched, he reached in and grabbed a packet of wet wipes that someone had left in the glovebox, before disappearing back into the dark and foreboding woods to do his dirty business.

"Initially," he had explained to us later, "I was worried that CSI might find my deposit and think it was somehow related to the bizarre and ghoulish ceremonies that had been taking place. However, a few minutes later, a very different set of concerns obliterated every other thought from my mind."

Lloyd then described the slow burning sensation he had experienced. The slight discomfort that had started as a warm glow had steadily increased to the blistering heat of the surface of the sun... and in the very place on the body where the sun doesn't actually shine at all. Initially, Lloyd had wondered whether he had unwittingly squatted over some stinging nettles when he had released the beast. He even began to wonder whether the devil himself was taking revenge on him for defecating on his unconsecrated ground. Eventually, he returned to the vehicle to get some more wipes to try and sooth the burning pain and it was only then, when he switched on the interior light, that all became clear. It wasn't actually the work of some toxic plant or the sorcery of Beelzebub, but rather it appeared that the agony he was experiencing had been self-inflicted. Picking up the packet and examining it in the light, he soon discovered that he hadn't been using a pack of wet wipes at all – these were industrial-strength, highly chemical dashboard cleaning wipes!

I was still chuckling at the memory of my colleague's misfortune when he returned to the room after completing his current ablutions.

"Sorted?" I queried. "You found an actual toilet and actual paper to use this time?"

"Pristine toilet and two-ply paper to hand," came the response. "The show home is well-equipped. Mission accomplished... of sorts."

"Of sorts?"

"Well," was his shamefaced reply, "it seems the water hasn't actually been connected yet."

Before I had time to comment, I heard a dull thudding outside. I looked out to see a male kicking violently at the front door of the target house. It was our man!

We raced down the stairs, three at a time, bursting out onto the street, catching our suspect by surprise. Hearing our front door swing open, he looked back and hesitated for a second before deciding to make a run for it. He sprinted across the front garden, vaulted over the small perimeter wall and then ran off down the street. He had about forty yards on us as we raced along after him in the middle of the deserted road. I racked my baton as I ran, whilst Lloyd gave updates on the radio guiding units to our location.

Gwain was fast, and not weighed down by twenty pounds of body armour and steel-capped boots. We hurtled down the street and onto Avery Walk, but he had already fled down an alley and was now on Lucknow Street. He was gaining ground on us, so I shouted after him in a bid to get him to give himself up.

"Stop! Or we'll release the dog!" How was he to know that we didn't have one?

He appeared oblivious to my shouts, but I knew that it was only a matter of time before the other units descended on the scene. Suddenly, a police car, blue lights flashing, rounded the corner at the other end of the street. Gwain was trapped. In a panic, he suddenly darted to the right and scaled the gates of St Christopher's Park. Gotcha! The park covered a large area which included woodland, a small lake, extensive flower gardens and a play area; our target was contained – at least for now, but we needed to act quickly. As soon as resources had been deployed to cover the exits and everyone was in position, we went in.

Hauling ourselves over the gate, Lloyd and I dropped down onto the gravel beneath. Again, we shouted for

Gwain to give himself up before starting to systematically search the grounds. However, the park was too big an area to comb effectively and after ten minutes of fruitless searching the decision was taken to call out the helicopter.

It wasn't long before we heard the familiar sound of the rotors chopping through the air. A police car, parked at the gate, illuminated its blues to guide the chopper in. The helicopter's high-intensity beam soon lit up swathes of the park. After five minutes, we were informed that they were switching to infrared mode. Gwain may have been able to hide from the helicopter lights under benches or the budding foliage on the trees, but in infrared mode his heat source would be easily picked up. He would soon be ours. We all waved our arms to identify who on the ground were police, and with that the helicopter changed modes. The first scan picked up a couple of rapidly moving heat sources that were most likely foxes running from the scene. The second sweep identified the small glow of nesting birds on the island in the lake. Then, on the third look, a call came down from above.

"To the officer standing by the play area, start walking to your left." I started pacing as directed.

"Now stop. Move to your right. That's it. Now stop. Directly in front of you: what have you got?"

"It's a large holly bush," I reported, illuminating it with my torch.

"We're picking up a large heat source coming from it."

I couldn't see anyone, but if the helicopter said he was there, he most probably was. I thought I'd bluff him out.

"Gwain, I know you're in there! Come on out, the game's up!"

After a couple of seconds I heard rustling, and then an arm, followed by a leg, emerged from the foliage. I wasn't sure whether he would still be as mad as an un-medicated honey badger, especially after being immersed in a prickly bush and I held my baton at the ready. Just a few seconds more and our absconder appeared in the full glare of my torch, scratched and bleeding. From his demeanour, it looked like his brush with the *Aquifoliaceae* plant had taken all the fight out of him. He was also much smaller than I expected – hardly the ogre that I had pictured in my mind following his wife's character assassination.

We're all guilty of it to some degree: bestowing physical attributes to the criminal class that they almost never possess. If you've ever fallen victim to a burglary, you probably imagined that some man-monster selected your house and studied your routine for days before making his move; rifling through your precious things and carefully selecting his haul. The reality is that usually some smack addict, weighing six stone wet through, on seeing an open window or trying a door and found it unlocked has chanced his arm, stealing the first thing that comes to hand.

I slapped the cuffs on Gwain and informed him he was under arrest for threats to kill. He must have recognised my voice as he immediately began apologising for his attitude on the phone.

"I was angry, but it was all talk. I said some things that I meant, but should never have said."

Maybe it wasn't such an apology after all.

"I don't think that came out right. Look," he continued, "I'm not usually a violent man. I'm a lover not a fighter." That was the second time I had heard that tonight.

"Your wife doesn't seem to go for the fighting sort," I replied.

"How would you feel, though?" He seemed to be winding himself up now. "I'd just paid four grand for a new set of tits for her, and now some other guy is playing with them!"

I had an involuntary flashback to Mrs Gwain pushing out her pneumatic assets when I had taken the initial details.

"And I should have known something was up when she started making me wear condoms," he bemoaned.

Condoms? In the plural? I was about to tell him that you were only supposed to wear one at a time, but instead I decided to tell him to save it all for the interview back at the nick.

Lloyd, meanwhile, came hobbling over from the other side of the park, complaining that he might have pulled something. That's the trouble with foot chases – you don't get to warm up beforehand. It's nought to sixty in a matter of seconds, like a greyhound out of a trap. It's all too easy to strain a muscle in those circumstances, although I don't suppose that extra biscuit had helped him. Bisc-etiquette karma, I thought to myself.

As I led my prisoner towards the gate, Jacob and Ffion from the night shift came over and offered to take him down to custody whilst I got on with my arrest statement. I gratefully agreed, and twenty minutes later I was back in the office, sat in front of a screen, merrily typing away.

"Ah, PC Donoghue." Carol Dunbar, B shift's inspector, walked into the room, obviously pleased that our offender had been brought to book. "Would you like to debrief me?"

I told her that I'd love to. Fifteen minutes later, she had an even broader smile on her face.

"Excellent result! When I saw it on the log, I thought it was going to be a bit of an..." she paused, checked behind her, and then, curling her fingers in the shape of bunny ears, mouthed the words, "*excrement* job." She seemed pleased with her little funny.

I liked Inspector Dunbar, despite her use of air quotes. There was something naive and innocent about her – like a librarian in police uniform. She was not long out of university and on the Accelerated Promotion Scheme but, with her delicate mannerisms, it seemed more like she had come straight out of Hardy's Wessex.

I suspected that on her days off she probably expressed herself 'via the medium of dance'.

"And where is your colleague?" she enquired, clearly wanting to share the love with him, too.

As she spoke, a flustered Lloyd rushed into the office with a pair of rubber gloves, a bottle of bleach and a roll of bin bags all tucked under his arm. He quickly grabbed the key to the show home and exited stage left.

"He's a little busy at the moment," I explained and, despite my personal hatred of them, I raised my arms and prepared to make a set of air quotation marks. "He's busy with one of those *'excrement'* jobs that we were just talking about."

# CHAPTER 7

# The Grinch

"Is that your BMW parked out there?" The young man pointed towards the road.

Mrs Garfield peered at the man standing at her front door. He was tall with short, dark hair and slightly built, some might even have said gaunt-looking. From what little she could see, she'd probably have put him in his mid-twenties. She tried to get a better look at him but it was too dark, his face only semi-illuminated by the 60-watt light that was half-heartedly spilling out of the doorway from the hall. She had lived in the village all her life and prided herself on knowing everyone, including their children and now their children's children, but this man was a total stranger to her.

Mrs Garfield glanced at the hall clock: it was after ten in the evening; an odd time for someone to call. She had actually been dozing on the sofa when the persistent knocking had woken her and it had taken a moment for her to orientate herself. She leant out of the door and stared past him in the direction he was indicating.

"Oh no, that's not mine," she answered when she saw the vehicle. "It belongs to old Mr Edwards next door. There's not a problem is there?"

"No problem," replied the male, and set off down the footpath.

"You probably won't get an answer..." she began, but it was too late; he was already out of earshot.

*How strange*, she thought, slowly clicking the door shut. As she began turning the lights off in the lounge, she could already hear the man banging on Mr Edwards' front door. She shook her head as she made her way upstairs. The whole terrace was occupied by pensioners and they wouldn't take kindly to being woken up at this time of night. Mr Edwards was particularly hard of hearing, and she was sure the whole street would be awake before he realised there was someone at his door, if at all. She could still hear the hammering as she started to brush her teeth. *Some people just have no consideration for others,* she sighed to herself as she rinsed her toothbrush under the tap. Eventually, the banging stopped.

"Is that your car?" demanded the male as Mr Edwards opened his door. His tone betrayed the fact that he was clearly angry at having to wait so long for an answer.

"Steady on!" countered Edwards indignantly. "And what sort of time do you call this?"

"Is that your car?" the male repeated, raising his voice.

"What's all this about?"

"Just answer the question. IS THAT YOUR FUCKING CAR?" The man was now screaming in Mr Edwards' face.

"YES, IT FUCKING IS!" Edwards shouted back, mimicking the crudity of the question. He was angry at the attitude of his caller yet curious to know what was so urgent at this time of night. Had there been an accident? Had this male crashed into his parked car? Was he trying to tell him, albeit bluntly, that someone had damaged the vehicle? He looked across at his car but couldn't see anything untoward. "What's it got to do with you, anyway?"

"Give me the keys!"

An awful rush of realisation suddenly swept over Edwards as it dawned on him that this wasn't simply some rude upstart: this man was here to steal his vehicle.

He was being robbed on his own doorstep! He went to slam the door shut, but the thief immediately jammed his foot in to stop it closing.

"GIVE ME THE FUCKING KEYS!"

Edwards kicked the intruder's kneecap, causing him to withdraw his foot in pain. He seized the opportunity to slam the door, the night-latch clicking it locked. He made for the phone on the hall table, but, before he could get to it, he heard a smash. He turned to see the intruder punch his fist through one of the small glass panels in the door, sending shards of glass flying into the hallway. Immediately a hand came through and began grasping blindly for the lock. Edwards momentarily froze, thoughts racing through his head: had he time to ring for help? Should he lock himself in the kitchen or make a run for it? Where were his bloody car keys anyway?

Aware that he had already wasted valuable seconds, he knew he had to act now – a moment later and the intruder would be in. Instinctively, Edwards picked up the nearest thing to hand – a letter opener lying on the hall table. As the intruder found the handle, Edwards drove the long blade hard into the back of the robber's hand. He heard a scream of pain but, undeterred, the assailant continued to turn the lock.

The blood drained from Edwards as he realised he had crossed a line. He had stabbed the thief and now that same thief would have no compunction in using violence against him. He had wagered that his tormentor would run away when he realised someone was prepared to fight back. He had gambled… and lost. The thief wouldn't just be after the car keys now; he'd also want revenge. If he managed to get into his house, he would certainly be on the receiving end of a savage beating. He quickly discarded the letter opener, casting it down the hallway – the last thing he wanted was for it to be prised out of his hand and used against him. Edwards now threw his weight against the door in a vain attempt to keep it shut, but the male was bigger and stronger. Inch by sickening inch, the door was slowly pushed open. He tried to shout for help, but nothing came out.

A second later and with an almighty shove, Edwards was sent staggering back into the hallway. The intruder was now standing in the doorway, silhouetted against the night sky, about to enter his house; his Camelot. Edwards knew there was only one thing for it now. Taking him completely by surprise he lunged at his assailant, grabbing him around the chest in a bear hug. Something in his mind had told him that he'd never be able to run away – not with his seventy-year-old knees – yet if he could only close the distance between them both it would prevent his enemy from being able to throw any decent punches. Hanging on for dear life, Edwards gripped the intruder tightly and used his arthritic old knees to best effect; repeatedly jabbing them into the thug's thighs and groin. He felt the blunt impact on his abdomen as the male punched him in return, but they were so close together that the blows had little effect.

BANG! The intruder then changed tack, and started to use his greater strength to smash Edwards against the wall. BANG! With every impact, he could feel the wind being squeezed out of him. BANG! He hung on grimly, but he could already feel himself tiring. His aggressor was a third of his age and much fitter. BANG! Edwards knew he couldn't hold out for much longer, but he was determined that he wouldn't let this bully have an easy victory. He could smell the man's rancid breath and hear his jaws snapping shut as his assailant tried to wrangle his head around to bite at his ear. The old man then felt a blinding pain as his opponent smashed his own head into the side of his face. The shock of the pain seemed to galvanise the old man's strength, and for a few more seconds he was able to mirror his attacker's every move and thwart any further blows by keeping his head close to his. BANG! Edwards' grasp was loosening – he knew he was spent. BANG! With his mouth already dry and his arms wilting, he could feel himself letting go.

Suddenly, there were shouts at the door. Dear God, if this was the intruder's accomplices he'd have no chance. The man was flexing his chest now, almost breaking Edwards' grip. BANG! Another smash into the wall and Edwards gave in; his attacker was free. *Goodnight Vienna* he mouthed as he brought his arms up in front of his face, bracing himself for the flurry of punches and kicks… but none came. Instead, the man backed out of the house and sprinted off down the path and into the night.

Mr Edwards waited a second, and then cautiously looked up to see his neighbour, Mrs Garfield, standing in the doorway, wielding her metal walking stick. Behind her were a group of four or five vigilante pensioners from further up the street. He took a look at the ageing posse, and then spent a few moments gathering his thoughts, swallowing hard to draw some moisture back into his mouth.

"I suppose you'll all be wanting a cup of tea, then?" he growled, before falling back against the wall and sliding down onto the floor.

\* \* \*

At the very time old Mr Edwards was facing his terrifying ordeal, we were racing to the scene, aware that a crime was in progress but with no knowledge of the full facts. The only information that we had was that a member of the public had rung the police on the non-emergency line, reporting a suspicious male in the street. A further call, this time on the 999 system, had then been received to report sounds of a disturbance next door. We arrived five minutes later, pulling up in the street with our sirens and lights blazing…

I've lost count of the number of times I've arrived at an incident to be surrounded by a mob demanding that

X, Y or Z be locked up straight away, only for them to then take umbrage when I've tried to clarify what X, Y or Z is alleged to have actually done. We can't just go around locking up people for no reason! As Lloyd, Gwen and I alighted from our vehicles we were instantly ambushed by the elderly ensemble, all firing their version of events at us, all shouting to be heard, all demanding to know why we weren't racing off to catch the culprit, all shouting a varied mix of confusing, conflicting and confounding facts and fiction.

Apparently, the intruder had attacked Mrs Garfield first before attacking Mr Edwards. Some said the male had got away with a car, while others claimed he had only taken the keys. Mr Edwards had been beaten senseless. Mr Edwards had beaten the intruder senseless. The intruder was trying to rape Edwards. Edwards had been stabbed, or was it the intruder who had been stabbed? A couple walking their dog in the street earlier in the evening had looked *very suspicious*. A group of youths who had been hanging around on the street corner during the day *must* have something to do with it. One resident had had a note from the postman this morning saying she wasn't in... *when she most certainly was!* The assailant himself was either a youth in his teens or a male in his forties, was pale in appearance, had a swarthy complexion or was possibly *foreign looking*. There had been sightings of a white van hanging around the area, as well as a dark hatchback which had been revving its engine in the next street all day. There were also reports of a guy on a motorbike who said he was delivering pizzas... *but who has pizzas in this street?*

Gwen and Lloyd quickly made their excuses, saying they would take the van and comb the surrounding streets, leaving me to try and sort the wheat from the chaff. I quickly sought out our caller, Mrs Garfield, and asked her if she could give me her condensed version of events. A minute later, I had established the basics of what had happened, had a description of the felon and was able to deduce what he was to be arrested for. I relayed this information to my colleagues before contacting Comms to ask if a dog section was available to assist in the search. I then went to speak to Mr Edwards in order to put some more meat on the bones.

"Good luck," whispered Mrs Garfield, placing her hand on my arm. My bemused expression following her comment had obviously illustrated the fact that I sought further explanation. "Let's just say he's a bit..." She left a pregnant pause while she searched for the right word. "Let's just say *difficult*. The children round here call him The Grinch."

I thanked her, steeled myself, and then went to confront the monster. As I entered the front room, I saw that one of his neighbours was already with him, dabbing his head with a damp tea towel. He quickly shooed her away.

"Get away with you, woman! Worse things have happened at sea!"

I wasn't sure how much of the bluff and bluster was for my benefit. I was sure that he had been lapping up the attention when I had entered. I introduced myself and asked his full name for my records.

"Hilary Edwards."

"Hilary? You don't hear that name every day!"

"I do," he countered gruffly.

I decided to stick to the facts, and managed to get to the part where the caller had put his foot in the door before we were interrupted by the sound of someone in the hallway.

"Uncle Hilary?"

"I'm in here!" he bellowed, before turning back to me. "Here comes the Gingeraffe," he sighed, rolling his eyes.

A tall redhead, who looked to be in her thirties, entered the room. She stood momentarily at the door before running over and kneeling at his feet. "I've just heard! Thank goodness you're alright!"

"This is my niece, Rose," he explained. "She's recently divorced."

"Wido…" she began, shooting him a perplexed look.

"Widowed! Widowed! That's right. Either way, she's not much fun right now."

Her expression changed to one of absolute confusion. "Why would you even say that…?"

I gave her a sympathetic look, and then asked our host if we could get back to the matter at hand. My colleagues were scouring the area and would be expecting an update soon. Just as I had got him back on track, there came the sound of further footsteps in the hall and seconds later a young woman, with a toddler dressed in pyjamas in tow, burst into the room.

"Grandad! What's happened? Someone said you've been attacked!"

Hilary then launched into his story, telling the young woman that he would have beaten the intruder from here to kingdom come if he hadn't been held back by the woman next door.

I sat impatiently, clicking my pen, waiting for a break in proceedings so I could continue my questioning. My opportunity came when Rose began to play with the infant.

"How old is he now?" she asked the mother.

"About eighteen months," interjected Mr Edwards abruptly in a bid to close that avenue of discussion. He seemed annoyed that the limelight had been diverted from him.

"Four!" the mother exclaimed. "He's four, Grandad!"

"What am I?" he countered. "His bloody biographer?"

As the mother grumpily folded her arms, Rose started to giggle.

"Oh dear, that's funny," she blurted out. "I haven't laughed as much since my husband died!"

"You laughed when your husband died?"

Hilary's comment was met with a stony silence from his niece. This was her cue to petulantly fold her arms, too. Both women seemed to acknowledge that their support wasn't being appreciated. The young mum took hold of the child's hand and addressed her relative. "C'mon Rose, let's leave The Grinch to it. We've tried to help!"

And with that, the mother, the four-year-old and Rose all flounced out. It was all I could do not to let out a little cheer. I appreciate the need for police to remain victim-focussed in these matters, but trying to get a logical, coherent version of events is difficult enough, and it's not helped by constant interruptions from third parties, however well-intentioned they may be.

"So, are you going to catch him?" Hilary was back on track.

"I've no doubt we will," I reassured him. "I'm sure we'll get a result from his DNA." It seemed that there was a *high* possibility of getting a positive DNA match due to the *low* IQ of the robber.

Our criminal had conveniently left his DNA in the blood splattered liberally up the door and wall, but others have been more imaginative. Chad had dealt with a case recently where a burglar had left his DNA in a teddy bear. Aroused by the thrill of burgling a house, the felon had satiated his sexual arousal by cutting a hole in, and then having penetrative sex with the toy. It remains unclear whether they were first alerted to this fact by the bear smoking a cigarette when they found him, but, regardless, the crime scene investigator did recover the semen from his fluffy innards. However, there were no winners in this sorry case: the burglar was charged and, sadly, the bear was ritually incinerated by its owner. Apparently, there is no bleach on earth strong enough.

In this case, Mr Edwards' intruder hadn't even tried to hide his identity. Crimes such as these are on the increase, with criminals appearing not to care if they are recognised. Several times a week we deal with reports of a thief walking into a shop, blatantly picking up a crate of lager and then brazenly walking out. They know they'll be caught, but seem to rely on the fact that they'll more than likely get off with another warning from a magistrate loath to add to our already overcrowded prisons. In the meantime, they've already enjoyed what they wanted: the alcohol or, in this case, a set of wheels for the night. It's the criminal's interpretation of getting goods on credit.

"Hello, anyone home?" A shout came from the front door followed by the sound of yet more footsteps in the hall. I was beginning to despair that at this rate I'd never get all the details of the crime, when the door was pushed open to reveal a couple of familiar faces.

"These are the paramedics, Hilary," I explained. "I've asked if they could give you a once over."

"Is that your police car outside?" one of them asked, addressing me. "Looks like someone's just thrown a slab of concrete through the windscreen."

"I hope you're joking!" I replied. "I signed for that vehicle!"

I raced outside to inspect the panda, and then stood staring despondently at the damage. The screen was shattered; the offending paving slab lying on the passenger seat.

It's not uncommon for police vehicles to be vandalised. Sometimes when we attend a job we return to find the tyres slashed or the occasional brick through a window, but it's usually committed by opportunistic vandals who then slink off into the shadows. This was different, though – there were words written in blood on the bonnet.

'I'LL BE BACK'. It was decoratively finished off with a bloody handprint.

Obviously, our suspect was still in the area and was goading us. I notified Lloyd and Gwen, informed

Comms and requested an update on the dog section. Chad and Geezer radioed quickly to advise me that they were heading up to our location from Sandford. As I sat brooding over the next move, the paramedics emerged from the property.

"Mr Edwards is fine. A few bruises here and there, but otherwise he's in rude health."

"Very rude," I added, "judging from his exchange with his family."

"ILL BE BACH?" read one of the medics.

Admittedly, I had used artistic licence when I had interpreted the message. Without any punctuation marks, and the way in which some of the letters had been formed, it could just as easily have been a random comment about an unwell composer from the eighteenth century.

"He needs seeing to about his blood loss," commented his colleague as they climbed back into their ambulance.

I was going to quip that it was too late – he died in 1750 of a stroke, but thought better of it. The paramedics were right: despite him terrorising the neighbourhood, we still had a duty of care towards our culprit. I added it to the list of reasons why we needed to find him sooner rather than later.

As the ambulance pulled away, a brick came flying through the air, narrowly missing my head before smashing into the wall behind me. I took cover behind the car while I tried to work out where it had come from. I got on the airwaves and announced that the suspect was back. I could hear sirens in the distance as another brick smashed into the side of the panda.

"We're here. Where is he?" Lloyd and Gwen were on the radio. They pulled up at the end of the street and were quickly out on foot. Geezer arrived at the other end, blocking the exit with his car. He too got out of his vehicle and began a systematic search, shining his torch into every backyard in the terraced row. Chad had been dropped off in the neighbouring road, and was busy checking the numerous cuts and rat runs that led off the lane.

Another brick landed close to Geezer, causing him to let loose a barrage of expletives. It was clear that our suspect was on the move, changing positions to get better viewpoints and better fields of fire. It was a dark, moonless night and the labyrinth of backyards and gardens would offer a thousand hiding places as he made his manoeuvres; whilst the barking of the local dogs masked any sound of his movements.

Soon our own police dog added to the din. The handler had him on a long leash as he came running down the road towards me. Meanwhile, my colleagues and I began climbing over fences and hedges, zeroing in on where the latest missile might have been launched from. Up and over walls, checking yards and then moving on. If we could contain our target, we could limit the amount of damage he could cause.

From the sound of each impact we would try and gauge where the object had been thrown from and move closer. Then a cry would go up and a shadowy figure would be spotted running across a road and the search would relocate. However, as more and more locals spilled out onto the streets roused by the noise, it became increasingly difficult to establish whether we were chasing our suspect or just an innocent spectator. I also became convinced that one or two of the bystanders were using the opportunity to throw the odd bottle in our general direction – just for the sheer hell of it – which only added to the general confusion.

Furthermore, each time we scrambled over into another yard we made ourselves clear targets as we were silhouetted against the night sky, and had to duck as yet another unidentified object flew overhead. Our attacker had started out throwing bricks, but now he had resorted to hurling anything he could lay his hands on. It seemed that as our quarry sought to evade us he had been forced to adapt his ammunition to what he could grab nearby… and thankfully bricks were in short supply.

Ten minutes later and we had narrowed down our search to a row of terraces on the edge of the village and it wasn't long after that we all converged on a single backyard. This had to be where he was… finally cornered. Tentatively, we entered, with Lloyd making his way to the back door of the property. The house was in darkness and the door was locked. Geezer kicked the shed open and checked inside – nobody there. Gwen then proceeded to check behind the damp sofa lying abandoned in the yard – nothing; behind the sheets hanging on the washing line – no luck. There was only one place left. I made a silent approach before suddenly flinging open the top of the wheelie-bin lid. I shone my torch into the darkness to reveal two startled eyes reflected back at me. I stood back and shouted my instructions.

"Come on out, we have you astounded."

"Shouldn't that be surrounded?" corrected Gwen quietly.

"I know," I replied, "but just look at his face!"

As he emerged, his eyes betrayed the fact that he hadn't expected to be caught so soon. He had been certain that he could lead us a merry dance all night long. Then, just as we were being lulled into a false sense of security, our prisoner made a valiant last stand, suddenly producing a bottle and an empty mackerel tin that he launched at us. But a well-directed pepper spray from Lloyd saw him sink back down into the bin. Rather than drag him out of his hiding place, it seemed easier just to wheel him back to the van and tip him out. This resulted in another struggle – a particularly smelly one – but he was eventually housed in the van's cage, ready for onward transportation to custody.

Whilst Chad volunteered to wait with my vehicle until the recovery truck came, I got a lift back to the station with the dog section. When I arrived, I peered through the bars of the custody suite to see who was on duty. Tonight, it was Brian Firby.

It is widely believed that working in custody does an odd thing to sergeants. In the outside world, they may be the nicest people you could possibly meet, but put them on a twelve-hour shift in the pokey and they turn into humourless grumps. Multiply that by years of custody duty, and you have someone who would make Ebenezer Scrooge seem cheerful.

Sergeant Ingarfield once told me that it was like being Jonah – stuck inside a whale. You can hear all the fun that people are getting up to outside, but you're trapped inside a concrete behemoth with bars on the windows as though you are a criminal too.

"What's that disease where the tiniest sound can annoy you to the point of rage?" he asked me.

"Marriage?" I suggested.

"No. That other one – the other one. I feel like I've got it when I'm in here. Cocky males and lippy women, all making their demands: shouting continually; none of them exercising their right to remain silent; the constant banging on the doors; the incessant pressing on the cell buzzer; everyone wanting my attention. Sometimes I think if I died and went straight to hell, it would take me a week to realise I wasn't still at work."

I bore this in mind as I rang the custody bell. I could see Firby shoot me a disapproving glare as he looked up. He seemed to take it personally when I brought prisoners in – as if I was doing it to ruin his day! He signalled that he would be with me in two minutes – at least I think that's what he meant.

I used the opportunity to go outside and liaise with Gwen and Lloyd who had just arrived with our charge. It had been an eventful journey, by all accounts. I told them that I would explain the circumstances of the arrest to the sergeant if they could bring our prisoner in (well, it seemed pointless for us all to get messed up when they were already liberally covered with the contents of the wheelie bin). They reluctantly agreed, telling me that I owed them one. I went back inside to see if Firby was ready to let me in.

"How are you, Sergeant?" I enquired.

"Living the nightmare, living the nightmare," he replied. "Well, Donoghue, what are you lumbering me with tonight?"

"Angry male with a list of offences as long as your arm, Sarge."

"It's always the same with you. Why don't you ever bring me someone who's in a good mood?"

"This one might entertain you all shift with his self-defecating humour?" I suggested.

"I think you mean self-deprecating," he replied, shaking his head.

"No, self-defecating," I asserted. "He soiled himself in the back of the van on the way here, and he thinks it's funny."

# CHAPTER 8

# Death Comes to Sandford

"Can anyone do me a quick favour?"

Inspector Dunbar poked her head around the parade-room door accompanying her request with a warm, friendly smile.

"It's just that we're going off duty shortly and we need someone to deliver a death message."

"I'd be more than happy to," I volunteered. Well, who could refuse when she'd asked so nicely?

She gave me a decidedly odd stare, and told me to pop through to her office. I sat there for a few seconds to try and work out what I had done to deserve such a look. The horrible truth then dawned on me: she wasn't thinking what a nice, pleasant individual I was, willing to help her in her hour of need; no, she now regarded me as some kind of sick sadist who actually *enjoyed* telling people that their loved ones had just died.

Why had I sounded so enthusiastic when I had piped up? Damn you hindsight! With my colleagues shaking their heads in disbelief, I did the walk of shame out of the parade room and along the corridor.

The truth is that everyone dreads delivering a death message. It's probably the singularly worst thing we ever have to do throughout our entire careers. Books unread, words unsaid; a life half lived. How do you tell a person that someone close to them is dead: that the hopes and dreams they shared will never be realised; that they will never hear their loved one's laughter again, and never be able to tell them how they really feel? Sometimes I say: 'I can imagine' when I break the news, when really, I can't.

During police training there are no workshops on how to deliver the devastating news or words of advice from the force chaplain. The responsibility lies entirely on the shoulders of each individual officer. I just hope that I broach the subject as tactfully as I can, and with as much compassion and empathy as I can muster. But what do you do once the tears have dried? How can you possibly lift them from their darkest pain? How do you tell them that no one is ever really gone – they just stop being there?

Delivering that fateful message is an awful burden, and Inspector Dunbar now believed it was something I looked forward to! I knocked on her office door and she ushered me in, inviting me to take a seat whilst she went and got the details of the job.

As I sat alone, I began ruminating over the folly of my impetuous decision. Thankfully, it had been some time since I had last carried out this painful duty. Gwen had been the last on the shift to carry out the unpleasant task, although I was intrinsically linked to the whole episode.

It had been late spring, and the report of a particularly nasty collision on the bypass had come in over the radio. It had been pelting with rain all that morning, and a juggernaut that had been thundering down the hill had ploughed straight into the side of a small works van that had pulled out of a side junction. I was the first officer to arrive at the crash site and had been met by a scene of utter carnage.

The road had been littered with smashed vehicle parts, and tins of paint that were being carried in the van had spilled their garish colours across the wet tarmac. The lorry had jackknifed and was blocking both carriageways. In the sheeting rain the driver had sat at the side of the road, crying and covered in blood. The van had been on its side in a ditch; its driver slumped over, dead at the wheel. His passenger had been located thirty feet away, having been thrown from the vehicle and then smashing through a fence to land unceremoniously in a field; his body twisted like a collapsed marionette whose strings had just been cut. Amazingly, he had survived – but only just, and was being cared for by some brave passing motorists.

Backup had arrived in due course and little by little the scene had been contained, diversions set in place, witness details taken and vehicles recovered. It was the air ambulance who had finally taken the patient to hospital, where he had been reported as critical but stable. Eventually, from the unpleasant task of going through his blood-soaked pockets to find his wallet, I managed to establish who the dead man was, but it was left to Gwen, who had never even set foot near the incident, to carry out the hardest task of breaking the sad news to the deceased's partner. Perhaps for the wife, the day would have started out like any other, but as she waved him off that morning she could never have envisaged that that would be the last time she would ever see her husband.

Having located the address, Gwen told me that she had walked down the garden path to the front door with the usual trepidation that we all feel when we have to deliver the awful news. Prior to knocking, some officers attempt to identify a neighbour or friend who is willing to come to the house and support the bereaved; someone who can stay with them while the news sinks in. In this instance, none of that proved necessary as the wife merely laughed in my colleague's face, and told her that she had been planning to leave her husband for ages and he'd just saved her the trouble. Gwen left as the black widow began enthusiastically dialling the insurance company to find out how much his life-policy payout would be.

"Mrs Lavender, the lady who died today, lived in one of the outlying villages." The inspector had returned, breaking my train of thought. "It took a while to work out if her death was suspicious or not," she added, handing me the incident log.

Neighbours had notified police, expressing concern that they hadn't seen Celia Lavender for a number of days. An officer had been summarily tasked to attend the address to check on her welfare. After knocking, and checking both the front and back doors and getting no reply, he had then checked the windows, but all were locked and secure. Standing on his tiptoes, he had then proceeded to peer through each one, cupping his hands against the glass to get a better look, but nothing seemed amiss. Eventually, he had pushed open the letter box to look inside, and that's when he had detected that telltale odour of a decaying corpse.

Entry was duly forced and the body was found in the hall at the foot of the stairs. She was an elderly lady and the cause of her death seemed consistent with a fall (in actual fact, more people die from falling down the stairs than being murdered). Her neck appeared to be broken, giving strength to the theory. There were no signs of a struggle, no marks on the body and no traces of blood were found. There were no signs of a break-in either; the house was secure. Nothing appeared to be disturbed or missing. The keys to the doors were still in the locks on the inside and all the windows were closed. With no other extenuating factors that would have been it: case closed; an unfortunate, accidental death. And yet there was something strange about this job – something that no one could explain.

Bizarrely, both the body and the rest of the hallway were covered in coils and coils of brand new bright-yellow garden hose. It was everywhere. It was clear that the deceased hadn't tripped *over* it – the hose was on *top* of her. The only logical explanation was that it must have been placed there *after* she had died. But why?

If someone else had been in the house when Mrs Lavender had fallen down the stairs, why hadn't they reported the incident? Why go to the trouble of placing the coils of garden hose over the body? And how did they get in and out of the property?

CSI had attended and had checked over the scene, inch by inch. CID had been out in force, pondering over the significance of the garden piping, and checking previous records to see if there had been any other killings with the same modus operandi. Neighbourhood officers had knocked on doors up and down the street, trying to establish if anyone had seen anything. Everyone had drawn a blank.

Then, just as the detective inspector had ordered the whole scene to be gone over again with a fine-tooth comb, a delivery van driver had turned up at the address and casually asked if he could have his hosepipe back. He had soon found himself down at the station to explain. An hour later, he had been de-arrested and taken back to his vehicle after it was discovered that he was guilty of little more than stupidity.

It turned out that he had tried to deliver the hosepipe to Mrs Lavender's house but getting no reply, as she was already lying dead in the hall, he had decided to post it. Instead of leaving it around the back of the property or posting a note through the door as any normal-thinking person might have done, he had posted it through the letter box. Unravelling the hose, he had fed all fifty metres – one hundred and sixty-four feet – bit by bit through the opening, where it had resumed its original state, coiling itself up on the other side of the door, the hallway and all over the prostrate form of our victim. To add insult to injury, it wasn't even the right address!

With everyone satisfied that there was no mysterious hosepipe killer on the loose, officers then resumed the routine aspect of any sudden death: establishing who the immediate family were.

Sometimes, however, identifying next of kin can be easier said than done. Usually, people don't die leaving beside them a convenient list of who to contact in the event of an emergency. Even when people do keep a diary or have an address book, in the section at the front where it says: *who to contact in the event of an emergency*, most of the time it's either blank or some wag has written: *an ambulance*. I've done it myself, but I don't really know why; maybe I thought it would give the coroner a little giggle when I was laid out cold on a mortuary slab. I made a mental note to start acting like a sensible human being... perhaps in the new year.

There was no useful information in Mrs Lavender's diary, nor had any family member arrived at the address while the police had been there. The hour-long search to establish details of any living relative had resulted in officers hunting high and low through decades of accumulated documents, papers, letters and notes that had been shoved in cupboards, drawers, boxes and tins. Personally speaking, the main reason why I don't really want to die is that I don't relish the thought of a complete stranger rifling through all my stuff. Nowadays, some people even have what is called a 'Porn Buddy', tasked with locating and destroying any such dubious material before loved ones find it; obviously, their primary role being to *delete browser history* straight away!

However, the searchers were not going to give up that easily, and had eventually come up trumps when they had looked in the favourite hiding place of all old people: the biscuit barrel. Along with a savings book and a wad of cash was an old envelope marked *NOK*. It contained the name *Emily* and an address in Sandford.

"I'm sorry, but we don't have an awful lot more information." Inspector Dunbar sounded quite apologetic as I looked up from reading the log. "We've no idea of Emily's surname, relationship to the deceased or even her age."

Five minutes later, I was in a panda car heading to the address. I had managed to establish that it belonged to a private care home for the elderly, but I still had no idea whether Emily was a resident or a member of staff. The reason for my visit would require a very careful and tactful explanation, and I certainly hoped that there wouldn't be more than one person by the name of Emily present. On arrival, I pressed the button on the intercom and waited patiently. Eventually, I was buzzed in...

"How do I know you're a real policeman?" The smartly dressed woman, whom I estimated to be in her late fifties, resplendent in a crisp white blouse and dark-blue pencil skirt, was questioning my credentials.

I was standing in front of her dressed in full police uniform, but it was still a legitimate question. It was only a few weeks ago that we had swapped our ties and smartly ironed white shirts for black open-necked polo shirts, so perhaps I no longer fulfilled her expectation of what a traditional British bobby ought to look like.

"I have some ID here," I explained, reaching into my pocket and showing it to her. I flipped open the wallet to display the silver constabulary crest on one side and my warrant card on the other.

"Anyone could have got a badge and stuck it on, and I don't know what the warrant card is supposed to look like. That could be any old thing you've made at home."

Fair point. I don't suppose many people would know what our actual identity cards look like, although I think she was grossly overestimating my technical abilities to make one.

"Well, my police car is outside," I joked.

She peered out of the window. "You could have hired that from a props company – just like your uniform."

"Why don't you ring the police switchboard and they can confirm that an officer has been dispatched here?" I suggested.

"Oh, I'm not falling for that one! You could have one of your accomplices answering it and saying any old thing to me!"

I was racking my brain to think of some other way that I could prove I was genuine, when I heard a buzzing in my earpiece heralding a call from Comms. I apologised for the interruption before answering the call. They wanted an update from an incident I had attended the day before. I informed the dispatcher that I was unable to speak at present as the information they needed was sensitive and I wasn't alone; he told me that they would call again later.

"And what was that?" demanded my interrogator.

"I'm sorry," I apologised again. "It was just the control room. I'll get back to them later."

"No, the gobbledegook you were just talking. That was just utter gibberish."

I played back in my mind what I had said: *'Go ahead... Say again... Verbal altercation... a bilking... Wait one, not state 12. Standby... Much obliged.'*

Admittedly, 'police speak' can sound incredibly strange to anyone listening in to one side of the conversation as we change from clipped formalities into code and then occasionally stray into something that sounds like it's straight out of a Dickens' novel. In an attempt to win her over, I explained what it all meant.

*Go ahead* = Hello, pleasure to speak to you. How can I help?

*Say again* = I'm sorry, I didn't quite understand what you were saying there. Could you repeat it, please?

*Verbal altercation* = It was just an argument and there was no violence used by either party.

*A bilking* = A term used to describe a situation where a customer makes off without paying for goods or a service.

*Wait one* = Steady on, stop what you're saying for a second.

*Not state 12* = I'm not actually alone at the moment and someone who is not supposed to listen into what I'm about to say might overhear.

*Standby* = Give me a few seconds and I'll go and find somewhere out of earshot of anyone else.

*Much obliged* = Oh, you'll give me a call later when I'm free from this detail? Thank you very much.

It's the *'much obliged'* that sounds Dickensian. Who on earth nowadays says they're *'obliged'*, let alone *'much obliged'*? Well, we do – on the radio.

"I mean to say," she continued, despite my explanation, "you didn't say *'roger'* once!"

Recently, we had actually been told that there was far too much *rogering* going on, and it was now officially banned from the airwaves. I was going to tell her that there were a number of reasons why police radio-speak had to be brief and to the point, and not least because we are charged by the telecommunications company that runs the network for every word spoken. In order to demonstrate to her that is how every officer speaks on the radio I pulled out my earpiece so she could listen to a random transmission. At that very moment, it burst into life:

*"I have espied an inebriated gentleman creating rather a debacle within the confines of the shopping emporium. On the balance of probabilities, it would appear he has over imbibed on a hefty ale they call the Special Brew. I will now attempt a tête-à-tête with the rascal and endeavour to procure the furnishment of his details. Roger Diddly, over and out."*

Oh no! Of all the people to be on the radio at that very moment! I quickly plugged my earpiece back in.

PC Rupert Fawcett was known to all and sundry as 'The Actor' or I should say 'The ACK-TOR' as it was pronounced in an overly exaggerated theatrical manner, as though he were a seasoned Shakespearian luvvie. Every utterance he made was over the top – why use one word when three could be delivered with a huge dollop of melodrama? Speculation was rife that he was on commission from the network providers. How else could you explain his verbosity?

I was just about to tell my inquisitor that this wasn't the best example to judge me on, when she indicated that she was satisfied with proceedings.

"You see, *HE* used *roger!*" she declared emphatically.

In actual fact, he had used *Roger Diddly*, but, if it got me her seal of approval as a bona fide police officer, I wasn't complaining. I dread to think what 'The ACK-TOR' *actually* says when he is tasked with delivering a death message. I had visions of Monty Python's parrot sketch:

*"Your relative has passed on! He has ceased to be. 'E's expired and gone to meet 'is maker! 'E's a stiff, bereft of life, 'e rests in peace! 'E's pushing up the daisies, 'e's kicked the bucket! 'Is metabolic processes are now 'istory! 'E's shuffled off 'is mortal coil and joined the choir invisible! HE IS AN EX-RELATIVE!"*

"I do apologise, Officer." My host brought me back from that horrendous thought. "It's just that we need to establish one's credentials prior to any interaction with residents." She then went on to explain that a number of the people at the home had some peculiar 'issues', as she delicately put it.

Satisfied that she was now on side, I explained my unusual quest to her. I soon established that there was only one Emily at the home, and my host agreed to facilitate a meeting with her.

"I must warn you," she added, "Emily is one of our more challenging residents and has her own particular style of communicating."

"That won't be an issue," I replied confidently.

"She will only speak to you via the banana phone."

"Banana phone?" I repeated incredulously.

"We've been trying to get to the bottom of it for some time, but it must be the result of some form of psychological trauma." She reached over and picked up one such fruit from a bowl on the reception table. "If you will," she said, and then proceeded to demonstrate talking into the banana, holding it as one would a phone.

133

"Do I really have to?" I pleaded, but she was adamant.

"If you want to communicate with her, it's the banana phone or nothing."

Just as my instruction was coming to an end, a young woman approached us from along the corridor.

"This is her," was whispered urgently in my ear, and I grabbed a couple of bananas from the bowl in preparation.

I must admit that she looked younger than I had expected, and not quite as I had envisaged either, with her baggy cardigan and tousled hair.

"This is Hitler," my host announced, nodding in my direction. "Hitler, this is Emily. Emily, this is Hitler."

I gave her a confused look, but chose to ignore her comment for the time being; instead I presented one of the bananas to Emily, the other I placed at my ear.

"Hello, Emily," I began, speaking into the bendy yellow phone.

Emily just stood there, arms tightly folded across her chest. I proffered her the banana again, but she just looked at me as if I was stupid.

"What on earth are you doing?" she enquired.

I shook the banana at her again, but she declined to pick up the receiver; instead she unfolded her arms and slowly pulled her cardigan aside to reveal an identity badge. After squinting to read it clearly, I discovered that it read: 'Manager'.

"You're not Emily, are you?" I asked quietly.

"No," came the monosyllabic response.

"And there is no such thing as the banana phone, is there?" I continued, barely above a whisper.

She shook her head.

"And this lady I've been talking to isn't really in charge, is she?"

"No," she replied.

"You're in charge, aren't you?"

She nodded.

I slowly replaced the bananas in the bowl and turned around in time to see the bogus host scuttling off down the corridor. I wasn't altogether convinced that my 'looking for the best in people' was really working out for me.

"Come into my office," invited the young woman, "and I'll get you a cup of tea. I think you need it after that."

We proceeded through to a large room with a desk at one end and a small conference table in the centre. As I sat there, waiting for my drink, I explained how stupid I felt. The young woman didn't disagree but at least sympathised, telling me that Mrs Cunningham was very plausible, and made out to all new visitors that she was staff. I explained that I had been totally taken in; after all, she had looked the part – she even had glasses and wore her hair in a bun. I conceded that I had also inadvertently informed her why I was visiting the home.

"That'll be all round the place by now," I was informed. "Gossip is like currency in a place like this."

"That's why I was hoping that we could go and see Emily as soon as possible," I requested, "before she hears the news from someone else."

"You don't need to worry about that," she replied. "She won't be hearing the news from anyone. I'm afraid Emily passed away yesterday."

A distinctly sombre mood now descended.

"It was most tragic," she continued. "We held a surprise party for her birthday. We didn't know that she had a weak heart."

I sat in silence, not really knowing what to say or where to look.

"I can take you to her room if you like," she volunteered, trying to sound upbeat. "They're clearing it out now. Maybe you might be able to find some information regarding any relatives or contacts, although we thought she didn't have any family."

I was led through a maze of corridors to where a couple of staff members were stripping a room back to its basic state ready for the next occupant. Aha! So the handles on the side of the mattress are there to help move it? And to think I've been using them incorrectly for all these years!

Outside the room sat a box of personal effects belonging to Emily. The sum total of someone's life had been reduced to a handful of cards and pictures. We took it back to the office and I went through the contents with the manager, but it offered up no clues. At her suggestion, I went to have a chat with some of Emily's fellow residents at the home to see if I could shed any more light on her life.

As I left the office, I noticed an extract from the poem The Roaring Days by Henry Lawson, framed on the wall. It seemed fitting somehow:

> *'The night too quickly passes and we are growing old, so let us fill our glasses and toast the Days of Gold; when finds of wondrous treasure set all the south ablaze, and you and I were faithful mates all through the roaring days!'*

The conversations I had with her faithful friends and confidantes about Emily's roaring days were both funny and touching – like an over-friendly clown. They shared the high points of her life with me and we had a giggle over how amusing Emily could be. It seemed to be a cathartic experience for everyone concerned. They say that laughter is the best medicine, and it certainly seemed to be – with the exception of the woman with the weak bladder. I suggest she sticks to her usual medication.

It was revealed that Emily, like most of the home's patrons, had led a full life. They had all seen and done so much. As children some had been evacuated during the war and had experienced rationing. Others had served their country and fought in conflicts, witnessing history in action. In contrast, what tales of life would I have to tell when I grew old? That I used to talk on a phone that was actually *attached to a wall*; that I used to have to answer it *when I didn't even know who was ringing me*; that I used to *tell someone the number that they had rung* when I picked up the receiver? By comparison, I felt as though mine was a life only half lived!

Whilst I had enjoyed my time chatting, just as her friends had enjoyed telling their tales, it hadn't actually helped me with my task. I had failed in my duty. The only next of kin I had been able to find was Mrs Lavender – her of the killer stairs. I was saddened to think that no one would collect the personal effects of either woman and that no family would mourn them. They would soon be forgotten and their once-treasured artefacts put out with the rubbish.

By the time I had finished and thanked the manager for all her help, the residents were in the dining area having their evening meal. I had a quick look in before waving goodbye... old people certainly have a way of making eating a salad look sad. As I prepared to leave, an elderly gentleman waved me over. I approached him and crouched down by his chair; perhaps he had the missing piece of the jigsaw – that vital piece of information I was searching for?

"Excuse me, could I have some more pudding?"

I smiled and informed him that I didn't actually work there.

"I don't give a shit where you work," he growled. "Can I just have some more pudding?"

I glanced over at the manager and she gave me a sympathetic look before coming to my rescue. She assured him that she would sort some out for him. I then quickly made my escape.

On the way back to the station I pulled the police car over. It had been a day of sadness, disappointments and embarrassments for me. If only there was some kind of magic liquid that could erase bad memories. I decided to ring Miss Jones to ask her if she would like to meet for a drink when I finished work. School would be over by now and she would already be at home.

"I'm just about to wine down," she told me when she answered the call.

"Do you mean *wind down*?"

"Nope."

It seems that she had had a hectic day, too.

"Drink responsibly," I joked.

She immediately countered with, "Responsibility is why I drink!"

"Look, I may be too late, but I was just wondering if we could meet up for a drink when I get off duty?"

"Actually, after the day I've had with the kids at school I could really do with some decent adult conversation!"

"Charming," I muttered as I put the phone down, "You could have just said no."

# CHAPTER 9

# Girls Who Cry Need Cake

"Reports of a disturbance at the Sandford Manor Hotel."

The call hung in the air, awaiting a response. I sat nervously waiting to see if any units responded. I counted down the seconds of radio silence and after a suitable amount of time had elapsed I took my chance.

Today I was on the diary car, travelling from one prearranged appointment to another. Officially, I wasn't allowed to deviate from my duties – a superintendent's authority was needed to countenance such an outrage – but, up to now, the high had been 25 degrees and the low had been a report of a dog fouling the footpath. I needed something to liven up my day, and what better than a trip to the haunt of the rich and famous.

The exclusive Sandford Manor Hotel was where the well-heeled gentlemen of the county held their balls, and this evening was no exception as it was hosting the social event of the year: the summer charity ball. The town's elite would all be there, dressed to the nines in their designer evening dresses and James Bond-style tuxedos. This was as good an opportunity as any to break the monotony of my shift and in the process see how the other half lived. I would seize the day! Officially, I was supposed to be on my meal break, so surely nobody could complain.

Hopefully, I could *carpe* the most out of my boring

*diem*, and, hopefully, still be able to *carpe* my sandwiches after I'd sorted things out at the hotel. With any luck, no one would even notice I'd been away. It was probably some minor hullabaloo over who had polished off the last vol-au-vent.

Within minutes, I had blue-lighted across town and was now making my way up the long drive to the hotel. Sports cars, limousines and top of the range 4x4s were parked in every available space: in lay-bys, passing places and on the grassy verge all along the welcoming tree-lined approach. As I drew closer, I could almost smell the opulence.

I saw the first of the revellers in their satin gown and Armani dinner jacket stumbling their way back to their car. The champagne must have been flowing. I wondered if there had actually been a heated tête-à-tête over the Moët itself: do you ask for a glass of 'Mo-aye' or 'Mo-wett'? It seems that the wrong pronunciation has taken a firm grip, as whenever someone actually does say it correctly – 'Mo-wett' – they usually attract slightly patronising looks or embarrassed glances.

Drawing level with the couple, I was suddenly snapped from my champagne reverie back into police mode: either the woman was wearing an unusual outfit, or those were bloody smears all across the front of her saffron-coloured dress. The male who accompanied her carried his jacket over his arm, his bow tie hanging undone, which is the usual rakish way to wear such attire at the end of an evening, but he also seemed to be clutching his face. I stopped to find out what was wrong, but they just indicated towards the main building. I changed gears and accelerated the last twenty yards to the hotel. Instead of couples milling around outside as I would have expected, the place was deserted.

As I pulled up directly outside the entrance, glass crackled under my tyres. I stepped out amongst the broken champagne flutes and spilt beer and made my way towards the entrance, my hands feeling for my pepper spray and baton. Something definitely wasn't right here.

I glanced in and was greeted by the sight of utter devastation. The usually pristine reception was littered with broken glass, the marble floor wet with drink and blood. Bloody footprints criss-crossed the atrium, interspersed with blood-splashed magazines and brochures that were strewn about the floor. The large ornamental vases that stood either side of the main desk had been toppled, and a table lamp, along with the glass table on which it once stood, had been smashed into a thousand pieces. Paintings hung at odd angles on the walls; another lay in the middle of the floor, its frame broken and canvas ripped. The reception itself was devoid of people; not a soul in sight. I had switched off my emergency lights and two-tones when I had turned into the driveway, so I returned to the vehicle and gave a squawk on the sirens to try and attract someone from the hotel.

"Thank God you're here!" A door slammed as the duty manager rushed out from the bar entrance. "Where's everyone else?" he queried breathlessly, glancing over my shoulder. I decided against telling him that I was the only officer available.

"What's happening?" I asked urgently. "Is anything still on-going?" I had no idea what the 'anything' was, but I needed to know if I had to break up a brawl or stop some drunken maniac in his tracks.

"No, it's over. There's been a fight."

"Is anyone injured?" I demanded.

"The place is a total wreck. They've smashed everything."

"Injuries?" I asked again. "Has anyone got any serious injuries?" Whenever you arrive at an incident, everyone has their own agenda, their own priorities. Right now, as far as I was concerned, the damage could wait – the most important thing was saving lives.

"The fighting's over," he replied again, ignoring my question. "I don't even know how it really started either. Oh my God, it's just a wreck in there!" He waved his arm in the general direction of the hotel, looking as if he was about to burst into tears.

"Look, you need to listen to what I'm saying: I need to know NOW: does anyone have any serious injuries?" He appeared shell-shocked, but time wasn't on my side. I needed to establish facts – and fast, starting with casualties. From the amount of blood in reception, someone was clearly badly hurt. As he was still panicking, I took control of the situation, making my instructions as straightforward as possible. "Find your staff and get them to check the place to find out if anyone is injured."

"Yes, yes, of course." He acknowledged my request and set off to find his co-workers who seemed to have abandoned their posts.

Just as I pressed the transmit button to update Comms, my attention was drawn to a man staggering through the reception supported by a woman who I presumed to be his wife. In one hand she held his jacket, the hem dragging on the ground and in its wake clearing a trail through the gory mix on the floor; the other she used to bolster her husband. Her dress was covered in blood, but it was his shirt that drew my attention. It was soaked crimson-red; so wet that it was sticking to his skin. The white towel which he was holding to his neck was rapidly starting to discolour.

"Can you get an ambulance?" she pleaded. "My husband's been stabbed."

I took hold of him and led him to one of the benches outside before telling him that I would need to see the wound in order to assess his injury. Slowly, he peeled away the towel to expose his bloodied neck. Initially, it just looked like a mass of blood but then, a second or two later, a great flap of skin about the size of a fist flopped down exposing the red-raw innards of his throat. I felt physically sick. I instructed him to replace the towel and to stay still, whilst reassuring him that I'd get him immediate medical attention. There was nothing in my first aid pouch that could help – he needed to get to a hospital fast. I'm no medical expert, but even I could tell that this could potentially be a fatal wound. Things didn't bode well, judging from the amount of blood the victim had already lost. I was taking no chances, and got straight onto Comms informing them that we had a major incident on our hands. I needed an ambulance, all available officers, dog units, the sergeant and CID here urgently. The entire building and grounds needed to be sealed off. Nobody was to enter or leave.

"Where do you want everyone, John?" replied the dispatcher, coolly and efficiently.

Contrary to what some people may believe, there's no Battle of Britain style war room up at police headquarters; no female officers in A-line skirts with long sticks pushing models of police officers around a gigantic model of the county. In fact, for some Comms operators, Sandford is just another dot on the map and it's usually left to the officer at the scene to deploy resources where he sees fit. I raced back into reception and picked up one of the dirty brochures from the floor, flicking past the adverts for summer fun days and Christmas parties until I found the site plan. I wiped my forearm across the page to clear the mess and gore before studying it closely. There was a main road for access and egress to the hotel, while to the west, a secondary service entrance led out onto a quiet country lane. Those were the obvious ways in and out of the place, but this was a rambling country estate and there were acres of parkland and woods that an offender could use to make good his escape. Getting officers to these areas would be a logistical nightmare, but it had to be done; even if it meant trekking for miles over open fields, marshland and woods. In order of priority, I identified the key points where I wanted officers to be placed, hoping that enough troops could be mustered to meet my requirements.

"Get the helicopter up, too," I added. It would be able to spot anyone making off over rough ground. There wasn't a moment to lose!

I still needed to get further basic information about what had happened; some idea before Supervision began clamouring for a situation report, but, before I could even get back to the victim, the radio was already buzzing in my earpiece.

"John, I need an update now." Barry was on the radio.

"Sarge," I whispered into the mouthpiece, "we've one with a serious injury who needs urgent medical treatment. I've literally only just arrived on scene, but it looks like there's been a major disturbance. That's over now, but I'll need more backup to secure the scene. We're looking at a serious wounding or potentially a murder if he doesn't pull through. You'd better get down here."

"I'm on my way now with DS Slade." He left a pause before he spoke again. "Aren't you supposed to be on the diary car?"

"I'll explain later," I replied and terminated the call.

I returned to the injured man; he didn't look good. I didn't want him to even try to communicate nor move a muscle if he could help it. The towel was now saturated a deep red, blood dripping from its edges. Instead, I asked his wife what she knew, but she appeared to be pretty much in the dark about everything. She explained that the evening had been pleasant and uneventful until the last half-hour when the air had just seemed to thicken with tension. There had been a commotion at the bar, although she had no idea what it was over. Punches had been thrown and, whilst some had tried to calm the situation down, others had joined in. It had all escalated so quickly. Most revellers, however, had just tried to get away and protect their loved ones. Her husband had steered her into the reception out of harm's way, but then the fighting had spilled out into the lobby. They had taken shelter against a wall but couldn't avoid being buffeted by those fighting. The next thing she knew, her husband had slumped into her arms and blood was flowing from his neck. Assisted by the receptionist, she had dragged her husband to the toilets, where she had tried to stem the blood-flow. When she emerged, she explained, I was there.

As she spoke, I tried to note down the basics in my pocket notebook, but my hands were still wet with the victim's blood and my pen tore through the paper. I darted back into reception to assess where events had taken place. Distressed guests were now emerging from their hiding places and were walking through the foyer, leaving a further trail of bloody footprints, and destroying my crime scene. Where was my backup? I needed to seal off the area fast. Unceremoniously, I shouted for everyone to move out.

I summoned the receptionist, who had now returned, and told her to position staff at the doors of the main entrance, the bar area and stairs, and to stop people coming through. When I got back to the injured male, paramedics were already in attendance and lost no time in getting him into the back of the ambulance. Andy and Gwen arrived shortly after and instantly set to work; Andy accompanying the victim to hospital whilst Gwen began trying to establish who else had witnessed the incident.

By the time the call came through from Comms asking for a description of the suspect, the roadblocks were already in place. Time was of the essence if we were to have any chance of apprehending the attacker. The only reliable fact we had was that the assailant was one of five hundred guests, wearing either a ball gown or a dinner jacket.

The duty manager had reappeared, and I told him I needed to view the CCTV. He got onto it straight away.

The cameras would have recorded the entire incident in the bar and lobby, and hopefully would show the knife attack itself. As he trawled through the footage, I pressed the manager for more information. This was a charity ball at the most prestigious venue in the county: how on earth had it come to this? Looking embarrassed, he rubbed the fingers and thumb of his right hand together.

It seems, like most things nowadays, it was down to money. A lot of the people who had made their fortune by more dubious means now sought to ingratiate themselves into polite society; and what better way to achieve that than via a function such as this? The ball had started out many years ago as a select gathering, but once the corporate owners of the hotel realised that some were willing to pay any price to become involved, the event grew and grew. Nowadays, the great and good in Sandford society were joined by the greedy and the mean.

I've often been told that rudeness and aggression are little more than expressions of fear: fear of not fitting in; fear of not getting what you want; fear of being discovered. Lace that insecurity with alcohol and it becomes a volatile concoction. He told me that an argument had developed in the bar between some of the 'newer' guests and punches had been thrown. Soon a drunken fight had developed into a full-scale Wild West saloon brawl. And somewhere in the melee, our victim had sustained his horrendous injuries.

"I saw it happen," interrupted the receptionist. "I saw the guest who slit that poor man's throat."

I looked at her in stunned silence for a second. This was the break we needed. "Fantastic!"

She shot me a disapproving glance.

"I meant fantastic that you saw it," I quickly clarified. "Not fantastic that he was almost killed."

This seemed to appease her.

"Well," I prompted, "who was he?"

"I don't know his name," she replied, "but he's got a

room booked. I'll have to check the records, but he was a massive brute of a man. He looked like the son of Godzilla!"

"I know who that is," pronounced the manager confidently. "Liam Bell."

I was glad he had butted in so quickly, as I was about to suggest 'Jesuszilla'.

The identification of the suspect had arrived at the most opportune moment, given that Supervision had just pulled up outside, closely followed by Jessica, Lloyd, Ron and a dog unit. I was summoned to brief the sergeants with what I knew. When I told them we had a suspect, DS Slade informed us that he was already aware of him. Apparently, Liam Bell had once been an enforcer for a drugs gang and was well known for his extreme violence towards those who didn't pay up quickly enough.

These days, however, Bell was better known as an aspiring business owner. But, before you start thinking that at least he gave up his old criminal ways to become a pillar of society and budding entrepreneur, think again. Bell went into the skip-hire business – a tough enough environment to compete in with its stringent legislation, but slightly easier to succeed in if you don't worry about technicalities such as the law.

Not only did Bell not allow the vagaries of licences and insurance to bother him, he also had his own particular way of securing business: if you happened to be having some building work done, you might wake up one morning to find a skip outside your house. If you tried to explain to Bell that you hadn't ordered a skip, you were informed, in no uncertain terms, that you had now. If you already had one outside your property from another company, that skip would be removed during the night and replaced by one of his own. And it wasn't unusual for the owners of legitimate skip-hire companies to arrive at work to find the tyres on their vehicles slashed or their engines spiked. Bell's trademark was to pour water in the fuel tank; a far more effective way of disabling a vehicle than using sugar or salt, as fuel floats on water and stops the diesel from reaching the engine.

All in all, Bell was a nasty, violent, unscrupulous thug, but the motive for attacking our victim still wasn't clear. I rang Andy and asked if he could check with the victim's wife whether they were involved in the building trade. Meanwhile, the manager had located the relevant CCTV and we all squeezed into the reception's rear office to review the footage.

Fortunately, the cameras were high quality and clearly showed some pushing and shoving that had started in the bar. An added bonus was that faces were clear and distinct. There was no audio, but it wasn't needed: facial expressions were enough. There! That was the first punch, quickly followed by another. Soon the place was in uproar as staff gave up trying to calm things down and innocent guests made a stampede for the exit. It was a hard core of only six or seven men fighting, but, so far, there was no sign of Bell.

Fights tend not to be static affairs and we switched cameras as the melee spread, like a travelling tornado, the ten yards or so through into the reception. I could make the victim out now, turning his back on the fighting to defend his wife. We switched onto the second reception camera to get a better view of the pair; still no sign of Bell. Even though the footage showed only three or four minutes from the outset of the brawl, the room already looked like a war zone. Suddenly, we got our first glimpse of our suspect coming into sight from the left-hand side. We quickly swapped cameras to get a sharper, more detailed image of him. Bell paused for a few seconds, surveying the scene, before a wave of recognition spread across his face as he eyed his victim.

As the footage played on, Bell bent down and disappeared from sight. We flicked from camera to camera – he was back in sight again, only this time he had something in his hand.

"Pause it there," instructed Slade. We squinted at the monitor to try and get a clearer view.

"I think it's a champagne glass," proposed Barry.

"That's it!" declared Slade. "A champagne flute."

The footage was started again. Bell walked towards the reception desk, shielded his eyes and then smashed the top of the vessel on the wooden surface, leaving him with just the jagged glass stalk in his hand. He then made a beeline for the victim, punching a couple of brawlers en route to force them out of his way. He was now standing directly behind our man.

Hastily, the manager swapped cameras again in order to facilitate a direct, full-on view, and just in time to see Bell place his arm around the front of the victim's neck, violently dig the champagne flute stalk into his throat before dragging it forcibly down and across. As the blood started to spurt, Bell quietly slipped into the bar and out of sight.

"Right," declared Slade, "the other offenders can wait – we can identify and pick them up anytime. Tell the officers on the cordon that Bell is our suspect, and circulate his description. Search every vehicle that's leaving and take details of anyone who's seen anything."

As Barry updated the team at the perimeter, Slade indicated for the dog handler to get his attack dog out of the back of the van. A few seconds later and he was back with police dog Max straining at the lead, eager for some action.

"The rest of you," he added, "are with me." We set off behind him, accompanied by the manager and the receptionist with a passcard to the room he was booked into. There was no time to lose: we didn't want him disposing of any evidence or fleeing the scene.

Room 312. We didn't bother knocking; just quietly slipped the passcard into the slot and then barged in, our pepper sprays and batons at the ready. The room was bare. We checked under the bed and in the wardrobe.

Nothing. As I approached the bathroom, I considered opening the door slowly and deliberately, but instead opted for violently booting it open in case he was hiding behind it. The room was empty, but his wash kit and bloodied shirt were still there. He couldn't be far away.

Systematically, we began searching each room along the corridor and then the other rooms floor by floor. Knowing Bell's style, I wouldn't have put it past him to have informed an innocent couple that he was now occupying their room – whether they liked it or not. Barry coordinated our activities from reception, watching on the CCTV system as we checked each section of the hotel. Each time we cleared an area we lost another officer as they were posted in the corridor to ensure Bell didn't sneak back into any of the rooms we had just checked.

So far, we had been met either by guests alarmed at our intrusion, or empty rooms. We had been checking them so quickly that if you had been in the vanguard on one search, you were bringing up the rear by the time the next room had been entered. I had just finished one negative foray and was again apologising to the occupants, when I heard a cry go up from next door. It must be Bell!

I ran but couldn't even get near the door as my remaining colleagues were already jammed in the small opening. They were slowly squeezing in, foot by foot, trying to enter the room before fanning out. We didn't want to be wedged into the doorway, unable to swing our batons if Bell did attack us.

"Where's the flute, Bell?" demanded Slade.

"The fucking what?" Bell seemed genuinely confused.

"Where's the throat-slitter, Bell? The throat-slitter!"

Both parties were shouting. From Bell's demeanour and reply, I could sense that he wasn't going to give in without a struggle.

Bell was now brandishing the weapon, holding the throat-slitter aloft as if to emphasise his negotiating stance. He was standing against the far wall, the bed between him and us. He had one leg up on the mattress and was bouncing up and down on his other foot. His face was contorted with anger and hatred, the sinews in his neck pulled taut.

"I came into this world kicking and screaming and covered in someone else's blood," he spat, "and I don't mind going out the same way!" With that, he heaved himself forward and then launched himself at us.

Something shot past my leg and met Bell mid-air. I heard a scream as Max made contact with our attacker. There then followed kicking, screaming and, undoubtedly, blood. There were also anguished cries of: "Pull the dog off!" from Bell, but the dog handler merely retorted that Max preferred a squeaky toy as a reward for catching a criminal. I could still see Max shaking his head back and forth as Bell struggled beneath him.

I waited in the corridor with the manager and receptionist whilst my colleagues arrested a subdued Bell. Usually, I wouldn't have gone near the suspect to avoid any cross-contamination issues, but, with officer numbers as they were, sometimes needs must and my presence was still required in case Bell became violent once again. Minutes later, our offender was led out in cuffs, pausing only to tell the manager that he thought the function was 'shit', and that he wouldn't be coming back. Unsurprisingly, neither staff member seemed to be overly hurt by his critique. As he spoke, I was forced to consider whether it was acceptable to throw a breath mint into someone's mouth whilst they were talking.

Soon I was back at reception with Jessica and Gwen, where I learned that as an added bonus the police helicopter had directed officers on the ground to two males who were making their way across the open fields to the south of the estate. They weren't connected to the incident at the hotel but had been breaking into vehicles in the car park. Andy had also radioed from the hospital to inform us that the victim was stable, and that his wife had revealed that her husband had had a recent confrontation with a man who had parked a skip outside their house. Could this be the motive we were looking for?

The reception and the main bar remained cordoned off as crime scenes. The band was still packing up their equipment in the main ballroom, but couples were now leaving the hotel in droves. I held a door open as a shell-shocked couple walked through, thanking me profusely for my help. A woman followed shortly afterwards and shot me a pleasant smile. Her husband, who was just behind her, gave me a disapproving look as if I had been trying to make a play for his partner. It's a sad indictment on society when politeness is such a rarity that it's mistaken for flirting... A third duo followed in their wake and barely looked up at me. I made a mental note that if I ever became king, it would be made law that you could take anyone down with a leg swipe if they didn't thank you after you held a door open for them.

Meanwhile, the manager was outside the front of the hotel asking guests if they had enjoyed the evening. It struck me a little that it was like saying to the President's wife as she left Ford's Theatre in Washington: "Other than that, Mrs Lincoln, how did you enjoy the play?"

I gazed soulfully into the distance for a few minutes until an irate man started to shout at me, breaking my chain of thought. Apparently, I had been inadvertently staring directly at his wife the whole time. I apologised and quickly moved back inside.

"We're just waiting for the CSI to arrive," I explained to the receptionist, "then you can get this area cleaned up. Will it be much of a struggle?"

"A struggle?" she repeated. "You don't know what a struggle is until you've tried taking a turtleneck sweater off a big-headed toddler! Don't worry about it. It won't take us long to sort once you're done. Look, you've had a busy time – would you and your friends like some of the leftover food? I'm sure the manager wouldn't mind."

"That would be lovely," I replied and went to tell my colleagues the good news. Gwen was manning the cordon tape but it appeared that Jessica had gone to the little girls' room. In next to no time, one of the catering staff came over to ask what we wanted to drink. I opted for a coffee, Gwen requested a tea.

"And what is your other friend having?" enquired the caterer.

"I don't know," I shrugged, surprised by her line of questioning. "Probably a number two."

Our discussion was cut short by the arrival of Jane, the crime scene investigator, or, as we like to call them, the SOCO – scenes of crime officer – just so they don't go all Hollywood on us. We all stood back as she approached as hell hath no fury like a CSI whose crime scene has been compromised.

"Colonel Mustard in the dining room with a candlestick," she boldly announced as she entered the reception. My colleague and I glanced at each other with perplexed looks on our faces.

"It's not my professional opinion on the scene and I've not been playing Cluedo," she enlightened us. "It's just a note from Gwen's diary from last weekend."

As Gwen started to colour-up and stutter a defence, Jane ducked under the cordon tape and extracted a camera from her bag.

"And remember, Gwen," added Jane flatly, "it's worth laughing at my jokes because if anything bad does ever happen to you, I've got the chalk and I can trace your body thinner or fatter than you really are, depending on how well you and I get along."

My colleague looked slightly confused.

Jane sighed and started to click away with the camera. "I see I'm going to have to start wearing glasses and tie my hair in a bun just so people will know the exact moment I lighten up."

"So, any good jobs recently?" I enquired. The CSIs were always good for tales of the strange and bizarre; pouring over the minutiae of every crime scene they go to.

"Well, I've got a bag of something in the van that I found at the last job that would bring tears to your eyes, John."

"Onions?" I guessed.

"No, butt plugs."

I winced and made my excuses, telling her I'd see if there was an extra cuppa going. When I returned five minutes later with a black coffee, the manager himself had arrived with a large plate of food to keep us going. I think it's fair to say that all of us had missed out on a meal whilst we were at this incident and were ravenous. We were just about to tuck in when a young couple arrived at the outer reception cordon. They stood, transfixed, looking in on the mayhem for a few seconds: Jane, in the middle of the floor on all fours in her white paper suit, taking swabs from a pool of congealed blood, surrounded by broken glass and shattered furniture; the rest of us standing by the 'crime scene' tape, cups of tea in hand.

"We're here to book in for our wedding tomorrow," explained the young man in a shaky voice. The girl simply burst into tears. I was about to suggest that he use the tradesman's entrance tonight, but the manager obviously had other thoughts: ever the consummate professional and keen to prove himself after his earlier breakdown, he instantly took charge of the situation; taking my plate from me, which I had already loaded with a slice of Battenberg, he thrust it towards the young woman:

"Girls who cry need cake!"

# CHAPTER 10

# Dead Cow Walking

We left a trail of footprints in the grass, still wet with dew, as we strolled through the meadow on an idyllic summer morning. Specks of colour punctuated the lush green canvas: bright-blue cornflowers, shimmering yellow buttercups and large, brilliant-white daisies with their giant heads that seemed to follow the sun as it climbed in the sky. Elsewhere, the wild Flanders poppies danced in the gentle breeze; their delicate red petals quivering with the slightest breath of wind. We chatted about anything and everything as we walked, our carefree laughter carrying in the air, alerting the rabbits to our impending approach; their tails rising and falling as they hopped away into the distance where the green field met the blue sky.

The sun played on our backs, its rays warming our necks, while the birds in the hedgerows provided the score to this perfect day. The fresh country air completed the feast for our senses. On approaching the opening to the next field, I glanced over at my companion and our eyes met. As I slowly placed my hand on top of the gate her hand gently came to rest on top of mine. Involuntarily, she let out the faintest of sighs. I quickly recoiled my arm in horror.

"Don't get any funny ideas, you nutter!"

"It was an accident!" she replied indignantly, and then pursed her lips to make her mouth resemble a cat's bum.

155

"I'm old enough to be your dad's younger, good-looking friend," I told her. "And anyway, we're on a job!" Now that the ground rules had been re-established, we continued on our way in an awkward silence. This wasn't some aimless ramble in the countryside – we had serious business to attend to: we were here to fight crime.

The cost of crime to Britain's rural economy is around £50 million per year. Isolated farms and homes are particularly vulnerable to organised gangs. High-value farm machinery is often targeted and smuggled out of the country to developing nations. Pesticides are also high on thieves' shopping lists. Illegal waste sites and fly-tipping, as well as arson and criminal damage to fences and crops, are all major issues, too. Poaching is yet another big problem, but the activity that has seen the biggest increase by far is theft of livestock. The nature of modern farming makes this a difficult problem to combat as animals are often grazed in fields far from the farmstead. It is not uncommon for police to hold identification parades in order for farmers to identify their own sheep from a group that has been recovered. One farmer even took to dying his flock bright yellow to deter would-be rustlers. Today, however, we were on the hunt for cows – but not just any old cows – Jessica and I were looking for ghost cows!

Most people are familiar with the concept of car-ringing or car-clocking, where criminals switch details or wind back the milometer so, effectively, you don't get the car you thought you were buying. Cow-ringing or cow-clocking is exactly the same thing – but with cows.

Basically, all cattle should be tagged in each ear and have their own individual passports. This is to ensure that the authorities know that the animals are properly looked after and that their movements can be tracked to establish when they enter the food chain; therefore, should there be any issues, they can simply trace where a problem animal has come from and take the necessary action.

With cow-ringing, unscrupulous farmers simply remove the tags and send them back to the authorities, claiming that the animal has died. Then, when he is actually ready to sell the animal, he'll provide a false set of tags and documentation to certify that the cow is much younger that it actually is – and get a better price at market as a result.

However, it's not just a question of hard-pressed farmers trying to supplement their income; the implications of this fraudulent practice are far greater: as these 'ghost cows' don't officially exist on paper, no official checks are made on their welfare; they don't get visits from the vet and, to avoid prying eyes, many are kept well away from the farm often in appalling conditions. As a direct result, the dangers of infected animals entering the food chain are increased significantly.

We'd been given a tip-off that a farmer was operating the scam up near Todd's Plantation. Not wanting to make it obvious that we were onto him, we had decamped from our vehicle several miles away and were now proceeding over meadow and field on foot.

We trudged through the next field in silence. Our approach needed to be stealthy as cows have huge brains and incredible senses. They can detect odours up to five miles away, have near panoramic vision and can hear higher and lower frequency sounds better than humans.

I wasn't sure whether Jess was quiet because she had done her bovine homework, or was sulking after my rebuke; either way, it suited our purpose. We weren't that far now from where the ghost cows were meant to be and as I carefully opened up the next gate my colleague slipped past me, shooting me a sullen glare. I put my finger to my lips, indicating that she should maintain her silence, yet she responded by flailing her arms about, shouting loudly and swearing liberally.

I stared at her in shocked disbelief, until I realised the

cause of her outburst. She seemed to have been suddenly surrounded by a squadron of angry bees, intent on harassing her; swooping and dive-bombing her in the process. I'm no expert, but bees always appear to be proud little insects with a strong work ethic and I didn't think they'd take too kindly to being sworn at; if anything, it seemed to be making them worse! I toyed with the idea of wading in to try and assist her but decided against it, and instead opted to get my phone out – not to call for help, but to get a photo of the whirling dervish in action to share back at the office. If I framed it right, I could probably get the rows of wooden hives positioned along the edge of the hedgerow in the background of the shot. There was no use in telling Jess to stand still, so I had to compose the shot as best I could as she ran back and forth like a loon. Actually, I did try asking her to pause for a second but she subjected me to the same shocking abuse she had the bees. Very rude. Consequently, I moved in closer and was just about to capture my masterpiece when, suddenly out of nowhere, I felt a sharp pain in my left eye. It seems a kamikaze bee had disregarded my neutral stance in this confrontation and had gone in for the kill. I guess this is what the term 'suffering for your art' must mean.

As my assassin injected me with his poison, the pheromones that alerted the other bees that there was a threat in their midst were released, signalling his colleagues in the vicinity to go in for the attack. As other bee-fighter squadrons were rapidly scrambled from their nearby bases, I thought discretion was the better part of valour and called to Jess to follow me in order to facilitate a tactical retreat, otherwise known as running away. Five minutes later found us on a rough country lane, panting heavily as we tried to catch our breath.

"My God!" exclaimed Jess looking over at me. "What happened to your eye? It's swollen up like a tennis ball!"

"I think I've been stung," I replied quietly. I could feel it starting to throb.

"Well, you will let me know if you develop any superpowers, won't you?"

Before I was able to formulate a sufficiently acerbic response, I spotted someone who might actually have some sympathy for my predicament. A beekeeper in full garb, looking like a cross between an astronaut and a champion fencer, was advancing along the path carrying a smoking oil can. It might just as well have been a smoking gun!

I was aware that beekeepers pump smoke into the hives to make the bees sleepy before they collect the honey, but I could only assume that he had carried out this task just prior to us coming across their colony, meaning that the bees had woken up to discover that they had been burgled. The angry little creatures had no doubt begun searching for the suspects, when who should innocently walk past but me and Jess. The rest, as they say, is history. I decided to ask the gentleman for assistance, believing that he'd be sure to know what to do about my now very painful bee sting. I was also certain that I'd get a far more sensible response from him than I had from my most unsympathetic and unhelpful colleague.

"You mean to tell me that you've been disturbing my bees!" the beekeeper demanded angrily when I explained the situation.

"It sounds like a question," I ventured, "but from what I've just told you, I think you already know the answer. And we weren't disturbing them... it's not as though we're some kind of marauding honey badgers – we were just quietly walking past."

"You fuckers!" This wasn't really the wording of the apology that I was expecting. Evidently, it wasn't only his oil can that was fuming. "I've a good mind to take off this suit and make you pay for it!" he yelled, throwing his can to the floor with a clatter and putting up his fists.

"You want me to *buy* your beekeeper's outfit?" I

queried. My joke fell flat and only served to make him even more irritated.

"Tit for tat!" he exclaimed as he took his big protective gloves off and threw them down. "Tit for tat! Those bees won't settle for ages. Well, you've ruined my day – I'm going to ruin yours!"

"Wait, wait. Calm down! There is no tit, there is no tat. I've been stung in the eye by one of your employees. I should be the angry one – not you!"

I could see him staring directly at me, and then he lifted his helmet to get a better view. He leant in closer and then tilted his head, screwing up his eyes as he studied my face. I was sure I saw him wince.

"Bloody hell! You need that seeing to!" Without another word, he picked up his belongings and turned and stormed off past us in the direction of his killer bees. I just stood there, more confused than ever. I always thought beekeepers would be chilled-out individuals, like Sylvia Plath or Maria Von Trapp. I never imagined them to be wound up like a spring, but I guess we all have our moments.

"What a rude man!" Jessica broke her silence as he disappeared into the distance. "There's nothing worse than bad manners!"

"Well, I suppose genocide comes a close second," I ventured. She conceded that I probably had a point.

We continued our way down the path wondering what it was that had made the Bee Man so tetchy. Naturalists and conservationists have long been aware of the importance of bees, and it's said that if they disappeared off the surface of the globe, mankind would only have four years of life left: no more bees would mean no more pollination which would mean no more plants, and so no more animals, and, ultimately, no more man. Moreover, for our beekeeper time is honey. Having said that, an average bee only makes a twelfth of a teaspoon of the stuff in its entire life, therefore even if my bee died after its malicious attack on me, it wasn't going to drastically affect either the future of bee-kind or the honey harvest. Winnie the Pooh should be the one he should have a grudge against, if anybody. He's the one who seems to think that it's socially acceptable to just stroll into someone's house without question and demand all their honey; but of course everyone loves that bear, so his various foibles go largely ignored, along with the shenanigans of his little pig friend and that mad, stripy bastard. If ever there was a case of double standards this was it!

We hurried down towards the village and past a pile of household rubbish that someone had tipped at the entrance to a field. I made a mental note to report it when we got back to the office but, for now, all I wanted was to return to civilisation and have my eye seen to as the pain was increasing with every minute that passed.

"Oh my good God!" declared a familiar voice. "It's the start of the zombie apocalypse!"

By now we had reached the outskirts of the village, where we were met with this less than charitable greeting by the vicar of St Augustine's Church.

"What on God's green earth has happened to your eye?" he enquired as we drew nearer, finally showing some sympathy for my injury. "And you, young lady, whatever has happened to your hair?"

"I was stung by a bee," I replied, trying not to wince with pain as I spoke. "As for her hair – it's always like that."

I explained to Jess that I had met the vicar last year when he had reported a theft at the church; another victim of rural crime.

"Thieves broke in and stole everything that wasn't nailed down," he explained to my colleague.

"So at least they left Jesus," I added in a bid to cheer him up. He responded with a *Mona Lisa* smile.

He had since turned God's open house into Fort

Knox, complete with bars on the windows, new locks and a state-of-the-art CCTV security system. Signs next to the parish notices and order of services read: 'Someone besides Jesus is watching you... and neither that someone nor Jesus is going to be happy if you break the law.' Above it was a pair of eyes staring out at the reader. I'm not sure if they were supposed to be the eyes of Jesus or that omnipresent 'someone'. Regardless, it's been proved that a pair of eyes peering down at a thief at a crime hotspot appears to intimidate potential criminals into moving on rather than carrying out their nefarious deeds.

Initial trials of the scheme saw a pair of eyes on a poster overlooking an honesty box for tea and coffee in a university common room. When the posters were present, students paid up almost three times as much as when the posters weren't there. When signs were put above cycle racks in Newcastle upon Tyne thefts fell by sixty per cent. Perhaps that is why in countries that are dictatorships there are pictures of the leader everywhere so that the population has the feeling that Big Brother is always watching them. Not that I'm suggesting that God is a dictator...

"Where're my manners?" declared the vicar before asking if we'd like a cup of tea and a cold compress for my eye. We sat on a bench in the graveyard at the front of the church while he called for his wife to do the necessary. Ten minutes later, a woman emerged from the vicarage carrying a tray laden with tea, an assortment of biscuits and a thick wad of damp cotton wool.

"Jesus Christ!" she exclaimed when she saw me, before quickly putting down the tray and making a sign of the cross. She apologised profusely for her reaction and then offered me a garibaldi. At their request, I then relived the entire bee incident, almost knocking over the drinks as I portrayed Jess as some kind of raving madwoman, attempting to fight off the bees. The whole re-enactment took a distinctly sober turn when I described my encounter with the angry Bee Man.

"I think he's bipolar or lactose intolerant, or something," reflected the vicar's wife as she tried to account for his violent reaction. "He's certainly a character!"

"I'd actually describe him as another type of C," volunteered the vicar thoughtfully, gazing down towards his shoes. It was perhaps a little strong for a man of the cloth, but I gave a little chuckle and nodded in agreement.

"Curmudgeon!" he proclaimed enthusiastically and without any trace of irony. The lapsed Catholic in me immediately began to feel guilty about the word I'd actually just had in mind.

We finished our tea, thanked the vicar and his wife and were about to set off back down the country lane to our car and onward to medical assistance for my eye, when Jess shook me violently by the arm and nodded in the direction of the graveyard.

"Isn't that your arch enemy?"

I had to stare intently into the distance before I could be sure. He had put on a few pounds since I'd last seen him, but there could be no doubt: the male happily digging out a new plot at the bottom of the churchyard was definitely the man in question. Maybe 'arch enemy' was a slight exaggeration, but I certainly didn't have much time for him after an unhappy encounter a few months back.

Seeing me looking at him he smiled, put down his spade and started to make his way over towards us. I recognised his gait – I still wasn't sure whether it was a pimp walk or scoliosis. Either way, it was definitely him.

I had first met him last February. I had gone to a report of someone acting suspiciously in the deserted pedestrianised town centre late one evening and, as I approached, he had jumped out of the shadows and started shouting aggressively at me for no apparent reason. I was taken by surprise and had automatically reached for my pepper spray. A tense stand-off had then ensued whilst he ranted incomprehensibly at me and I in turn endeavoured to calm him down. I eventually managed to establish that he was sleeping rough, and that he had thought I had come to lock him up and steal the cardboard box that was his makeshift home. I tried to explain that I hadn't even known he was there until he had jumped out at me, and that I didn't have the slightest design on his box.

Twenty minutes later, we were sitting on a low brick wall as he poured out his life story. He apologised for his outburst and admitted that he was ashamed of the person he had become. He had once been an aspiring teacher in a successful school, and then one day, to cope with the stress of the job and to relax, he had tried a reefer of cannabis. From then on, he had happily smoked the drug every night – until, however, his supplier had introduced him to cocaine. Not long after, and in search of a bigger hit, he found himself taking heroin. He revealed that his drug habit had taken years to progress to that stage, but no time at all for his life to quickly unravel. Within six months he had lost everything: his wife, his house, his job, his friends and finally his self-respect.

Eventually, he had found himself living on a big roundabout on the outskirts of a town down in the south of the country. The land had been covered in trees and he had managed to set up camp, hidden from view and undisturbed by human contact. If you didn't mind the constant drone of traffic, it was a peaceful enough place to live he explained.

By day he would venture into the city and do odd jobs for cash. When he wasn't working, he'd just sit quietly on the town hall steps, watching the world go by. He had become a regular fixture and all the local bobbies would enquire about his health and welfare whenever they saw him. They developed a good relationship with him and the regular beat officers would tell probationers that he was the detective inspector on an undercover operation. He played along with it and each time a new recruit sidled over he'd usually asked them to fetch him a cup of tea. Bemused members of the public would exchange puzzled glances whenever they clocked a young officer scurry away and then return five minutes later to surreptitiously slide a cup over to the homeless man sitting on the stairs.

Things had gone swimmingly for a number of years until his requests had started to become more excessive. It was fine asking for a cuppa and maybe a pasty, but when he began demanding a three-litre bottle of industrial-strength cider the plug had been pulled on the whole exercise.

Then one day he had returned to his roundabout home to find that the council had cleared the entire area. The trees had been cut down, his makeshift shelter had gone and all his worldly possessions had disappeared. There had been nothing else for it but to seek pastures new. And that was how he came to be sleeping rough in a cardboard box in the centre of Sandford shopping precinct.

As he sat there, cold, hungry, unshaven, and with tears in his eyes, I don't know what it was but something about his story touched me. I told him there were people who could help, but he informed me that he had: 'been there, done that, bought the T-shirt and then sold it again to buy more drugs'. I told him to wait there before hurrying over to the all-night Tesco superstore.

I checked my balance at the cashpoint and then went on a mini spending spree. I got a sleeping bag from the camping aisle, a thick jumper, a couple of pairs of thermal hiking socks and a woolly hat and gloves from the clothing section before heading to the food aisles for chocolate bars, sandwiches and a pasty. I even got the security guard to make me some coffee and poured it into the flask I had just bought.

"So what's all this in aid of?" queried Al as he handed

the flask back to me. I explained that it was for the homeless guy who was sleeping rough in the precinct.

"What are you bothering with him for?" he continued. "You can't solve everyone's problems."

"Have you never heard the story of the starfish?" I asked him. When he shook his head, I asked him if he was sitting comfortably and then I began:

"Once upon a time, there was an old man who lived by the sea. Every morning he would go for a walk on the beach. One morning, after a great storm had passed, he came across thousands upon thousands of starfish that had been washed up on the sand, littering the beach as far as the eye could see. As the sun rose in the sky the creatures began to dry out and die.

"In the distance, he noticed a small boy approaching who every so often would bend down, pick something up and then throw it into the sea. As he drew level with the young boy, he wished him good morning and asked him what he was doing.

"Throwing starfish into the ocean. They've been washed up and can't get back by themselves. When the sun gets high, they'll die unless they are put back into the water.'

"There are thousands of starfish on the beach. I'm afraid you won't be able to make much of a difference,' the old man replied.

"The boy picked up another starfish and threw it as far as he could into the sea. Turning and smiling at the old man, he said, 'I made a difference to that one!'"

Unfortunately, my uplifting story had gone to waste as Al had got bored midway through and had pottered off mouthing: "Yeah, yeah, Grasshopper," as he went.

Undeterred, I wheeled my trolley full of booty out through the main doors. I removed all the tags so that he wouldn't be accused of shoplifting if he ventured into the store and then, feeling full of righteous goodwill, set out to find my starfish. The shopping cart rattled as I pushed it across the pavement – I had one with three wheels and a hoof as usual, causing it to veer off in random directions, but, eventually, after clattering over the broken paving slabs I finally arrived back at where I had left my new friend. He was gone.

I spent an hour scouring the town for him but he had disappeared off the face of the earth. And I was left with a trolley full of clothes that didn't fit and food I didn't want...

I despondently returned to the supermarket. Al listened to my tale with interest this time before calling over several of the night shift shelf-stackers so they could all hear my story... and then laugh at me, too. When the laughter had finally died away, he told me that someone matching the homeless guy's description had come into the store about five minutes earlier, used the washrooms and then left.

"I told him that he couldn't just use the toilet as they're for customers only, but he just told me to go and scoop his shit out and give it back to him if I was that bothered about it. He then instructed me to go forth and multiply. He was very angry and aggressive. He looked bedraggled – quite thin and gaunt, with a strange walk. Does that sound like your fella?"

"It does," I replied sadly.

"I saw him leave. He got into the back of an old minibus and was driven off."

Fast-forward five months and now here he was in the churchyard, having the audacity to look fit, healthy and happy. And after all I'd almost done for him!

"Ah, have you met Byron?" queried the vicar, conscious of my staring. He waved in the general direction of my nemesis. "I found him homeless on the streets of Sandford in late February when we were on one of our soup kitchen runs. We brought him back here and he's been working with us at St Augustine's ever since. He's a changed man."

"Pleased to meet you, Officers." Byron now

approached with his hand outstretched. He had obviously heard the vicar's comments and was keen to demonstrate how his life had been turned around since that fateful day in February. "I've a healthy lifestyle now, too, thanks to the vicar and his lovely wife. I used to be an addict but the only drug I need now is God's love... and methadone."

Clearly, he didn't recognise me, or he was playing some kind of one-upmanship; subtly pointing out how the offer of a home and meaningful work was better than my contribution of coffee and a sleeping bag. Well, your loss Byron – if that really is your name: it wasn't just any old sleeping bag – it had a soft, durable polyester cover and eco-sensitive polyfibre filling. Mind you, I concede that it came in a monkey design, but, in my defence, they only had children's sizes left in stock.

"I was at a low point in my life when I first came here and..."

"Yes, very sad," I interrupted, "but sorry – I've got to go." I pointed at my eye. The pain had now become unbearable.

Jess, looking slightly startled, thanked the vicar and his wife once more, and wished Mr I've-turned-my-life-around all the best before getting up to leave.

"You'll need that eye seeing to," added Byron leaning in, his big hands moving towards my face. I flinched and moved my head out of reach of his grasp. I wasn't at all keen on having his dirty great paws explore my delicate eye socket.

"I used to be a biology teacher," he protested, clearly affronted by my unwillingness to be his crash test dummy.

"We'll swing by the ambulance station on the way," whispered Jess in an effort to placate the beast. He seemed satisfied with that, and I was secretly relieved that I wouldn't have to resort to any stronger rebuttal of his kind offer – the vicar was looking at me oddly enough as it was. We started to briskly walk down the road and, five minutes later, we were at our car. By now I wasn't feeling at all well and I was grateful when we pulled up at the ambulance station.

"… and that, Romeo, is why we always check the pulse first!"

Steve, one of the paramedics, was in full flow, holding court as we walked into the restroom, working the crowd like Eva Perón. As he finished, his audience burst into fits of laughter.

"What's all that about?" I asked.

"It's a Shakespearian medical joke – you wouldn't get it. Star-crossed lovers: he thinks Juliet is dead and… JESUS CHRIST!" Steve had now turned to face me and recoiled in horror when he saw me.

"Aww, come on, I don't look *that* bad!" I protested.

Actually, I think I probably did look that bad. I was also feeling incredibly unwell. I squinted at him as he came in and out of focus.

"Hello, Jessie," beamed Steve catching sight of my colleague standing at the door and seeming to forget all about his patient.

"I think you've got the Jessie there," she replied, nodding over at me. "It's only a sting."

"Oh, fair play, Jess," replied Lysa, Steve's colleague, as she wandered over. "It does look pretty nasty."

I caught a glimpse of myself in the mirror for the first time: one half of my face was normal, whilst the other half looked like the Elephant Man. The eye itself looked like a tennis ball with a horizontal slit in it. It all looked rather red and angry, too.

"It was a bee, you said?" clarified Lysa.

"They can be vicious little things," added Steve. "We got called to a woman who got a particularly nasty sting while she was out playing golf."

I shook my head in dismay, but this was all new to my colleague.

"Whereabouts was she stung?" queried Jess, walking right into his trap.

"Between the first and second holes," he replied.

She adopted the furrowed brow and mouth-like-a-belly-button expression while she pondered over his answer.

"We'll need to get that sting out," explained Steve, appearing to go back into professional mode, although I wasn't entirely convinced.

"Why do I get the impression, Steve, that you're thirty-five per cent listening to me but sixty-five per cent waiting for an opportunity to insert a pun?"

"I apologise," he muttered. "I'll get Kate to deal with you. It'll be good experience for her. She's a student nurse on attachment with us."

"Thanks," I replied. At last he was taking this seriously.

"Kate!" he shouted loudly, "Come over here and take a look at John's Jap's eye."

I rolled my remaining good eye in despair.

A fresh-faced young girl in an immaculate uniform responded, jumping up and making her way over. After the introductions were made, Steve left us to it.

"So you're John!" she stated as she stood in front of me, snapping on latex gloves. "I've heard a lot about you."

"All good I hope," I quipped cheerily.

"No," came the flat reply.

I glanced over at Lysa, but she purposely averted my gaze and made a tea-based excuse to escape into the kitchen with Jess.

"It looks like the little blighter has left his bum spike in your eye," she declared, manoeuvring herself towards me with a set of tweezers. "And he won't be feeling too good himself either at this moment in time."

She repositioned herself and asked me to sit facing the light. "You know, your chances of being killed by a bee are about one in six million." I'm not sure if the information was intended to reassure me or to make me feel like even more of a baby because I'd winced when she touched my eye.

She explained that the honey bee has a heavily barbed sting, which is why they are so hard to get out. When I asked her how she knew so much about the subject, she told me that her father was a beekeeper up near Todd's Plantation. I didn't wait to find out if she also had a long lost uncle, who had once been a biology teacher before turning into an ungrateful drug addict, and quickly changed the subject.

"Ta da!" Kate stood triumphantly holding the tweezers aloft, displaying the tiny barb for all to see.

As Lysa returned with a tray of tea, Steve reappeared holding a can of insect spray which he handed to Jess.

"Is it good for bees?" she asked, taking hold of the aerosol.

"No, I think it kills them," he replied.

"Very funny," she commented as she studied the instructions. "It says here: *do not spray near eyes.*"

"Just go for the whole body," he clarified. "You can't be that accurate!"

Kate then stepped in and put up a vigorous defence on behalf of the little creatures, but I assured her that it wasn't necessary as I had no intention of returning to the scene of the crime: the late shift could search for the phantom cows. As we prepared to leave, Lysa gave Jess strict instructions to look after me, telling her to care for me like I was her pet Tamagotchi. Jessica responded with another of her perplexed faces; the reference going over her head by a couple of decades.

Having finished our cuppas, we got up and began making our way to the exit. Placing my hand on the door handle, I turned around to say my goodbyes and felt another hand rest on mine. I looked over to see Jessica's horrified face.

"You've only gone and done it again! You fruitcake!"

# CHAPTER 11

# Let Sleeping Dogs Lie

"All units, there is a report coming in of a major disturbance in a block of flats on the Red Estate; further details to follow."

No sooner had the Comms operator finished her broadcast than we raced out to our cars. We had been in the night shift briefing when the call had come through, but we had all been expecting an incident like this since setting foot in the station earlier that evening. It had been a gloriously hot, sunny day and for most people that entailed having a barbeque and a few drinks in the back garden, yet for others, those well-known customers who seem to monopolise our service, it meant drinking to excess and fighting.

As I drove through the town with sirens screaming, further information came through: knives and baseball bats had been seen. Jess was in the passenger seat and was busy shaking her pepper spray and checking her baton in anticipation. By now the radio was alive with other units calling up, all eager to assist; all travelling from far and wide to descend upon this one location.

By the time we arrived on scene, officers were already there, hammering on the thick metal doors that led into the foyer of the block of flats. I could hear shouts and cries from within echoing in the stairwell, as well as the sound of windows being smashed and baseball bats bouncing off walls. After what seemed like an eternity, a woman came staggering out of the main door and then fell to the ground. As officers stormed in, Geezer knelt down and began administering first aid. Suddenly, and mere inches from his head, a vacuum cleaner smashed onto the concrete pavement causing dust and pieces of plastic to explode all around him. At first I could only hear Geezer coughing somewhere in the middle of it, but, eventually, as the cloud cleared, I was able to make him and his patient out, both covered in fine grey powder.

I looked up in time to see a head disappearing into an upstairs window. Jess had seen exactly the same thing. We dashed into the flats and sprinted up the stairs past colleagues dodging blows and grappling with angry residents, while others were making strikes and applying cuffs.

It was three flights up before we saw the open window on the landing. A door to one of the adjacent apartments was slowly closing. That was all the evidence I needed. A good kick and the door swung open, crashing into the wall. The man inside looked back at me wide-eyed – a startled rabbit, panicking and desperately looking for somewhere to run to.

Before I knew it he had charged at me, his head crashing into my stomach. He caught me off balance and sent me reeling backwards into my colleague, resulting in us both toppling back against the safety railings before sprawling out onto the landing. Like a shot, my assailant was up and back in his flat, slamming the door. My initial kick must have knocked the door slightly off its hinges as he was struggling to fully close it. Hearing him fumbling with the safety chain on the other side, it was now my colleague's turn to do the honours. Now back on her feet, Jess leant back against the railings for leverage before raising her right leg to smash the flat of her boot at full force into the wooden door, sending it flying open and ploughing into the suspect's face – his nose splattering in an explosion of blood and gristle. He staggered backwards into the room. If this had been a cartoon, we'd have heard tweeting noises and seen stars floating around his head. However, he wasn't finished yet; his eyes darted around the room, searching for anything he could use as a weapon. A split second later, he had snatched a bottle off a low table and held it menacingly in his hand, raised and ready to smash down on anyone who dared approach him. A tense stand-off ensued as we each quickly weighed up our options.

We stood in the doorway – me with my pepper spray poised and pointed at his face, Jess with her baton drawn, held above her right shoulder.

Our suspect remained in the lounge, clearly ready for a fight; the neck of the bottle still grasped firmly in his hand. Next to him was a table littered with glass bottles of various sizes and different alcohol content; all of which could be used as makeshift weapons.

We were at an impasse. We could spray him with the irritant and rush at him, but, even if it blinded him, he could still swing wildly with the bottle, smashing either me or my colleague across the skull. Alternatively, he could charge us again and, although we could eventually overpower him, he'd almost certainly cause us injury as he went down. But if Jess and I waited too long, it would give him the opportunity to scan the room for further potential weapons; and if he retreated into the kitchen, he'd have a veritable arsenal to choose from. If we withdrew, there was the possibility he might barricade himself in the room and then we would have to wait for negotiators and Uncle Tom Cobley to arrive.

"Listen, you're trapped in your flat," I told him. "There are police everywhere. You're going to be coming with us – one way or another. You can put up a struggle and get carried out, or you can give up now and at least leave with a little dignity. What's it going to be?"

It's solely down to the offender which choice he makes: whether he is physically carried out kicking and screaming by three or four officers, bloody and bruised, eyes watering and nose running from the effects of pepper spray, hands cuffed and legs bound with restraints, or else he calmly walks out to the waiting police vehicle; either way, the end result is the same.

He stared defiantly back at me. It was the first chance I'd had to get a clear look at him. He was in his late twenties, six-foot tall but thin and wiry. One of his fists was tightly clenched, the whites of his knuckles showing, while the other still firmly grasped the bottle. He was baring his teeth at us. He was a perfect anthropological study: the archetypal angry young man.

"Well, what's it going to be?"

I got my answer when the bottle came flying through the air and smashed against the door frame above our heads, showering us with lager and shards of glass. Just as quickly, he grabbed another bottle and threw it. We ducked as it flew past our heads and exploded on the landing. Reaching out for a third, Jessica dived through the room in time to bring her baton down on his outstretched hand as it hovered over the table. As it made contact, all I heard was a sickening crunch followed by a piercing scream.

He instinctively recoiled, bringing his hand into his chest, whilst shielding it with the other. He began to whimper, tears filling his eyes and rolling down his cheeks to mix with the blood from his shattered nose. Collapsing to his knees, he started to rock back and forth as a dark patch on his light grey jogging bottoms grew larger; a sure sign that he had wet himself.

"I'd like to go out with a little dignity," he informed me between sniffles.

I told him that was a sensible choice, although in all honesty and judging by the state of him, that ship had definitely already sailed.

I glanced down at Jess who had slipped on the wet floor during her heroic lunge.

"I didn't know you could do the splits."

"Neither did I," she replied uncomfortably, whilst struggling to her feet using the table and my belt to assist her. She allowed herself a minute to regain her composure before eventually getting her cuffs out and applying them to our bottle thrower. As we led him down the stairs, we met Gwen and Andy, who had custody of the handcuffed and pensive-looking occupants of the flat below. The woman, who celebrated the fuller figure, appeared to be in her early forties. She had a shaven head and the customary homemade ink dots on her face and each knuckle, as well as some additional artwork that could easily have graced a heavy-metal album cover. Evidently, she was keen to show off all her other tattoos – her red vest top and shorts hiding little. Her husband looked almost identical, but without the huge breasts.

"Alright, Donna?" our prisoner mumbled as we passed them on the landing, "Alright, Phil?"

"Alright, Ralph?" she replied sotto voce, whilst her partner merely grunted a reply. "You finished with the hoover we loaned you?" she added as an afterthought as we started down the next set of stairs.

"I was bringing it back when I got a bit distracted," he muttered, looking back over his shoulder. I felt him tug on the cuffs as he quickened his pace in a bid to get out of earshot before she had the chance to ask him to elaborate.

"Oh, it's you!" the woman called cheerily as we began our descent. "Evening, PC Donoghue. I'm glad you're here!" I looked back to see her trying desperately to get my attention.

"We're old friends," she added by way of explanation to my colleagues who were now looking on, rather surprised at the enthusiastic level of her greeting on seeing me.

"Not really *friends*," I corrected her, in an attempt to downplay the whole affair. "I locked you up once. It's really not the same thing."

I had actually arrested Donna at the start of the summer holidays for being drunk and disorderly. Early one Friday evening, a shy, well-dressed young woman had dashed into the local Tesco to make a last-minute purchase. Perhaps the vicar was calling round to her house and she needed to make some delicate triangular sandwiches, or maybe she fancied an alternative slice for her G&T; whatever the reason, she bought a cucumber.

Unfortunately, outside the shop was a drunken Donna Shanks who, on seeing her walk out with the fruit (yes, it is actually a fruit), had proceeded to bombard the poor woman with a string of loud innuendos, declaring to shocked onlookers that they should be more than a little nervous if they were served a salad in this lady's home. The young woman had clearly felt intimidated and was visibly mortified. Just as she was looking as though she wanted the ground to open up and swallow her, a knight in shining armour came to her aid or, to be more precise, I arrived on the scene. I had ordered Donna to leave the woman alone, to stop her crude remarks and go home. Instead, however, Donna had told me to 'go fuck myself' before trying to take a swing at me. So, not really a friend of mine at all.

"I'm only going to talk to PC Donoghue," she informed my colleagues loudly as we all stood on the landing of the flats. As I let out a sigh, Gwen and Andy smiled broadly. In case you are wondering, being the 'only person they'll speak to' doesn't actually carry any kudos at all – far from it, as it usually means that you're the one who is saddled with putting together the entire arrest package. I half wondered if Andy had put her up to it... but, before I could inform her that both these other officers were also excellent listeners, she was off again:

"You know me, PC Donoghue, if I'm in the wrong, I'll admit it." True: she had confessed to haranguing the poor Cucumber Girl, but that was probably only because she had thought she was the wittiest thing since Dorothy Parker. "Well, I've done nowt wrong today – it was her downstairs who started it!"

While Jess led our prisoner outside, I asked Donna what it was she wanted to tell me, thereby reluctantly taking over the mantle as the officer in charge. It had been absolute pandemonium when we had arrived, and I hadn't the faintest idea what had caused it. I had been happy to remain blissfully ignorant when I was just backing up my colleagues, but now that I had unwittingly become the OIC, I needed a clear handle on the situation.

"Well," she continued with more than a glint of madness in her eyes, "after what she said to me, I swung at the bitch, but the coward ran back into her flat! I was up for a one-to-one fight, but she weren't having none of it!"

I'm not sure where in any sane world this could be classified as 'doing nowt wrong', but I let her continue. She had become quite animated as she acted out the scenario, swinging her arms about as far as the handcuffs would allow. "Well, I kicked the door in and wellied the fuck out of her! I managed to get a good few uppercuts in, too, before the rest of them laid into me!"

"Excuse me, Officer," her husband politely interrupted. "You don't mind if I give my wife some legal advice, do you?"

"Certainly," I replied. "Go ahead."

He slowly turned to face his partner. "SHUT THE FUCK UP!"

Turning back to me, he thanked me for my consideration. My colleagues then led the couple out to the waiting vehicles for onward transportation to the cells.

As I made my way down the steps, avoiding the debris in my path, I surveyed the scene around me: every single window in the stairwell was smashed; doors had been kicked in; fixtures and fittings broken; weapons, which included knives, pickaxe handles and baseball bats, were lying discarded on the ground, either hastily thrown away when officers arrived or else forcibly taken from the assailants with the aid of our own batons. Now that the last of the protagonists had been removed, the whole place seemed eerily silent.

The door of the ground-floor flat was hanging off its hinges and so I quickly glanced inside. As I entered, a greyhound that was sitting on the sofa casually looked up and then went back to eating its owner's pizza. Well, I guess it was better than it going to waste. I went over and patted him on the head, telling him that he was a good boy, before pulling the front door shut as best I could and leaving.

I still had no clear idea of what had happened. All I did know so far was that we had five people in custody, a further two who were under arrest and on their way to hospital, and we had a crime scene of utter carnage.

Back at the station, the interviews weren't throwing much light on the affair either. The gentleman who had given his wife his expert legal opinion now followed his own advice and stated: 'No comment' to every single question I asked him; or, in other words, he offered up no defence at all. In reality, this tactic is not actually the clever move that most criminals seem to think it is. As I led him back to his cell, he asked me if I'd get him a cup of tea.

"No comment," I replied.

I did actually make him one – milk with two sugars, just in case you were wondering. Police have to play to a different set of rules.

When interviewing the teenager from the fourth-floor flat, I asked him if he had understood the caution. He looked at me blankly.

"Do you understand what lying is?" I continued, in a bid to clarify his level of understanding.

"Yes. It's like when you ask me if I was involved in the fight and I say no."

"That's right. Were you involved in the fight?"

"No."

"So, are you lying now?"

"Yes."

"Do you know the difference between right and wrong?"

"Wrong is the fun one."

"So, is what you did right, or wrong?"

"Yes. Errr... I mean no. No, I mean yes." His decision-making powers seemed to resemble that of a squirrel deciding whether or not to cross the road.

A third stated: "I didn't do anything, but, if I did, I was drunk."

"I'll mark you down as a 'yes, I was involved in the mass brawl', then?"

"Yeah, suppose so."

The fourth prisoner complained that he had just come out of his flat to see what was going on because he had heard a commotion, and was shocked to have been arrested. He claimed that he only had the kitchen knife in his hand on the off-chance that someone might have had some cake. I raised my eyebrows at his solicitor as if to ask if that was really the best explanation his client could come up with, but he just shrugged and gave me a look as if to say that he would get paid, regardless of the outcome.

Meanwhile, Ralph, the guy who had dropped the hoover out of the window, maintained that he hadn't realised that there was a fight ongoing, and that he had simply been attempting to empty the dust bag when it had slipped out of his hands. He'd had a few hours in the cells to ponder over his predicament, and it was clear that he was now having regrets about his rash behaviour – in more ways than one: he began enquiring about the people at the bottom of the block of flats who had been showered with the dirt and debris.

"They were taken to hospital," I explained to him,

"but they're picking up nicely now... which is more than I can say for Donna's hoover."

He suddenly became very pale, the colour draining from his face. I think he was far more worried about what his neighbour, Donna Shanks, was going to do to him when she found out, rather than any punishment we could give him.

The two prisoners who had been taken to hospital had now returned and were being questioned over their version of events.

'Her downstairs', who had allegedly made the offensive comment to Donna, and had been covered in hoover dust whilst being treated by Geezer, was next to be interviewed. It was plain to see that she had been on the receiving end of a beating, but she was unwilling to tell me much about it. She did, however, let it slip that Donna had knocked on her door and demanded to be let in.

"So when she told you to open up, what did you say?"

"I told her that my parents never loved me and that I have a whole range of daddy issues."

I detected more than a hint of sarcasm in her reply. She then showed me her middle finger and flopped back in her chair with her arms folded across her chest, signalling that this was the end of our little chat.

Her partner was in next. He had also been to the hospital where he had been treated for a head injury. From the outset, though, I had the feeling that I wasn't going to get much sense out of him either: when someone starts moaning in faux sexual ecstasy when you're searching them in the custody suite, it's a pretty good indication that they're not taking the whole procedure at all seriously. It was also pretty disconcerting for me!

In interview, he categorically denied being in the block of flats even though we had clearly found and arrested him there. He told me he was offended by the accusation that he had been present, to which I then replied that I was offended at how easily offended he was. I reminded him that we had found him in the flats with a head injury, had taken him to casualty in cuffs, that an officer had been present with him for the entire duration of his hospital stay and that we had brought him back to the cells in those same cuffs. Undaunted by the facts I had just put before him, he maintained his story that it was all a case of mistaken identity. He told me that we'd have to agree to disagree, I informed him that I didn't agree to that. In hindsight, I don't think we really bonded that well.

It was eventually left to Donna to furnish me with the details. And furnish me she did, as only someone who is convinced that they are in the right can. When she had finished unburdening herself, it became apparent that the instigator in all this – the individual responsible for sparking off the whole debacle – was still at large. In fact, officers had walked straight past him when they had first raced into the block. It appears that I had even spoken to him but had failed to act; instead, I had just left him snacking on stolen pizza. Yes, it seems that the main offender in all of this violence and mayhem, the one responsible for the arrest of every resident in an entire block of flats including the two that had to be taken to Accident & Emergency, was the greyhound!

The canine, it transpired, belonged to the woman *downstairs*. When Donna, who lived *upstairs,* had come home that evening, she was understandably upset to almost skid in one of the dog's deposits that had been inconveniently left on the communal landing. Outranged and disgusted, Donna had gone down and banged on the door of 'her downstairs' and demanded that she clear up the mess. In all fairness, the woman had complied and, following some verbal haranguing, had picked up the poo with her bare hands. However, a brown watery stain remained on the lino... and when 'her downstairs' had asked if she could borrow a cloth to clean up the mark, that's when the fun and games had really started.

"You want to borrow MY cloth to clean up YOUR dog's shit juice?" came the shocked reply.

"Well, if you don't mind."

"IF I DON'T FUCKING MIND!"

Donna had flown into an apoplectic rage, grabbing the baseball bat that she keeps behind the door (in case anyone unexpectedly throws a ball at her, Your Honour) and swinging it at the woman before chasing her down the stairs. The woman had taken refuge in her flat but Donna had once again banged on the door, only this time it was to demand that she came out and fight her. When she refused, Donna stated that she had then kicked the door in and, to coin a phrase, 'wellied the fuck out of her'.

Instead of calling the police and leaving us to deal with the situation, the victim's partner had led a spirited counter-attack, accompanied by their teenage son, a pickaxe handle and a large kitchen knife.

Making a tactical withdrawal up the stairs, Donna had been joined by reinforcements in the form of her partner and another neighbour who didn't really know what was going on, but didn't want to miss out on any of the action. Complete bedlam had then followed.

However, despite her full and frank confession, Donna was unrepentant. She remained adamant that the level of violence used was totally justified in light of the initial offence.

"It's disgusting! Dog shit in public areas should be stamped out!"

A noble sentiment; if not without a messy outcome.

I gathered together my interview notes, the statements from my colleagues, the list of exhibits and details of the weapons seized and then spent the next hour or so compiling them all into some kind of coherent report for the Crown Prosecution Service.

A short while later and I was back in the custody

suite. As I called her back to the desk, Donna seemed genuinely surprised to learn that I was charging her and the rest of the residents with violent disorder.

"I'LL SEE YOU IN COURT!" she shouted after me as I left. Judging by her tone, I don't think we are friends anymore.

I'm not entirely sure why, but criminals seem to think that this is some sort of threat to us. In reality, a visit to a magistrates' court is like a school reunion for most police officers, as well as being a morning away from the usual routine. To be honest, I was also quite looking forward to hearing what the judge's reaction to 'Poo juice-gate' would be.

I had dog overload, and decided to clear my head with a quick drive around Sandford in the company of Gwen before I began putting together my court file. No sooner had we reached the town than Comms were on the radio again, informing us that a passer-by had reported an extremely drunk man staggering along the road. We were tasked with making sure that he was safe, and hadn't become another road traffic statistic. We looked at our watches: it seemed a bit late for a night-time reveller – the clubs would have closed a long time ago.

We eventually located our straggler in the old part of town, taking two steps back for every three steps forward – and one step sideways. He was zigzagging all over the place, but was just about managing to remain upright by using the occasional lamp post for assistance; hanging onto it for dear life before swinging round it, each time propelling himself off in a completely new direction. We kept our distance, just checking that he made his way back home safely, and that no one saw him as easy pickings and tried to separate him from his wallet. Things were going pretty much to plan until he staggered up to the front porch of a house where he proceeded to rifle about for something. He had obviously found what he was looking for when he fished out his tackle and began urinating all over the front door.

"That is just disgusting!" exclaimed Gwen. "Isn't that where the Crawfords live?"

"You're right," I replied. "They're not going to be happy!"

Gwen unclipped her seat belt and started to get out of the vehicle.

"Where do you think you're going?" I queried.

"To arrest him for urinating over a stranger's front door."

"Just give it a minute," I urged her. I spoke from bitter experience: I'd gone to arrest a drunken male for urinating in the street and had tapped him on the shoulder only for him to turn around mid-flow and pee all over my boots. An extra sixty seconds wouldn't do any harm. We'd let him remove his privates from public view before moving in. However, our plans went up in smoke when the gentleman concerned fumbled in his pocket, fished out his keys and let himself in to the house.

"It's Geoffrey Crawford!" we both exclaimed in unison. "He's been pissing on his own front door!" That would certainly give Eileen something to complain about!

"He's a recovering academic," my colleague mused. "Maybe I'll pop round tomorrow and have a word when his head's a bit clearer. We don't want to disturb Eileen at this hour, either."

I was forced to agree. I thought it best not to wake Mrs Crawford at this time in the morning and risk setting her off.

"Let sleeping dogs lie," I muttered.

"That's a bit harsh," commented Gwen.

"No, I didn't mean it like that…" but it was too late. It had already been said.

Gwen started the engine and began turning the car around to head back to the station.

"After all we've been through during this shift," my

colleague informed me, and thankfully changing the subject, "I'm going to have a large glass of wine when I eventually get home."

I looked at her in surprise. "I thought you told me you were having a dry month?"

"I am," she replied. "I've got a nice bottle of Sauvignon Blanc in the fridge."

## CHAPTER 12

# All That Glitters...

"You called 999 for this?" I wasn't annoyed, rather just incredulous.

I was standing in a pleasant house in a quiet residential street in Sandford, where a woman, sprawled out on the sofa, had just informed me that her husband had accidentally taken the TV remote control to the pub with him. I made her repeat the tale just to make sure that I had understood it correctly: there was no theft; no domestic violence; no malice – he had just *accidentally* gone out with the remote in his coat pocket. Consequently, the woman had been left with what I would classify as a *mild inconvenience*: having to get up and walk to the television set when she wanted to change the channel.

"And you called the police on the emergency 999 line?" I asked again, still stunned that I had blue-lighted across town for this!

"Well, I tried to ring the 0845 number, but I couldn't get through," she responded defensively.

"The 0845 number?"

This was certainly new to me. To my knowledge, it was 999 for emergencies or the continental 112 that can also be used in the UK to request fire, police and ambulance services. There is also the 101 for non-urgent police incidents, but I had never heard of an 0845 number.

"Where did you get that from?" I asked, seeking clarification.

"Emblazoned on the door of your police station!" she replied emphatically. "It clearly says 0845-1730."

I thought about it for a few seconds before the penny dropped.

"I think you'll find that's the opening hours for the front office, madam."

"Oh."

Undeterred, she asked me what I was going to do about her missing remote.

I was a little confused by her question. This was by no means a police matter, but I then made the fatal mistake of opening up this whole debate by asking what she actually *expected* me to do.

"I want you to go round the pub," she stated, speaking slowly and spelling it out for me as if I were stupid, "tell him what he's done, get it off him and then bring it back to me."

In my defence, I think I was still partially astounded by the whole incident and so instead of walking out, I asked her why she didn't just phone him.

"D'errh!" she replied. "If I ring, he'll just tell me to wait until he gets back. If you go, he'll have to do as he's told!" She shook her head in exasperation.

"Look, madam, I'm going to stop you there. This is not a police matter in any way, shape or form, and I will not be collecting the remote control for you or indulging in any further conversation with you about it. The matter is now closed. I hope you enjoy the rest of your evening."

"So I'm going to have to get up and change channels like some sort of animal?"

I managed not to reply with a: 'Yes, like a barbarian!' I toyed with telling her that perhaps in future she should ask her husband to do the 'Macarena' before leaving the house, so she could check if he had the remote as well as his keys to get back in. Ultimately, I decided against it. I also decided not to dignify her question with an answer. I put my notebook away and prepared to leave.

"Whilst you're up," she shouted desperately as I reached the door, "put BBC1 on, will you? *EastEnders* is on in a second!"

I politely declined. As I walked out, I heard her scream something about how she paid my (expletive deleted) wages, knew my (expletive deleted) superintendent and would get me (expletive deleted) sacked. I quietly clicked the door shut behind me and headed back to normality.

Sadly, nowadays calls like this tend to disappoint rather than shock me.

Operator: "You're through to the police. How can we help?"

Caller: "I'm at the beach, there's a couple shouting. They're fighting now. Oh my God, he's hitting her over the head now... with a cricket bat!" The man was breathless, urgently relaying events as they unfolded; hardly pausing for breath. "A policeman has just arrived. He's taken the bat off the man. He's started hitting the man with his baton – no, the man's got the baton off him and is using it to hit the officer now! Jesus! A crocodile has just come along and stolen a string of sausages... "

He suddenly stopped speaking and there was an awkward silence before the operator finally spoke in a calm and controlled manner: "You're at the seaside watching a Punch & Judy show, aren't you, sir?"

Caller: "That's the way to do it!" and with that he put the phone down.

I'm from a generation where calling 999 was something sacred: only to be done in a real emergency! However, it now seems that some people ring 999 at the drop of a hat.

Operator: "Police emergency, can I help you?"

Caller: "Someone's stolen my... oh, hang on, there it is..." Click. Brrrrr.

The number of 999 calls has increased substantially over the years, largely due to the use of mobile phones.

Operator: "Police emergency, can I help?"

Caller: "Oh, don't mind me. I was just wiping cake crumbs off my touchscreen."

Often, for some people it's just too easy to call the police if things aren't going their way.

Caller: "This is an emergency!"

Operator: "You're through to the police, how can we help?"

Caller: "They've run out of McNuggets!"

Apparently, the caller was upset because she had already ordered her McNuggets *before* she was told they were sold out, and now the devils were asking if she wanted something else from the menu instead; but if she had wanted something else she would have ordered it in the first place! My heart went out to her – as did my colleagues' – when we charged her with wasting police time.

Operator: "Police emergency, can I help you?"

Caller: "You recently arrested my son for possession of cannabis. Well, it was actually *my* cannabis. I grew it and I want it back."

Operator: "Just give me your address, madam, and we'll send somebody round straight away."

She promptly received a home visit from the authorities where they also discovered a small grow of five cannabis plants, which we removed as well.

Operator: "What's your emergency?"

Caller: "I'm masturbating too much."

Operator: "Sir, that's not really a problem."

Caller: "Just one second," places hand over the receiver. "DID YOU HEAR THAT, MUM? NOW GET OFF MY CASE!"

And in a similar vein:

Operator: "You're through to the police."

Caller: "I want to complain about a prostitute I booked."

Operator: "About a prostitute you booked? Have I got that right, sir?"

Caller: "Yes! I want her done for fraud! She said she was in her thirties and had massive boobs."

Operator: "Sir, I don't think this call is appropriate..."

Caller: "Well, she was late-forties at best... and a saggy-titted monster!"

Everyone is different: some are cup half full, while others are cup half empty people; usually it doesn't matter – except that is when it comes to bra cups... well, this gentleman seemed to think so anyway. He was politely informed that the aesthetic qualities of a professional escort would not be something we would comment on.

Operator: "You're through to the police, how can I help?"

Caller: "Have you thought about buying a new boiler? We can supply and fit one cheaper than British Gas or any of the other leading suppliers!"

Operator: "You do know this is an emergency line?"

Caller: "But this is an emergency – the offer ends this Saturday!"

Regrettably, this wasn't an isolated incident: it's surprising how many sales calls actually come through on the 999 system. In businesses where salespeople are judged on how many prospects they actually connect and talk to, the emergency line is an easy target, and provides them with a tick in the box.

Other bizarre and inappropriate 999 calls have come in from people complaining about noisy seagulls; a daughter reported her parents for having loud sex in the next room; someone else rang in irate because they couldn't get a hot-dog tin open; another who woke up with the duvet over her head and panicked; and perhaps the most tragic case of all; the individual who was having trouble logging on to Facebook!

It must take a lot of patience to work in Comms and not just because of some of the idiots who ring in and abuse the system. The 999 operators frequently deal with people who are at their most vulnerable or are panic-stricken or in utter despair. Your worst day is their everyday.

For a number of reasons, whenever I have the opportunity, I'm always at pains to tell the Comms staff that I admire what they do. Not only are they the first point of contact for potentially hysterical and scared members of the public, which they consistently handle incredibly well, but, moreover, it's worth staying on the right side of the control room staff otherwise they can send you to some *really* rubbish jobs. Tonight, however, and despite my charm offensive towards them, I must have slipped up somewhere and upset someone, as I was contacted shortly after leaving the last job and told to attend an address where a woman had recently called the police asking for a curry.

Operator: "You realise that you're through to the police, madam?"

Caller: "Yes, I'd like a curry, please. Can you deliver it to 263 Odin Place on the Black Estate."

Operator: "This is an emergency line, not a takeaway, madam."

Caller: "Can you make it quick?"

Operator: "Madam, I really think that you should…"

Caller: "The sooner you can come round the better. I need it straight away!"

It was at this point that the operator began to realise that maybe this wasn't just another caller misusing the system, and perhaps there was more to it. Police receive a call about a domestic incident every thirty seconds, so operators are always alert to the possibility that amongst the spurious calls there may well be a genuine cry for help.

Operator: "Madam, just answer yes or no. Do you need police assistance?"

Caller: "Yes."

Operator: "Are you unable to talk freely because there is someone with you?"

Caller: "Yes."

Operator: "We'll get an officer there as soon as we can."

Caller: "Can you make that two naan breads? My partner is very hungry."

Operator: "Understood. We'll send a couple of officers out to you. I'm passing the information to my colleagues now; officers are already travelling to your location. If you stay on the line..."

A shout was heard in the background of the woman's address and the caller hastily put down the receiver.

Meanwhile, on the other side of town, I was instantly updated about the job and notified that Lloyd was also travelling to the address. I lit up the blues but kept the sirens off: I didn't want to alert whoever was in the house that we had been called until the very last second. Arriving in the street at the same time, Lloyd and I got out of our cars and jogged towards the address. A lack of house numbers on the doors of the properties made it difficult to identify where we were supposed to be: Odin Place is a maze of terraces. Eventually, I noticed a woman frantically waving us over from inside one of the houses.

As we ran up the path we could see into the front lounge: *EastEnders* was playing on the large TV screen that dominated the room and illuminating the figure of a male slouched in an armchair, swigging from a can of Carlsberg. The woman pointed discreetly towards the front door before picking up a baby and making her way towards the male. The door was unlocked so we let ourselves in and headed for the lounge, announcing our presence as we entered the room.

"WHAT THE FUCK ARE YOU DOING IN OUR HOUSE!" the woman yelled back at us, startling me. This wasn't the reception that I usually received when the cavalry arrived. "Fuck off! You're not welcome here!" She cradled the baby closer to her chest, whilst taking a couple of small steps backwards.

Alerted by her screams, the male had jumped up out

of his chair and was now on his feet. He turned to face us: he looked to be in his mid-twenties, of average height, although his build was scrawny; his greasy dark hair lay limp across his forehead, seeming to accentuate his close-set eyes. He hopped from leg to leg as if he was in a boxing match, pushing his shoulders back and jutting his head forward before he began demanding to know why we had just walked into his home.

"If you ain't got a warrant, then fuck off back where you came from!"

"Go on, get out!" The woman complemented his comments with contemptuous sneers. "Bastards! We fucking hate coppers!"

I looked over at the woman. Despite the vitriol of her verbal attack I could see she was frightened; her hands trembling as she held onto the baby tightly swaddled in a pink blanket. Her long black hair was matted, her make-up smudged, and it looked as if she had been crying. The left side of her face appeared red, too; consistent with a recent slap or punch.

Whilst Lloyd informed the male that we didn't need a warrant if we believed that a breach of the peace was occurring, I attempted to get the woman into a different room; away from her partner. She wasn't playing ball though and refused to budge; holding onto her boyfriend's arm and moving just slightly behind him.

"So who called you, then?" enquired the man, cracking his knuckles. "Come on," he repeated, "who is this mystery caller?"

We tried to get back to establishing what had been going on, but it was clear that he wasn't going to tell us anything until his question had been answered: who was to blame for our visit?

"Come on," he persisted, "who the fuck was it, then?"

I saw the woman glance towards her partner, her eyes betraying her fear; trepidation written all over her face as she waited to see how I would respond.

"A passer-by heard a disturbance and called us," I lied. "Now, if you can explain what it was all about, we can either leave you to your evening, or take whatever action is needed." This was another lie: I had no intention of leaving the couple in the same house tonight – not with the agitated body language the woman was displaying.

"Nothing's happened," she stated acerbically. Now that she knew that I wasn't going to drop her in it, she appeared to get a second wind. "We were enjoying a quiet night in before you ruined it, now fu..." She then proceeded to order us – in undiluted Anglo-Saxon – to leave their abode, adding some personal insults to her foul-mouthed diatribe. It was clear to me that she was terrified her partner would discover her duplicity, although her swearing and aggression made her a convincing actress.

Despite all our efforts, they remained uncooperative. We had been unable to separate them and neither would explain what had happened prior to our arrival. We were just going round in circles, stonewalled at every junction and I had had enough.

"How did you get that reddening to the side of your face?" I asked her.

She shrugged and averted her eyes. I asked her partner the same question.

"Can you explain how your girlfriend got that red mark on the side of her face?"

"The kid slapped her? How should I know?" He smirked and sat back down in the armchair. He then resumed watching television.

"It was the baby," she volunteered, furtively glancing at her boyfriend, yet her eyes told a very different story. That was enough for us.

"I'm afraid I don't believe you," I replied, addressing her, but speaking loudly enough so he could clearly hear. "And you," I said, walking over to block his view of the TV screen, "are under arrest for assault."

Lloyd and I had worked together long enough for him to read my mind and so before the male had time to react my colleague had handcuffed him and was pulling him out of the chair.

"He's done nothing!" the woman screamed – the baby's cries adding to the cacophony of noise. "Let him go, you bastards!" Obviously, she was maintaining her act until he exited stage left.

"Take me away, Officers," the male added cockily. "You've got nothing on me and I'll be back in the morning. At least I'll get some bloody peace and quiet and a decent night's sleep. I'm sick of the constant crying of that thing!"

He swaggered to the door, while she broke down in tears.

"That kid has ruined my life!" he shouted back to her as he reached the door. "All I ever do now is bloody babysit!"

"If it's your own child, it's actually just called 'staying in'," I corrected him.

"Whatever!"

As he was led out to the van, I informed the woman that we would be back to speak to her as soon as her partner had been booked into custody. It was her cue now to reply with a: "Whatever!" before shouting to her partner that she loved him and would be getting straight on to the inspector to complain.

"If I weren't in these cuffs, I'd smash your face right in!" The male began the customary tirade against us as soon as he was placed in the back of my vehicle. "You think you're big because you're in uniform, but when I see you when you're off duty, I'll fucking do you!"

The abuse continued non-stop for the entire duration of the journey back to the station, but we had heard it all before and it was water off a duck's back to us. They are known as 'handcuff heroes': those prisoners who are compliant before the cuffs are on, yet full of promises of how they'll fight you when they are actually handcuffed, and then are compliant again when the cuffs are taken off. It's easy to be brave when you know there will be no consequences.

"Hey boys, you couldn't let me have a quick ciggy before we go into custody, could you? C'mon, I'm gagging for one."

That's another thing that prisoners do: swing from caustic abuse to being your best friend when they want something from you.

"I didn't think you had any. You didn't have any when I searched you before you got in the van."

"No, but I thought you boys would have some."

"Sorry, neither of us smoke."

"You fucking faggots! I hope you and your whole bastard family die of cancer!"

And there it is again – swinging back to abuse. I didn't bother to point out to him the irony of his insult.

When we eventually reached custody, with our prisoner laughing all the way through the process and insisting that we had nothing on him, I informed the sergeant of the circumstances of the arrest. There then followed the obligatory threat of getting us sacked for wrongful arrest.

As Lloyd took the prisoner's fingerprints and mug shot, I had a quiet word with the custody sergeant. He was right: we had little more than a cryptic phone call to the police and a reddening of the face; nevertheless, I still had reasonable grounds to suspect that he had assaulted her. Despite the lack of concrete evidence, however, I was aware that there would be little objection raised as long as I could demonstrate that I had taken positive action in a suspected domestic abuse incident. Around ten per cent of all crime per se is domestic related; it's a figure every police force would like to see reduced.

Once our suspect was safely ensconced in his cell, I returned to the address to see if I could obtain some better evidence to back up our case... and hoped that I'd get a better reception this time around.

"Coffee?" she asked.

I gratefully accepted, and we stood in the kitchen while the kettle boiled.

"I'm sorry about all that language earlier," she began, taking the milk from the fridge. "I don't really think your colleague looks like a lanky streak of piss, and I'm sorry for dragging your lovely Cornish accent through the mud."

I accepted her apology, and explained that I was actually from Wales; hoping that I didn't really sound as she had portrayed me. They say imitation is the sincerest form of flattery, but it isn't when everything you say at an incident is repeated back to you in a ridiculous mix of Somerset and over-exaggerated Welsh valley patois; actually, imitation is not the best form of flattery if you're talking to a stutterer, either.

"It's just that I wanted my partner out of the house. He's always like that when he's been drinking, but I really don't want him to know that I called you."

I informed her that her partner would be in the cells overnight as we had to wait until he was sober before we could interview him. I then tried again to establish what had happened, but she was cagey with her replies. I tried to reassure her by telling her that we were taking the decision to prosecute him out of her hands: I had seen what I believed were injuries, and I suspected he was responsible.

"We can still prosecute him even if you, as the victim, stay silent, but it would really help if you made a statement."

But her response was that she loved him and didn't want to get him into trouble.

"He's not a nasty man, just a bit of a bad boy," she told me. I must admit that I hadn't really warmed to him – call me old fashioned, but wishing a deadly disease on me and my family is a bit of a mood killer. As for *bad boys*, it never ceases to amaze me how many girls say they like them... and how many of those girls eventually end up as single mothers.

When I asked her about her relationship, she replied that it was complicated which usually means either: *it's none of your business* or *I've got a story that will last for an hour*. Thankfully, at least in this case, she was willing to talk. A third of all assaults recorded by the police are DV related, so any time invested with a victim is time well spent. However, it soon became apparent that her life had been one long series of let-downs and acceptances of being hurt. She told me that she wanted to give him a second chance – again. To me, it seems bizarre that whilst there are so many undeserving people getting that perpetual second chance, there are plenty of others who haven't even used up their first. Of course relationships need to be worked at, but surely there must come a point when you realise that life is too short to be with someone who sucks all the happiness out of you. One of the hardest decisions you will ever face in life is choosing whether to try harder or walk away.

Someone once told me that love is a game where you are constantly trying to balance an increasingly unstable structure before it crashes down around you; but, then again, they might just have been explaining the rules of Jenga.

Actually, now I come to think of it, the person who gave me the Jenga advice chose 'I Still Haven't Found What I'm Looking For' by U2 as her wedding song, so maybe she was biased. In the end, she had broken up with her husband citing what she termed 'religious differences'. "I'm Catholic and he's Satan," she told me.

I think the moral of the story is that relationships are complex and need work, but, on the other hand, if you're giving your all and your all isn't enough, then perhaps you're giving it to the wrong person. If you love someone, let them go… and if they come back, then it's probably because no one else wanted them.

After an hour with the victim, discussing her fifty shades of regrettable life choices, we were no further forward. She wouldn't make a statement, refused to have her face photographed and even formally denied that there had been a domestic incident.

"Nothing will change unless you do something different," I told her, but she wouldn't budge. Even after I asked if she thought it was acceptable for her baby to grow up in an environment where she would hear and see emotional and physical abuse, she still wouldn't cooperate.

"Maybe I'll just brush the dog's teeth with his toothbrush instead," she sighed. I looked out of the window into the backyard to see something that looked like a cross between a border collie and a pit bull; he looked like he'd rip your arm off and then go for help. Well, I suppose that was one way of getting even…

Although it was cold comfort to me, at least she was now flagged up on the system and her partner was languishing in the cells. She also knew that support would be available to her now if she asked – she just needed to reach out and accept it. It can be frustrating, but sometimes there is only so much you can do.

I said my goodbyes and wished her luck before returning to my vehicle where I sat in silence for a minute or two. I knew I'd be back at the address again in the future – I just hoped that it wouldn't be soon. I also hoped that my victim wouldn't end up just another sad statistic; that she would realise that she wasn't trapped and that she could change things.

It had been a disheartening call, and I couldn't help feeling that, despite my best efforts, I'd only done half a job. Still, there was no point dwelling on it. Sometimes I wish that I could go back to a time when my only worry consisted of trying to stop the cassette tape before the DJ on Radio 1 started talking while I was recording the Top Ten.

I was still ruminating over it as I started the ignition, only to be interrupted by the sound of a private call coming through on the police radio. It was Kim in Comms telling me of another 999 call: this time a man reporting that a passing dog had urinated against his front gatepost.

It's estimated that of the almost six million 999 calls made to the police each year, about eighty per cent – a staggering four million – are judged to be non-urgent; well, maybe it was an emergency in this case – for the dog, anyway. The problem is that genuine calls that need our immediate attention – like the takeaway curry call – can sometimes be missed; lost amongst the trivial calls concerning weeing dogs, dirty touchscreens, missing McNuggets, confiscated cannabis and disappointing prostitutes. The point is: just because someone rings in on an emergency line it doesn't automatically qualify *as an emergency*.

As the old saying goes, 'All that glitters is not gold' – take glitter, for example.

# CHAPTER 13

# Brad the Impaler

BANG! The old wooden garage doors went in with one kick, sending splinters and scraps of old paint flying as they smashed against the inside walls. We stood, our batons raised, poised ready to attack, peering into the gloom only to see three shocked faces staring back. Horrified expressions immediately crossed our own faces as we surveyed the scene in front of us… and I was a little bit sick in my mouth.

An hour before I had been standing in the parade room, listening to the briefing for today's operation. There had been a spate of thefts from vehicles and, as a result, I had been brought forward and was working with Brad from B shift. We had been in an unmarked police car in the multi-storey car park at about six in the evening, monitoring a group of suspicious looking youths, when the fateful call had come in. A man out walking his dog on the industrial estate had reported hearing screams that not even the deaf could ignore emanating from one of the old disused garages. "It sounded like someone was being brutally murdered in there!" he added, describing the blood-curdling cries to a horrified Comms operator.

Even before the job had been fully passed over the open airwaves we were revving the engine and accelerating down the ramp of the multi-storey. It can be hard enough to make progress through traffic even when you've got your blues and sirens on, but in an unmarked vehicle you're on a hiding to nothing. Not all unmarked cars have hidden strobes in their grille or a blue light snowglobe that you can just lean out of the window and slap on to the roof at some jaunty angle; without these, you have no authority to break the speed limits, go through red lights or drive the wrong way down one-way streets; and other cars just assume that you're an impatient driver, therefore try and hinder you as you attempt to get past. Eventually, by beeping our horn and using every short cut and diversion that we could think of, we finally arrived on scene to the sound of sickening screams piercing the still air – and that was before we had even got out of the vehicle. We sprinted to the garage. Brad stopped and stepped back, drawing his right foot up to waist level before kicking out, sending his boot smashing into the door...

Once the dust had settled, and by the dim glow of a 40-watt light bulb, I was able to make out three figures. I blinked hard, half hoping that when I opened my eyes again the horrific vision in front of me would have disappeared. Unfortunately, it hadn't.

Before me were two of the town's habitual criminals: Drew and Chris Peacock; their presence was usually anticipated when something unlawful was occurring. However, what was unusual about this scenario was that their frail old mother was with them. What was even more peculiar was that Drew was naked from the waist down and bent over a table, his posterior naked and exposed. What was *really* strange, and frankly quite disturbing, was what Chris and his mum appeared to be doing to Drew's bottom – the thing that had caused me to do a little sick burp. Chris appeared to be holding his brother's anus wide open with a pair of dessert spoons, whilst his dear old mum appeared to have her hand inserted deep into the void; delving in as if she was at a fairground bran tub searching for a prize. Upon seeing us, the trio had frozen mid dip. I didn't really know what to say: should I order them to stop or just tell them to crack on and excuse myself, quietly closing the door behind me as I left?

My dilemma was solved when Brad broke the awkward silence with an understated: "What the…!"

Suddenly, it was a free-for-all as they each tried to justify their role in this bizarre threesome; all gabbling at high speed sounding as if they were speaking in tongues. Eventually, Brad called a halt to proceedings, signalling for them all to stop. He wanted to hear from them one at a time and since Drew appeared to be the centre of attention, it seemed only fair that he should go first.

A lengthy tale of woe then poured forth from our poor, unfortunate victim as he described, in detail, how he had received a visit from the taxman. According to Drew, someone must have dropped him in it by informing his unwelcome visitor that he had been cultivating an illegal cannabis grow in the lock-up. The taxman had searched the building high and low, but had failed to find any evidence of the plants. He then maintained that the collector, frustrated and angry that there was no tax to collect, had flown into an incandescent rage, grabbing a car's suspension strut – that just happened to be conveniently lying about – and forcibly ramming it up his anus and violently kicking it into place. The man had then left, slamming the doors shut and leaving him all alone in this awkward pickle.

At this stage, I think some explanation is in order before you begin panicking that your Self-Assessment form might have got lost in the post. Let me reassure you that HM Revenue & Customs hasn't resorted to such draconian tactics… at least not yet; rather it appears that the criminal fraternity are also advocates of the monetarist system of economics and, just as the government tax us on our earnings, so some of the bigger crooks tax the smaller villains on theirs – their illegal earnings that is. In this case, the tax collector in question was Big Vince, one of the town's hard men, who not only has previous convictions for bottom-related activities, but is also not a big fan of paperwork either.

On discovering that the offending item appeared to be stuck *in situ*, our distraught victim had ruminated over his predicament for some time before phoning his brother, Chris, whom he insisted had some medical training.

Once again, I think I ought to clarify a few things before you have visions of Chris Peacock in a black V-neck St John Ambulance jumper, with a first aid satchel slung across his shoulders: Drew's idea of 'medical training' consisted of the fact that his brother used to be 'pretty good at playing Operation'. You may or may not remember the children's game, but it basically comprises of the comic likeness of a patient nicknamed 'Cavity Sam' who has a number of openings in his body filled with fictional and humorously named ailments made out of plastic. The rules require players to systematically remove these plastic ailments with a pair of tweezers without touching the sides of the cavity in which it has been placed, lest Sam's nose light up and an annoying buzzer sounds; so, I guess, *almost* the same training as St John's.

Alas, however, when he arrived on scene, his brother's paws proved too big for the particular cavity on offer and the buzzer, in this case replaced by Drew's anguished screams, was sounding far too often. There then followed a frantic phone call to their dear old mum, in the hope that she would have smaller and daintier hands. On arrival, she was instructed to do something no mother should *ever* have to do: attempt to extricate a foreign object that was embedded deep in her son's rectum. Chris, meanwhile, was subsequently relegated to 'holding open' duties, using the two dessert spoons his mother had brought with her.

We listened patiently, wincing and grimacing at the

appropriate times during his unfortunate tale. Drew appeared physically drained as the story came to an end and he looked up at us expectantly.

"You're a good liar, Drew," said Brad eventually, "but before you get too excited, I'm also a good liar. You've got a long way to go before you're in Pinocchio's league."

Actually, in this case, I wasn't so sure that Pinocchio was such a good example to use: I'd read that scientists had worked out that, assuming he was made of oak, Pinocchio would have weighed just over 9lb with a nose about an inch long; on that basis, if his nose doubled in length after each fib, the thirteenth lie would have put so much strain on his neck that it would have broken. Hardly the role model for liars that he makes himself out to be!

Before I could come up with an alternative suggestion, however, Brad was off again. "I'll give you the bit about your mum and your brother delving into your anus – I can see that, but I don't believe a word about Big Vince coming round." Unbeknownst to Drew, Big Vince had been locked up two days earlier and was still on remand; therefore, he couldn't possibly have been responsible.

"By the way," added Brad, turning his attention to Drew's mum, "I think you can probably take your hand out now." Mrs Peacock looked visibly relieved that her ordeal was finally over, and Chris withdrew the spoons with a clink.

Whilst Brad continued questioning Drew as to what had really happened, I used the opportunity to call for an ambulance in case there really was something 'languishing in the depths'. Twenty minutes later and Drew was still maintaining his innocence, although by now he had conceded that Vince hadn't been round and that there were no car parts involved.

Hearing a vehicle pull up outside, I gratefully went out into the fresh air and waved to the crew, before noticing the Red Cross symbol on the side of the ambulance.

"We often turn out to help the regular ambulance service if they are hard–pressed," explained the technician as he hopped out of the passenger side, clearly having noted my furrowed brow.

"It makes us sound like a Third World country," I replied, but, before I could elaborate, I was drowned out by the sound of my colleague yelling from inside the building:

"DON'T TRY AND SHIT IT OUT!"

I ran back inside, quickly followed by the Red Cross staff, to witness Brad pleading with Drew not to strain to force the unidentified object out.

"Your insides might come out!" cautioned my colleague in a bid to stop Drew from self-administering. Mrs Peacock hurried over to my side to ask what he meant.

"I think he's suggesting that he might suffer a rectal prolapse if he were to strain too hard," volunteered one of the medics. Mrs Peacock's face remained blank.

"I think we're worried he might get a little tail," I explained. She seemed satisfied with that.

"So what on earth has occurred here?" queried the other medic, scratching his head.

I think the stress of it all – not least the indignity of having to put her hands up her son's bottom – had become too much for Mrs Peacock. She broke her silence and told us that she was sick and tired of this farce, ordering Drew to get on with it and tell us all what had really happened so that we could all be on our way.

There is a golden rule in life that says: *Never do anything that you wouldn't want to explain to a paramedic.* However, it seems Drew had ignored this advice when he found himself bored with nothing to do on a slow Thursday afternoon.

"… so I just started to wonder what I could fit in my

arse – don't look at me like that! We've all done it!"

We all did look at him *like that*... because none of us had done it!

"What's in there?" I asked him.

"A tub of my mum's moisturiser," came the reply.

"I hope it's not my Nivea!" exclaimed a distraught Mrs Peacock.

Drew hung his head. It seems that research and development had eventually turned into shame and regret.

We had no desire to prolong Peacock's embarrassment, and satisfied that this wasn't a police matter, we got back in our car and left the job in the capable hands of the British Red Cross. We were just about to head back to the station for a well-deserved cup of tea – and to soak our eyes in bleach in an attempt to erase the awful sight from our minds – when Comms must have realised we were on the move again.

"Reports are coming in of a body being found near the boating lake beside the shop, can you attend?"

I went to hit the blues then remembered that we were still in an unmarked car. It was rapidly turning out to be one of those days! I should have realised this morning that something was awry when I rolled my car window down to let a spider out and a bee flew in. Five minutes later, just as dusk was falling, we arrived at the lake. An ambulance was already on scene, parked up on the grass, blue lights flashing.

"Dead?" queried Brad as we approached. We were already thinking ahead to what needed to be cordoned off, what other resources might be required and if there were any witnesses.

"Not quite as reported," replied Lysa, poking her head out of the vehicle. "He's collapsed – maybe had some sort of allergic reaction."

"Any idea what to?" I added, "Do you think he'll survive?"

"Well, if he doesn't, John, I'll be sure to invite you to an *Open Mike Night,*" she replied.

I couldn't really see the connection between the medical state of the patient and a date at the local comedy club... until I saw her slowly shaking her head. Perhaps her sarcastic tone should have been a clue.

"He's called Mike, isn't he?" I clarified. "And by *Open Mike Night* you mean the post mortem, don't you?"

She nodded to both. "We've only just got him into the ambulance, Sherlock. Give us a chance before you begin asking us to predict his future, will you! Those teenage girls over there found him." She pointed to a couple of females standing outside the shop.

"When we arrived they were giving him CPR, which was all very laudable except for the fact that he was already conscious and breathing. The bigger girl was sitting astride him and beating on his chest – we had to drag her off before she broke all his ribs. The other girl was busy French kissing him, by the look of it. We told them to stand over there and wait for you to arrive. You'll probably get more information out of them for the time being."

Point taken, I put away my notebook and we headed over towards the pair. At the most, they looked to be about sixteen or seventeen. They were stood idly chatting to each other, dressed in the requisite velour tracksuits and Ugg boots, which seems to be the standard uniform of most teenage girls in Sandford. I could have sworn I vaguely recognised one of them but, before I could be certain, she ran up and flung her arms around me.

"PC Donoghue! My favourite copper!" she exclaimed.

"Can you stop hugging me please, Kirsty?" I calmly requested, standing passively, my arms pressed tightly against my sides.

"It's just a grab unless you hug me back, PC Donoghue!" she added, inviting me to reciprocate.

"Well then, can you stop grabbing me, please?"

She eventually let go but, undaunted by my lack of cuddles, she bounced excitedly from foot to foot. "It's just that I haven't seen you for so long!"

"That's a good thing," I told her. "It means that you haven't been in any more trouble."

"PC Donoghue is lovely," she explained animatedly to her friend. "He locked me up when I glassed my boyfriend, and he was really nice to me."

All I can say is that if you ever find yourself going out with Kirsty Stromboli, don't forget to buy her flowers on her birthday. Her partner, Wayne, had described her in his statement as: 'temperamental – half temper, half mental'. His lack of petrol-station roses had been just the thing to tip her over the edge and all hell had broken loose.

"And what's your name?" I asked her friend.

"Anne-Marie," she replied shyly.

"Is that hyphenated?"

"No, she's just got a bit of asthma," interjected Kirsty. "And she can hear what you say, you know!"

I chose to ignore her comment and introduced myself and my colleague to the girls. Anne-Marie glanced hesitantly over to her friend and slowly began to approach Brad with her arms outstretched. He responded by indicating that, contrary to what her friend had done, it wasn't necessary to welcome every police officer you meet with a hug.

"Did you notice anything unusual when you found the male on the floor?" asked Brad after the basics of the incident had been established.

"I did notice a snake," volunteered Kirsty.

"What did it look like?"

"Shifty," came the reply.

"It could be an adder," I suggested. It is the only venomous snake native to Britain. They're not usually aggressive, but will react if trodden on or cornered. Then again, lots of households in the town have exotic snakes as pets – if one had escaped it could just as easily be one of those. We'd need to identify what type of snake it was if we were to establish what antidote would be required. I'd break the news to Lysa later that she might have to suck out the poison.

"Where do adders come from?" whispered Anne-Marie, as we began searching the nearby bushes. If we'd had more time, I'd have told her that it was when an abacus and a grass snake loved each other very much, but there was no time to waste. Ironically, in a bid to flush it out, we racked our asps and began beating the long grass.

"THERE IT IS!" yelled Kirsty, jumping back. "IT BIT ME!"

The snake was following her, almost jumping up in a bid to attack her again. She was hysterical; tripping over as she tried to escape. It kept after her, rearing up each time she tried to kick it away.

Brad and I rushed over and immediately started to beat the snake to death with our batons, sending it flicking in the air with each blow that struck. Alternate thwacks rained down on the serpent as we sought to put an end to its killing spree, but it seemed impervious to our strikes. Finally, my colleague took hold of the handle of his baton with both hands, raised it high above his head and then delivered the final *coup de grâce*, bringing it down hard into the centre of the snake. The two ends sprang up as its middle was driven into the ground before flopping back down again to leave the beast flaccid and spent on the grass. Brad the Impaler!

After our period of manic activity we now stood bent double, breathing heavily, our hands on our knees, positioned either side of the limp and lifeless corpse; satisfied that we had executed the demon and put an end to its trail of destruction once and for all.

"Get Google on your phone and I'll describe it," instructed Brad breathlessly as I put my baton away.

There wasn't a second to lose if we were to find out what effect the bite would have on our victims. The paramedics were still at the site, carrying out urgent checks on their patient. A glance over at Kirsty saw her pale and shaking, hanging onto her friend for support. Retrieving my mobile from my pocket, I saw Brad hook the thing over his asp and raise it up towards a street light to get a better view.

"It's blue," he shouted out to me. I punched it into the search bar.

"Blue Malaysian, Blue Bungarus, Blue rattlesnake, Blue Indigo... there's a few."

"Shiny texture."

I refined the search and rapidly scrolled through the results. "Eastern Indigo or Blue Coral snake?"

"It's rot and mildew resistant."

"I think they all are?" I fired back. "Can you describe the head?"

"Afraid not."

"Why, is it too badly damaged?"

"No, it's a frayed knot. How obvious do I have to make this? I'm describing a piece of blue rope. That's what we've just brutally murdered – some blue twine that someone has tied a granny knot at the end of." Brad now turned his attention to the girls. "You're saying that this thing *actually* bit you?"

"Well, my foot touched it!" replied Kirsty defensively.

"Let me get this clear," clarified Brad. "This is the shifty bit of rope that you saw earlier?"

"I think so," came the muted reply.

Brad let out a loud sigh. He asked to see the underside of Kirsty's boot and as she teetered about on one leg, he shone the torch on the bottom of her Ugg.

"The rope was stuck to the bottom of your boot with chewing gum... that's why it leapt about after you." He shook his head.

The girls just stood there looking shamefaced and despondent. I felt a little sorry for them – their hearts had been in the right place, even if the snake's hadn't. I tried to make them feel better by telling them that it could have been anything that had stricken down our original victim, before telling them the case of Valerius Maximus, a Latin writer who had lived in Rome centuries ago. He met his death when a tortoise was dropped on his bald head by an eagle who had mistaken it for a rock.

That seemed to cheer them up a bit and I could see that Anne-Marie was itching to tell me something, as she tentatively raised her hand.

"The girl in the second row: have you got a question for the panel?"

She looked around as if to make sure that it was her I was actually speaking to.

"I don't know if this is helpful at all?" she began slowly, "But when we found the man on the grass he seemed *really* keen for me to have this; he kept on trying to give it to me as he lay there. I couldn't work out what he was trying to say as his face was all swollen like a pumpkin. Maybe it's a clue to who tried to kill him?"

We looked at her dumbfounded. Why had she waited until now to reveal this vital information?

"Well?"

She held out her hand to reveal her secret.

"It's his bloody EpiPen!" we chorused in disbelief. Brad unceremoniously grabbed it from her and ran over towards the ambulance.

"Was it important?" asked Anne-Marie, looking pleased that she had been able to help.

"Yes, it was," I replied, patting her on the shoulder. "People carry them in case they go into anaphylactic shock – they deliver a dose of adrenalin. It's great that you've given it to us but, you know, you really should have mentioned it sooner."

"I forgot about it when we were looking for the

snake. It was just all so exciting." She looked as if she was about to cry and I wasn't sure if it was because she felt she had done something really good, or something really bad. I tried to think of something to console her but before I could say anything, Kirsty was in like a shot.

"I once watched a mime artist almost choke to death on a street corner and everyone clapped... for a couple of reasons."

Brad had now reappeared, and told me that the arrival of the EpiPen had answered a couple of questions for the paramedics and they were now ready to leave for the hospital.

"PC Donoghue! PC Donoghue!" pleaded Kirsty on hearing this. "If I give you my phone, will you take a selfie of me and Anne-Marie with the body before they go?"

"There's two parts to this answer, Kirsty. Firstly, if I take a picture of you both, that's not a selfie, and, secondly, no." What kind of mawkish society are we living in!

"Well, can you give us a lift home then, please?" she requested, bouncing up and down. "I've got to see to the little 'un."

With all that had been going on, I'd almost forgotten that she had a child. A wave of panic suddenly overtook me as I realised that the baby might have been left home alone while we had been chatting. She must have read my mind and reassured me, telling me that the baby's granny was looking after her.

"You'll remember her, PC Donoghue," she added, "you were scrapping with her outside the pub last Saturday. She told me all about it."

Before you begin imagining that I had assaulted some poor pensioner, let's just remember that this is Sandford: whilst Kirsty's mum might well be a grandmother, there is no need to picture her with a blue rinse and a tartan shopping trolley. Due to the high rate of teenage pregnancies in Sandford, you can be a grandmother in this town while you're still in your early thirties.

If my memory serves me right, this particular grandmother had peroxide blonde hair, was spilling out of her very low-cut top, was wearing six-inch stilettoes, had a very dirty mouth on her and some very sharp rings on her fingers, judging by the cut under my right eye.

"And how is your mother?"

"She says she's never drinking absinthe again. Oh, and she apologises for biting you."

"Well, pass on my regards to her and tell her that she's got a good right hook."

"I will PC Donoghue. She'll be pleased with that!"

"So, are you and Wayne still together?" I enquired, changing the subject – Wayne being the victim in the glassing incident for which I had originally locked Kirsty up.

"I'm available, if that's what you're asking," she responded with a wink.

"I wasn't, actually. So, what happened between you two?" Being glassed by your partner may seem like an obvious answer, but they had reconciled long before the matter had even reached court. In a nutshell, Kirsty and Wayne's volatile relationship can be best described as a Barbie and Ken doll being repeatedly smashed together until they burst into flames; yet, through it all, they had both kept on coming back for more. Maybe it was their shared business interest that had played a part in keeping them together: it turned out that they had a substantial illegal cannabis crop in their loft, which may also have gone a long way in explaining Kirsty's mood swings as it is currently estimated that one in four cases of psychosis is associated with smoking weed.

Clearly, some other heinous act had once again caused young love to flounder. Rumour had it that Kirsty had sent Wayne a photo message asking if she looked fat in her new leggings; apparently, he had texted back

'Noooooo!', but it had autocorrected to 'Moooooo!'. She had then flown into a mad rage and Wayne had had to jump out of a top-storey window to avoid being stabbed by his angry girlfriend, breaking both his ankles in the process. I decided not to mention it.

"Of all my mistakes, he was the mistakiest," she eventually declared after some considerable thought.

"I'm sorry to hear that. How's Witnay? Have you got joint custody?"

"She's fine, but I've told you, PC Donoghue, I've been out of trouble. I've given up the cannabis now!"

"No, I meant joint custody of your daughter. Does Wayne still see her?"

"Oh. Oh, yeah. Sometimes."

"I'm having a baby," piped up Anne-Marie, breaking the awkward silence.

"You're kidding!" I replied.

"Well, technically, she is," added Brad, looking pleased with his funny.

"Oh, so you're a bodybuilder now," I joked. She just gave me a confused look.

"We've pulled out the book of names," interjected Kirsty. "We're almost through to M and we think we're really close now to guessing who the father is."

Anne-Marie just smiled blankly.

"So, what are you going to call it, then?" asked Brad.

To a police officer, this is an important question. Whenever we attend an incident we need to record the names of all the children in the household and ensuring that we get the correct spelling can sometimes be a nightmare. In some cases it's as if the parents went to register the name as Emily, only to be told that name was already taken but they could have Emily_2480 or Emmalee. I am forever apologising for mispronouncing their child's made-up name.

Denmark is one of the few countries that still have a list of approximately 7,000 official names that parents can choose from. Elsewhere, it took a judge in France to stand up for common sense and tell the parents that they couldn't call their child *Nutella*, however much they loved the chocolate spread. *Anal, Anus, Monkey, Superman, Lucifer* and *Robocop* have all been vetoed in other places, along with *Talula Does The Hula From Hawaii*. In Venezuela, they even drafted a bill banning names that 'expose children to ridicule, are extravagant or difficult to pronounce'. I made a mental note to forward the article to our inspector – Dick Soaper.

We drove the girls home and then set off for our unfortunate victim's house. Lysa had asked if we could let his wife know that he was in hospital and also see if we could get any further information regarding any allergies he might have. We found the address nearby, and were let in by his daughter who took us through into the kitchen where the wife was chatting with a neighbour. We explained how Mike had been found near the shops and that he had now been taken to Sandford Hospital.

"I... I just sent him out for some milk," she informed us, the slight tremor in her voice betraying her concern. She looked over at her coffee cup. "I suppose... I suppose I'll just have to drink it black."

I wasn't sure if it was shock, but as we weren't getting any coherent responses from her mum, we asked the daughter if she knew of any medical history.

"I know Fleming discovered penicillin in 1928," she replied. "We did it in school today."

This was all becoming a bit surreal. We tried to reassure them as best we could by telling them that it seemed to be some kind of allergic reaction, but that he was in good hands; finally suggesting that they might wish to make their way to the hospital. We then made our excuses and left, heading back to the police station. Between Drew Peacock and his bottom-feeding, Kirsty and the angry rope, Anne-Marie and the EpiPen and Mike and his mysterious allergic reaction, we felt that we needed to get back to normality and people who would talk sense to us.

"You pair of numpties!" Barry could hardly contain himself as we told him about our escapade with the string snake, whom we had now christened Brian. "How long was it? How many feet?"

"None, Sarge. We told you it was a snake. It didn't have any feet."

"Absolute muppets, the pair of you!" He was merciless in his mockery. "Can't tell the difference between some string and a serpent? Maybe I should send you to get your eyes tested!"

We both skulked off into the parade room and sat in front of the blank computer screen wondering how we were going to word our sequel to Comms. After five minutes, we decided to go and get a cup of tea in the hope that it would get our inspirational juices flowing. A further five minutes on and I was part way through typing a report that Ernest Hemingway would have been proud of, when we heard a loud shout and the muffled sound of somebody stumbling back and crashing against the door to the toilets.

It would appear that as our sergeant was lifting up the lid of the toilet seat, a blue monster – aided by an elastic band sellotaped under the lid – had leapt from the watery depths and almost scared the living crap out of our fearless leader. As shouts of: "BLOODY BRIAN!" echoed down the corridor, we decided it was probably best if we left the station and resumed our patrols… as quickly as our legs would carry us!

# CHAPTER 14

# Possession

"The voices in my head are telling me to kill someone." The male sounded calm and collected on the phone as he talked candidly to the operator about his murderous intent.

"Is there anyone with you?"

"Just the apparitions that taunt and torture me every day. Do they count?"

"Stay there. We'll send an officer out to you straight away."

I've paraphrased somewhat but that's the gist of it. If someone rings the police to tell them that they have the urge to go on a blood-soaked rampage, someone has to assess whether it's a genuine threat or not; that 'someone' is your local, friendly, unarmed response officer.

Naturally, the operator would have probed further and carried out checks on the system to try and establish how credible the caller seemed, but you can never be certain of someone's intent until you actually speak to that individual in person. Today, the person speaking to the caller face to face would be me. I had been in the office, happily chatting to Samantha, the front-counter clerk, when Comms had passed me the call; she had heard every word.

"Chances are it will just be a cry for help... well, hopefully, anyway," I told her as I put the phone down.

"Seriously, though, is it?" she enquired, ashen faced.

"What if he's been told in a seance to lure a police officer to his house so he can massacre them?"

"Luckily, I don't believe in all that sort of nonsense," I told her.

"It doesn't matter what *you* believe in," she replied flatly. "It's what *he* believes."

There followed an awkward pause as I tried to think of something amusing to fire back. My first instinct had been to tell her that after learning Morse code when I was in the navy I'd had to stop eating Rice Krispies because of all the evil things they were telling me to do; however, one look at her face told me that my feeble attempt at humour wouldn't have gone down at all well. To be honest, after she had planted the thought of evil in my head, even I didn't find my little joke funny anymore.

"I just have this sixth sense," she confided, looking me directly in the eye and placing her hand on my forearm.

"Don't tell me: *I see dead people*," I quipped.

"No. I've just got a very bad feeling about this." She was genuinely concerned at the prospect of my going out to the house alone.

Comms were on the phone again, telling me that they had checked the caller's previous history and discovered that our would-be killer, Robert Taxil, had a couple of convictions dating back to over a decade ago and in a different force area for a series of bizarre sexual offences.

Past records had shown that Taxil was fond of posing naked in the window of his front room at the exact time in the afternoon that the local school came out. Furthermore, he also had a penchant for lurking in public toilets, waiting for an unsuspecting victim to appear; then, when they began relieving themselves at the urinals, he would suddenly leap out, catch some of their pee in a cup, shouting, "I'M THIRSTY!" before drinking it in front of their eyes. I must confess, I didn't know quite what to make of this information. Samantha raised a quizzical eyebrow; I had to hand it to her: he did seem odd. In fact, something about this whole thing just left a bad taste in my mouth.

It seemed that he was now living in our force area and had come back onto the police radar just this year for various petty thefts and criminal damage.

In January he had gone into Tesco, where he had proceeded to open can after can of lager, standing calmly in the aisle drinking them one by one until police finally arrived and he was led away.

In March he had smashed a window in the Catholic church with a brick. On this occasion he had sat on the floor, waiting patiently for officers to arrive.

Every couple of months after that there had been similar incidents. At no time had he put up a struggle or made any excuses for his actions – he simply allowed himself to be led meekly away. His behaviour had, however, raised suspicions, and one intelligence report stated that officers noted that Taxil appeared to be taking an overly keen interest in police procedures: protocol; which particular officers dealt with him; as well as what shift was on duty at those specific times.

"I'll give Lloyd a call," I told Samantha. "I'll see if he can come along, too, if that makes you any happier."

Half an hour later, and with daylight fading fast, I was waiting for Lloyd at the entrance to the long dirt track that led to Taxil's smallholding. I thought about what Samantha had said and locked the car doors. According to the satnav, my exact location appeared to be in the middle of nowhere, parked on an unnamed road.

I soon saw the headlights of Lloyd's van in the distance. As he pulled up, I got out and briefed him with the scant information that I knew. He nodded grimly in response. Getting back in my car, I shuddered in the autumn chill.

In convoy we made our way up the rough dirt track to the house, our tyres sending muddy water splashing up the sides of the vehicles as they bounced in and out of the potholes along the way. As we arrived, the bare trees seemed to cry murder as the sky suddenly filled with crows; their harsh caws protesting at our intrusion.

The open yard was dotted with obsolete farming equipment and broken-down cars that were half stripped and gutted and their windscreens ritually smashed. We got out of our vehicles and looked towards the house: it was in total darkness, looking ramshackle and foreboding, silhouetted as it was against the darkening sky.

Walking through the puddles, we made our way to the front porch. A set of wind chimes was gently clinking in the light breeze; and, as if things weren't already eerie enough, there was a rocking chair sitting a few feet away. I silently prayed that it wouldn't start moving of its own accord. The only thing that could have added to the air of trepidation would have been the sight of an abandoned funfair on the field opposite. I was thankful for small mercies.

The front door was open as if inviting us in. I entered and shouted for Taxil. We were met with a deathly silence. There was still enough light coming in through the windows to make out a spartanly furnished room littered with cups and dirty plates.

The light switch consisted of two bare wires protruding from the wall – I decided against sparking them. Instead, we proceeded cautiously, holding our torches up next to our heads so that our eyes followed exactly where the beams shone. The room itself was freezing – the temperature even colder than outside. Tattered curtains hung limply either side of the panes of glass; swathed in cobwebs. Old newspapers lay scattered across the table and floor, with various articles ringed several times in black ink; someone had obviously pressed so hard and circled them so frantically that the pages were torn where the biro had dug in.

We shouted again, but no one replied. Feeling unnerved, I racked my baton whilst Lloyd shook his pepper spray. Admittedly, sometimes it feels like a sorry state of affairs when you feel you have to prepare yourself for a fight when, ostensibly, you've come to help someone, but, on this occasion, and especially with Sam's words fresh in my mind, I couldn't help but think that at any moment a madman with a machete was about to jump out at me. I changed hands, moving my torch to my left and holding my baton poised above my right shoulder, ready to bring down on any would-be attacker; nevertheless, we were still at a disadvantage: the house owner knew the layout and terrain and, in most circumstances, action beats reaction. In circumstances such as these, every doorway and corner was a potential hazard.

Whilst I slowly pushed the door to the kitchen open with my foot, Lloyd quickly scanned the area with his torch. "There's something on the table," he whispered urgently. I entered the room, almost slipping over on the wet floor. I shone my torch down and saw that it was swimming with congealed blood. On the table was a pig's head; but this wasn't a bronzed, glazed pig's head that oft adorn the table of medieval banquets and where the animal looks like it has died merrily, whilst eating an apple: this one was a pale, sad-looking specimen; its ears flopped down; teeth broken and uneven.

"That's one little piggy who won't be having any roast beef," I muttered.

Lloyd just gave me a quizzical look. I didn't elaborate.

The far wall of the kitchen was lined with shelves containing various specimen jars filled with odd-looking animal parts suspended in a musky yellowish liquid that I suspected was formaldehyde. It looked like a Victorian freak show; and it made my skin crawl.

Now satisfied that the rooms downstairs were empty, we started up the stairs, calling out as we went but again there was no reply. As usual in this type of situation we made our way carefully, keeping our backs to the wall in case something was thrown down on us. Once safely at the top, we prepared to enter each room in turn.

The bathroom was dirty but functional. The only thing that indicated that someone slightly unhinged might be living there was that the toilet paper hung down *over* the wall-mounted holder instead of *under* it, but, then again, everyone has their own little idiosyncrasies.

Even from the doorway of the first bedroom we could see that it appeared to be set out as some kind of workshop: technical drawings of cars were strewn about the floor; scores of old keys lay on the desk amid intricate sketches of locks; we found soldering irons that were still plugged in, along with randomly discarded circuit boards.

The second bedroom was very spartanly furnished: a double bed that had a bare mattress with a sleeping bag lying on top and two dark wood wardrobes both heaped high with clothes and dirty shoes.

The remaining bedroom, however, seemed at complete odds with the rest of the property: it was decorated in a pretty, flock wallpaper, with pictures adorning the walls; porcelain dolls stared down from a shelf. The bed was carefully made and the drawers were full of neatly folded items. When we looked inside, the wardrobes were hung with women's clothing. On a nightstand stood an old-fashioned music box containing an assortment of rings, trinkets and old watches. The last few remaining notes played out as Lloyd replaced the lid. Something just didn't feel right here…

Back on the landing, we looked up and saw that the loft hatch was slightly open. My colleague sighed – he knew what that meant. I cupped my hands in front of me to give him a leg-up so that he could take a look inside.

"What's that?" Before he had even started to move the hatch cover, Lloyd had suddenly stopped dead in his tracks and motioned for me to stay silent. I heard a slow creak followed by a violent slam. "Downstairs!" We raced down to see a large recess in the centre of the living room floor; the old rug that had been covering it had been folded to one side and a heavy wooden door lay on top of it. We stood either side of the entrance to what looked like an underground cellar. We knew what had to be done, but neither of us relished the thought of climbing down into the unknown.

"Robert! Robert Taxil! It's the police. We're here to help. We know you're down there. Come on up and talk to us."

We were rewarded with an eerie silence.

"I'll go," I volunteered.

"Are you ok with that?"

"Danger is my maiden name," I replied. I'd like to have said something profound like: *never let your fears decide your fate*, but, in reality, the only reason I was offering to go into the basement alone was that I didn't relish the thought of that heavy door slamming shut whilst we were down there and trapping us both. Besides, out here in the middle of nowhere the reception on our radios was sporadic – it would probably be non-existent in the basement. Lloyd could stand guard at the top.

"We know you're down there! Don't make me come and get you!" In vain I tried one last time to persuade Taxil to show himself, but to no avail. I put my baton away and swapped it for the pepper spray; in a confined space it would be easier to wield. I gave it a little shake to wake it up and, with my torch in my other hand, I took a deep breath and took my first step into the void.

I'm not sure how old you have to be before you stop being afraid of going into a basement alone, but, whatever age it is, I haven't reached it yet. I gingerly placed one foot on each step in turn, shining the torch in all directions into the darkness before I was confident enough to proceed any further: it was pitch black down there.

"Are you there yet?" called Lloyd from above after a minute or so had passed.

"Almost," I lied, mentally reprimanding myself for being so overly cautious. Emboldened, I hurried down the last few steps. Reaching the bottom, my face was suddenly enveloped in a heavy black cloth. I quickly tore it away, flailing at it with my arms and legs. As the frame that had supported the material collapsed, a dark and dingy room was revealed; various boxes and paraphernalia were stacked around the edges, but a deliberate space had been cleared in the centre. On the stone floor, and covering the whole area, a diagram of a large pentacle had been drawn in what appeared to be dried blood. It consisted of a five-pointed star set within a circle, the points representing the five Wiccan elements: fire, water, earth, air and spirit. I had seen this symbol before, but only in books. Pagans believe that the circle represents eternity; however, it has a totally different meaning for Satanists. My blood ran cold.

In the centre, someone had placed a large Ouija board. It looked homemade, marked out with the letters of the alphabet, numbers and the usual words: 'YES' and 'NO'.

The board used to be part of a harmless parlour game until the early 1900s when it became synonymous with the occult, the supernatural and tales of demonic possession. Many mediums and paranormal experts believe that the Ouija board is a portal through which any spirit – good or evil – may come through. There are documented tales of people speaking in Latin and other obscure tongues while they have been using it despite never having previously studied or spoken those languages before. Whatever the truth may be, it's certainly no longer a game, and definitely not something that I'd ever mess with.

Suddenly, the hairs on the back of my neck stood on end as I felt someone staring at me in the dark. I shone the torch quickly around the room, shuddering as though someone had just walked over my grave. Perhaps it was just my imagination, but the temperature seemed to plummet and a distinctly musty smell pervaded the room. I didn't like this one bit. If there was ever a time to reprise my Catholic faith, this was it. I desperately tried to think of something positive that I had learnt at school to cancel out the sense of pure evil that seemed to have filled the room.

"*Yea, though I walk through the valley of the shadow of death, I will fear no evil: for thou…* JESUS!" I almost shat myself as a huge rat scurried out from underneath a pile of boxes stacked behind me.

Once my heart rate had slowed and my breathing was almost back to normal, I hastily searched the rest of the basement to make absolutely sure there was nobody else present, before being drawn back to the Ouija board. There were notes written in chalk next to it, alongside two large candles that had burnt down; the wax still soft to the touch. I called up to Lloyd to tell him what I'd found. There was no answer.

"Lloyd, are you there?"

Silence. I stood and looked up the cellar steps, expecting at any moment the wooden door to be pushed back into place, sealing me in my ice-cold tomb. I checked my radio – there was no signal. Just as I was preparing to sprint up the stairs and confront whoever or whatever was up there, I heard a snigger.

"I'm here!" he shouted back. He'd done that on purpose, the bastard!

"There's some sort of presence in the basement – I can feel it!" Somehow it made me feel better to verbalise my thoughts: to let whatever it was down here know that I knew they were there.

"Like Casper the friendly ghost?" he called back.

Easy to think it's all a joke when you are standing at the top of the steps! That said, even the tale of Casper takes an ominous turn when you realise that he's actually a dead child.

Not wanting to spend any longer than I needed to down in the basement, I quickly got out my notebook and began recording what was written next to the board. Many of the words had been rubbed out and some of the letters were not properly formed; as though the writer had written them in haste; some didn't even make sense, whilst others were indecipherable. I then discovered KILL and PIG, and hoped that they referred to the sad-looking creature in the kitchen, but I wasn't holding my breath. Eventually, I came across a chain of letters, all linked together. They snaked over the floor, unevenly spaced, but they definitely spelt something out even though some of them had been written back to front. Letter by letter I wrote them down until I finally managed to piece them all together.

D – O – N – O – G... DONOGHUE. That was me! My blood froze whilst goosebumps covered my arms. I could hear my heart beating fast, the blood pulsating through my veins.

To my left was a pile of old newspapers which were all copies of the same edition of the *Sandford Advertiser*. I immediately recognised the advert on the back: 'NOW IS THE WINTER OF OUR DISCOUNT TENTS' as I had a copy of the same issue at home. There had been a sale at the local camping shop over Christmas and the slogan had raised a laugh at the time, but I was certainly in no laughing mood now as I knew what else was in that paper: I turned to the front page to see the familiar photograph of me and my colleague, Andy, standing in front of a fire-damaged property, being hailed as heroes after saving a family from their burning home on Christmas Eve. In the copy in front of me now, however, someone had scratched out our eyes with some sort of sharp implement – someone who obviously didn't share the same admiration for our night's work as everyone else.

"I'm coming up now!" I shouted to Lloyd, grabbing

a copy and making my way out as quickly as I could without looking too undignified.

"What's that?" queried my colleague as I breathlessly reached the top.

"The newspaper that Andy and I were in. It's been defaced."

"Have they drawn a big cock on it?"

"They might as well have done!"

Although our search for our potential killer had proved negative, I felt certain he was here somewhere, watching us. He had successfully lured us to the house and now he was toying with us; waiting for an opportunity.

"I'M OUT HERE!"

Lloyd and I looked at each other as we heard the shout. It had definitely come from outside. Evidently, he had chosen his time and his place. We were finally about to meet Robert Taxil.

"AREN'T YOU COMING OUT TO SEE ME?"

Batons raised, we bolted from the house into the porch. It was pitch black outside now that night had fallen. We scanned the area with our torches but couldn't see anyone amongst the cars. We shouted for him to show himself before walking into the yard itself, turning constantly to make sure that he wasn't creeping up behind us.

BANG! The basement door slammed shut. We spun round to see the lights go on in the house and the tattered curtains being closed. Swiftly, we made our way back and re-entered the house where we were met by the sight of a man sitting in an armchair in the middle of the previously empty lounge, his face obscured by a grotesque rubber clown mask.

"Is that you, Robert?"

"You must be the elusive PC Donoghue," he replied. "I'm afraid I don't know the name of your colleague."

"Could you take the mask off?" requested Lloyd.

"Tell your colleague," answered the clown angrily, "that I will only speak to you, PC Donoghue."

"You haven't got a choice," responded Lloyd. "You don't have a choice who you will or won't deal with."

"Oh, but I do. I've waited a long time for this."

"Robert, you rang the police saying you were hearing voices. We've come out to see you. What can we do to help?" My question hung in the air.

"GET HIM OUT!" The clown pointed at the door whilst shouting furiously, indicating that Lloyd should leave, before changing his tone back to calm and collected. "Please don't make me take the passive out of my aggressive just yet."

"It doesn't work like that, Robert. You called us here – you deal with us both."

"Oh, don't be a spoilsport, PC Donoghue," he replied sarcastically. "I've made a lot of sacrifices to get you here today."

"I know. I've seen them in the kitchen."

"Ever the wit, aren't you?"

"Look, Robert, we can take you to hospital if you think you're hearing voices. There are people there who can help you."

"Has anyone ever told you that you have lovely eyes, PC Donoghue? I have the perfect jar for them."

I was just about to tell him that I was flattered but I wasn't of *that* persuasion when I realised what he had said. I decided to change tack: I had noticed a photograph of children playing in what looked to be the town park in Sandford; if I could get him talking on the subject then maybe I could establish some sort of rapport with him.

"So, which one's yours?" I asked, picking up the picture.

"I haven't decided yet." He was reptilian in his response. His reply, slow and deliberate, sent shivers down my spine. "And answer me this, PC Donoghue." He seemed to be becoming agitated again. "If someone is staring through my window when the curtains happen to be open, how come I am criminally liable for what they see?"

I knew what he was referring to, but I didn't want to get drawn on past incidents.

"Look, take the mask off before we talk any further." Without seeing his facial expression it was impossible to read him or have any idea what he might be thinking. I was also growing weary of his prevaricating. While Taxil and I had been talking, Lloyd had slowly edged his way further into the room and was now stood only a couple of yards away from the chair.

"So you want to see my face? Do you want to see my black heart, too? I'm afraid someone lowered the blind on the window of my soul long ago. My life is dissonant, PC Donoghue. I'm beyond help."

He seemed to be filibustering; playing for time, but I wanted this over.

"If I can help, I will."

"Our communion will never be blessed, PC Donoghue. Try as you might."

"We can take you straight to the hospital. What else do you want?"

"I'm bored now," he commented, ignoring my question and instead nodded towards the newspaper that I had tucked into my body armour. "I see you've found my artwork. You really spoilt my fun when you had to play the hero."

"That's it!" I barked, as I lunged towards the chair and getting my handcuffs out in the process. Like a shot, Lloyd had also moved, holding the man down as I applied the cuffs. "You're under arrest for arson with intent to endanger life. You do not have to say anything, but it may harm your defence if you do not mention when questioned something which you later rely on in court. Anything you do say may be given in evidence." It must have been Taxil who had set the fire. This meant we could now stop looking for the culprit.

Taxil made no attempt to struggle and nor did he speak: he simply allowed himself to be taken just like he had in the reports of all the previous incidents. Lloyd and I, meanwhile, were both shaking from the adrenalin still charging through us. I think both of us genuinely believed that we were in for the fight of our lives. The psychological tension that had risen steadily throughout the night now seemed somewhat of an anticlimax, although I wasn't complaining.

As I pulled off the clown mask, I resisted the urge to say: *'If it weren't for you pesky kids'* but, unfortunately, Lloyd couldn't contain himself and I could hear him exclaim: 'It's the janitor!' as Robert's face was finally revealed. Maybe this was our escape valve after the stress of the whole escapade, or perhaps we were just raised on too many episodes of *Scooby Doo*.

Robert Taxil, messenger of the spirits, practitioner of The Dark Arts and potential killer was a bit of an anticlimax too: he didn't look like an evil genius at all; in fact, he looked completely unremarkable. He was a balding, stocky, middle-aged man with a characterless face: a completely unremarkable personification of evil. We led him out to the vehicles and sat him in the cage in the back of Lloyd's van.

"We're taking you to custody, Robert. You've been arrested on suspicion of causing the fire on Christmas Eve as a result of what you said to me back there. You'll be able to get the help you need there, too. Have you any questions for me?"

He just smirked.

I told Lloyd that I'd follow him back to the station in the panda. Getting back in the car, I breathed a sigh of relief. I felt like the weight of the world had just been lifted from my shoulders. I also made a mental note to thank Sam in the front office: she hadn't been completely right as the worst of her fears hadn't been realised; still, it hadn't been a particularly pleasant job. Thankfully though, we all remained safe and unharmed. We had some positive results too: Robert Taxil wasn't going to be killing anyone tonight nor hopefully ever if we could get him the help he needed; and we'd found a suspect for the Christmas Eve house-fire – that would please CID. I got my notebook out again and wrote down the time of arrest. As the tail lights of Lloyd's van disappeared down the track, I started the engine and allowed myself a little smile and, if I could have reached, I would have given myself a pat on the back.

Suddenly: CLUNK! The central locking system on the vehicle activated. Glancing up, I saw a pair of eyes staring back at me in the rear-view mirror. A second later and I felt two cold hands around my neck. Next, I was pulled violently back as the pressure on my throat was intensified. The back of my seat was forced into my body as the strangler pushed his knees into it to gain extra leverage. Instinctively, I reached up to try and prise the hands free, but couldn't get a firm grip around them. I kept on trying, scratching my windpipe as I dug my nails into my neck to try and force my fingers around his. I began grasping at the front of my body armour, searching for my radio before grabbing it and pressing the talk button but, barely able to catch a breath, I could only gurgle. I tried to find the panic button, feeling desperately with my fingers, but I couldn't locate it before I was pulled harder back into the headrest. I pushed my foot down hard on the accelerator and the car shot forward. Within seconds we had cleared the yard and careered off the road and into a ditch. Undeterred, my attacker continued squeezing, slowly cutting off my air supply. I started kicking my feet and pushing even further back in my seat in an attempt to reach for my pepper; all the while trying to punch at whoever was behind me but I was getting weaker and my head becoming even lighter. I tried to pull at his hands again but there was no moving them: my strength was fading. I was becoming dizzy, my senses waning. In the darkness I saw a pinpoint of white light; gradually it grew bigger and bigger until everything became brilliant white…

Dunk! Dunk! Dunk! It was the sound of the car door handles being tried; then, a smash, closely followed by the sound of pepper spray being discharged. At once, the hands around my throat released and I slumped forward in my seat, gasping for breath.

"CUFF HIM! CUFF HIM!" Hearing Lloyd's urgent shouts, I turned to see my colleague leaning in through the smashed rear window and begin grappling with my assailant. I released my safety belt and twisted round, kneeling on the seat in order to slap my handcuffs on one of the attacker's wrists. He was flailing blindly against me, his eyes swollen tightly shut from the effects of the pepper spray and as I moved closer, my eyes also began to burn.

"GET THE OTHER ONE ON!" Half blinded, I grabbed at the tangled melee of limbs eventually seizing hold of the assailant's other wrist. I was about to apply the other cuff when I heard Lloyd frantically hissing, "That's me!"

Letting go, I climbed through the gap between the front seats to the back of the vehicle so that I could get better control of our prisoner. Locating the would-be murderer's other wrist, I swiftly clicked the second cuff into place. My eyes were stinging and my throat was burning from the residual pepper lingering in the air, but we finally had the attacker contained.

"Who is it, Lloyd?" I asked, still unable to see clearly. "Who the hell is it?" I felt light on my face as my colleague shone his torch into the car.

"It's Taxil!" he exclaimed.

We got him out of the vehicle and into the fresh air. Lloyd and I then stood whispering between ourselves, debating what on earth could have happened. My colleague explained that when he hadn't seen me following the van he had come back to investigate. It seems that the glowing white light had been his headlamps and not the Angel Gabriel coming to guide me to the Pearly Gates. Neither of us, however, could work out how our prisoner had managed to swap vehicles. I didn't want to believe in the possibility that evil spirits were working with him or that black magic really was at play. I much preferred it when Taxil was just someone who had issues – I could deal with that. We questioned him again and again over how, handcuffed, he'd managed to leave the confines of a locked cage in a moving vehicle and slip unnoticed and uncuffed into the back of my stationary panda car, but he just stonewalled us. I wondered if I should also arrest him for possession. We eventually led him back around to the van and opened up the back door again. But sitting in the cage, handcuffed just as we had left him, was Robert Taxil, smiling back at us. We did a double take: looking at our prisoner and then back at the man sitting in the cage.

"I see you've met my twin brother, Ian," he remarked. We shut the cage door and called up for more transport.

It was only over the course of the next block of shifts that we finally got to establish what the Taxil twins' master plan had been. It had never even occurred to us that there had been two people in that house. Nothing had shown up on any of the system checks: to all intents and purposes Ian Taxil didn't exist.

"The good news," our sergeant informed us, as Lloyd and I were called into the office, "is that you won't face any internal disciplinary action for crashing a police vehicle or for criminal damage when you broke the window." I couldn't quite tell whether he was being serious or not. He went on to inform us that both Robert and Ian Taxil had been interviewed and subsequently charged with arson with intent to endanger life and the attempted murder of a police officer. They had also both been admitted to a mental hospital for assessment.

Furthermore, CSI had since been back to the house to sift through the property for evidence of involvement in any other crimes.

"It seems that you and Andy held quite a fascination for the brothers. If you want I can show you what the forensic guys found, although I should warn you that it might have a mild laxative effect."

"I'll pass, if it's all the same to you, Sarge."

It transpires that after Robert's encounters with the police ten years earlier, their mother, in a bid to start afresh and keep her sons out of trouble, had decided to move halfway across the country to the smallholding near Sandford. Reclusive by nature, they had kept themselves to themselves and out of trouble for over a decade. A couple of years ago, however, their mother had died thus the restraining influence over the pair was gone. They found it difficult to cope without her and turned to any means they could to try and contact her in the afterlife.

"Clearly, judging by Robert's past," he continued, "he was, to a large degree, already messed up. Combine this with dabbling with a Ouija board and they soon became obsessed with the occult."

Burning down a random stranger's house on Christmas Eve was, they believed, the ultimate test they had been set by the spirits to convince them that they were serious in wanting to join the forces of darkness. Unfortunately, Andy and I had inadvertently thwarted their plan when we had kicked the door in and rescued the family. The Ouija board had then told them that the only way they could redeem themselves was by punishing the police officers involved.

"Well, that's just like me blaming everything that has gone wrong in my life on that unsuccessful wishbone pull back in 1987!" I protested. Barry raised his eyebrows to suggest that I was already preaching to the converted before he continued with his revelations.

The brothers had then devised a simple plan which

involved one of them committing a crime and then waiting to be caught. Meanwhile, the other brother would hide to see which police officer responded. If it was either me or Andy, their strategy was to hide in the police vehicle and turn the tables by abducting us. They had even learnt how to clone car keys so that when the officer locked the car via the key fob they could replicate the signal and let themselves into the car to lie in wait while the officer was tied up, dealing with the other brother at the scene.

Frustratingly for them, neither Andy nor I had been on duty during their orchestrated crime spree; however, they had used every opportunity to gather intelligence on us along with police protocol and procedures. They had even managed to calculate when E shift were on duty, allowing Robert to call at precisely the right time with his cry for help as this greatly increased the likelihood of their intended target being successfully lured out to their property. All that had been left for them to do was identify who had actually arrived at the house, before putting part two of their scheme into operation. What they hadn't bargained for was Lloyd turning up, too.

"I'd jump in front of a lightly tossed beach ball for you," my crewmate informed me when he discovered that his presence had probably saved my life. I was touched.

"And what about the animal parts in the jars?" I asked.

"Just a hobby, I presume," Barry replied. "Or maybe practice for when they caught you."

Well, that was just rude!

# CHAPTER 15

# Therapy

The dead man was sat back on the sofa, his mouth open and eyes wide, staring at the ceiling. His body was mottled and bloated; naked apart from a dirty dressing gown caked with dried excrement. The whole room stank of a pungent mix of faeces, body odour, decomposition and stale cigarette smoke. The cadaver had been there a few days before it was found and long enough for putrefaction to have set in: for the gases to build up; the body to begin to bloat and discolour; for the eyes to bulge out of their sockets and the tongue to swell and protrude; yet, thankfully, not long enough for the flies to discover it. I considered myself lucky.

Back in March, Brad the Impaler had attended a routine report of a concern for safety. Relatives hadn't heard from their uncle since before Christmas and, arriving on scene, Brad had immediately known the reason why. The windows had been thick with bluebottles and even after he had forced open the front door he had had to wait for several minutes to let the swarms of flies out. Pulling his fleece up over his nose and mouth, he had then ventured inside where he was welcomed by an overpowering stench. He found the body lying in the front room next to a gas fire that was still dutifully burning. The eyes and the tongue were gone, and a mass of writhing maggots were spilling out of the mouth and the abdomen; the fingers were mere black twigs; the skin like greaseproof paper. On the table were half-written Christmas cards never to be sent. But the flies, he told me, the flies were everywhere; tens of thousands of flies.

"He was like this when I found him," the woman told me as she stood in the doorway, bringing me back to the here and now. "We only went away for a week. We thought he'd be alright."

Stepping over the detritus strewn across the floor, I pulled open the curtains and surveyed the scene before me. In front of the sofa was a low table, its surface covered with overflowing ashtrays, dirty plates with the remnants of half-eaten food, an empty glass tumbler and a toilet roll. Thirty or so empty whisky bottles littered the carpet, alongside scores of crumpled-up cigarette packets. Dozens of takeaway pizza boxes were randomly discarded, seemingly thrown across the floor having served their purpose.

I navigated my way through the mess, my boots sticking to the floor with every step; then a crack as I stood on a plastic bottle, breaking it and sending its contents spilling over the carpet. An intense smell of ammonia filled my nostrils.

"It's urine," the woman informed me, pointing to a heap of bottles on the other side of the room. Nearby stood a metal-framed commode with a dirty red bucket suspended underneath.

"It's my father," she explained as she made her way over to the body. She stood in silence, looking down at him and shaking her head. "Why did you let yourself get like this?" she whispered, addressing the corpse. "You were so fit and healthy." He continued to stare into space, leaving her question unanswered.

"Just look at him now," she added, turning to look at me. "He hasn't shaved for days, there are food stains down his dressing gown, he hasn't even bothered to put any pants on, and it looks like he could swoop down and catch his dinner from a lake with those toenails…"

I remained silent. People have different ways of coping with death and who was I to tell her how to grieve, although I did find her personal criticisms of her dead father a little jarring. Before joining the police, I believed that relatives always cried when they were with the dead body of their loved one as that's what they do on television. In reality, however, I'd found that they tend not to be numb with grief or constantly reminiscing about their dear departed; instead they are usually inclined to talk about any disconnected subject rather than confront the reality of the situation. And it's not because they are 'hard faced' or uncaring either: it's just their coping mechanism; what gets them through. After all, death is not something that we can rehearse for. In my experience, most relatives appear calm and collected. I've chatted about anything and everything, laughed with them and even shared jokes or told them about my day. Ultimately, it's their call and I'll do what's necessary to make them feel at ease. In this case, I just allowed her to talk.

"Goodness me, that looks irritated!" she exclaimed. I instinctively glanced over but wasn't particularly keen on having some horrendous rash pointed out to me; then I realised that she was staring out of the window. I went over to see an unhappy-looking paramedic climbing out of his vehicle. He looked like he was in a foul mood – he would be even more hacked off when he discovered that he had been called out for someone who had died days ago. Paramedics don't usually attend if it is obvious that the deceased has been dead for some time.

He entered the flat, greeting us with a grunt, and began to carry out his procedures while the daughter outlined her father's medical history. It didn't take long as there was virtually none. Her father, it seemed, had always been fit and healthy and hadn't seen a doctor in decades. However, after retiring from work, he seemed to have lost his purpose in life and had slowly gone downhill.

"He had no interest in anything," she told me.

It seems it pays to have a hobby…

"He would just sit in the house all day watching television. Then he took up drinking and by the end of the year he was consuming a bottle of whisky a day." I had to ask her to repeat herself just to make sure I had heard it right as whenever I'm lucky enough to be given a bottle of Scotch it usually lasts me between two and three years!

Next he gave up cooking for himself and just lived on takeaways – the pizza delivery boy even had a key to let himself in. It seems it wasn't just Alice in Wonderland who kept eating and drinking hoping magically it would solve all her problems.

He was a heavy smoker, too. Apparently, he had always enjoyed the odd cigarette but, by the end, he was getting through forty cigarettes a day. Finally, around Christmas time, he decided that he couldn't be bothered to walk anymore. There was nothing physically wrong with him, but he had decided that going through to his bedroom or even walking the ten yards down the corridor to the toilet was just too much effort.

"I told him hundreds of times that if he wanted to live a long life he'd need to exercise and eat healthily, but he just didn't seem to be bothered."

On the other hand, in the course of my job I've seen the insides of lots of nursing homes and I have to say that living a long life doesn't always appear all it's cracked up to be.

"What's the story behind the televisions?" When I had first entered the living room it had struck me as unusual to find two sitting side by side.

"All he did was watch the telly," she replied. "All day every day. Day and night. He used to have one on for twelve hours and then switch it off so it wouldn't overheat, and then switch on the other one so he could keep watching."

"How long do you think he's been dead for?" she asked pensively.

"I'd guess about three days." The TV was paused on Wednesday's evening news, which seemed as good an indication as any.

"I'd go with that," interrupted the paramedic, packing up his equipment.

"Cause of death?" I whispered as I accompanied him out to his vehicle.

"Suicide," he replied grumpily. "A heart attack brought on by his lifestyle, I'd say. A long, slow suicide."

"Sorry about the wait," he added, getting back into his car.

"I was only on scene minutes before you," I told him. "It's fine."

"No, sorry for the *weight*," he clarified. "He's a large man. The funeral directors will have some trouble getting him out of the flat, especially around those tight corners. I'd stay and help but another job's just come in." And with that he was off, trailing rainbows of happiness in his wake.

I got on the radio and asked Comms to arrange for the undertaker to attend. Heeding the paramedic's advice, I also put in a call to Andy, asking if he would come and help move the body.

Returning to the house, I found the deceased's daughter in the kitchen making a cup of tea. We took it into one of the other rooms to drink whilst we waited for the undertaker to arrive. As we chatted, I learned that her name was Rosemary and that she lived just a few streets away from her father, whose wife had died some years before. She wasn't sure why her father had let himself go, but admitted that the years of caring for him had taken their toll on her. She had felt constantly stressed and the whole situation had impacted on her own personal life.

A week ago, Rosemary and her partner had gone away on their first break in years to try and salvage their battered relationship and had returned home to this. If anything, though, she had confided, it was a blessed relief that it was finally over. She'd had years to prepare for this eventuality and had known that this day would come sooner rather than later.

It's said that the first time that someone takes the time simply to listen, is the time that true empathy is born. I've also heard it said that if you reply with: 'Wow! That's crazy' that ninety-nine per cent of the time you haven't been taking in a word of what was being said.

Although I tried to be attentive as she poured out her troubles, every now and again my mind kept wandering back to what I had found on my doormat this morning. Preparing to leave for work, I had noticed a small plastic bag lying on the floor under the letter box. I had picked it up, feeling its weight and then held it up to the light before hurling it away in horror! Gingerly approaching it again, I had picked it up once more and studied it to make sure my first impression had been right: it was. Someone had posted me a bag of excrement! Why on earth would anyone do that? I immediately thought of the Taxil brothers but they had both been remanded and were in prison. But did they have contacts on the outside? Had they found out where I lived? Who else had a grudge against me? I'd locked up hundreds of people over the years – it could be any one of them.

"I said, don't some of the sights you see in your line of work give you nightmares?" I was instantly back in the room as Rosemary posed her question for the second time, raising her voice and clearly demonstrating that she expected a reply. "I mean, it can't be nice seeing all those unpleasant things. Do you have trouble sleeping at night?"

The reality is that I don't have any trouble at all – I sleep just fine. I wouldn't say that I have become hardened to the suffering and cruelty that I see, but it certainly doesn't affect me as much now as it did when I first joined the police.

"I've heard that a lot of emergency service personnel – police, firemen and paramedics – don't tend to talk about their emotions much," she added.

"I can't say that I'm surprised," I told her, but she didn't seem to get the joke.

"Have you heard of CBT?" she asked.

I told her I had heard it mentioned in connection with psychotherapy, but didn't really know much else about it.

"Cognitive Behavioural Therapy," she explained, "is a type of therapy that can help you manage your problems by changing the way you think and behave. It was originally used to treat depression but is now used in all sorts of ways. I got into it because of the difficulties I had dealing with my father and discovered that it helped me. It can assist with anything from post-traumatic stress to insomnia. In fact, I found it so useful that I'm now training to be a full-time therapist myself."

"Wow! That's crazy!"

"It's just that I thought I could try a little session with you now while we wait for the undertakers to arrive? It's not difficult – just a short, easy introduction to the therapy. We just talk through things. It's nothing to be worried about."

"It's very kind of you," I replied, "but I'm fine, thank you." It seemed a little bizarre that at a time like this she wanted to talk about my feelings rather than her own, but perhaps this was just her way of coping. I'm not comfortable talking about my feelings at the best of times and, to be perfectly honest, I still had the bag of faeces on my mind. Now, I might have been interested if she could have solved that little mystery for me.

"Suit yourself," she pouted, before disappearing off into the kitchen to make another cup of tea.

They say time flies when you're enjoying yourself and after what seemed like an eternity later I heard a knock at the door. I shouted for whoever it was to come in and moments later the door was pushed open and Andy appeared in the room, looking eager to tell me something. He asked where the body was and then went and closed the door, as though worried the corpse might overhear. He looked around conspiratorially to make sure no one else was listening and then, when satisfied that we were alone, he motioned for me to come closer.

"You know that job I went to this morning?" he questioned, eagerly. "Guess what it was all about?"

"You'll have to tell me," I replied. "You'd be amazed at how often I'm wrong when people ask me that question."

"Well, it was down as a domestic but, when I arrived there, I discovered the reason for the fuss was that the wife had come back to find her husband nailed to the dining room table!"

Wow! Now that actually *was* crazy! It transpired that whilst his wife was away on a business trip, the husband had invited one of his friends over and then, in the words of Andy, they had proceeded to 'abuse each other's genitals'. He used air quotes to accompany his revelation.

"Apparently, it's a real *thing*," he continued, making rabbit ears with his fingers around *'thing'* to emphasise the point. "It's part of the bondage and sadomasochism scene, by all accounts. They punch and slap each other's penises or penii – whatever the word is – and attach weights to their testicles, squeeze them, tie it all up with ropes… all sorts!"

When I mentioned earlier that everyone should have a hobby, this wasn't exactly what I had in mind.

"Anyway, it looks like their little games went too far and the friend ended up nailing the husband's scrotum to the table."

"Bollocks?"

"No, it's true! I thought they were supposed to have a safe word or something!"

"Like an ex-partner's name?" I suggested. That would certainly stop any romantic activity dead in its tracks, although I wasn't sure where the romance fitted into this particular pursuit. Andy frowned and continued with his tale.

"The visitor then panicked, leaving the husband attached to the dining table. He was stuck there for twelve hours until his wife returned from her trip. She went mental when she discovered him!"

Not least due to the fact that they had to eat off that table, one would have thought...

"Anyway, look it up on Google. Apparently, it's called 'Cock and Ball Torture' or CBT for short."

"CBT?" Rosemary had walked back into the room just as Andy was finishing his tale. "Did I hear you mention CBT?"

"Erm, yes," he stammered back, blushing profusely. "Have you heard of it?"

"Heard of it?" she replied enthusiastically. "It's my speciality!"

Andy was visibly taken aback.

"In fact, I'm hoping to go into it full-time if I can. I'd call myself a semi-professional at the moment."

His eyes grew large as he stared at her in disbelief.

"I even offered to give your colleague a quick session whilst we were waiting for you to arrive, but he declined. He's a bit of a stick in the mud, whereas I'm sure you're a lot more open-minded."

Andy glanced at me, a traumatised look on his face.

"Would you like me to have a go with you?" she continued. "It looks like you could do with some!"

"I don't think I'd really enjoy that," he responded politely.

"Oh, come on. You're not scared, are you?" she joked, toying with him. "What's the worst that could happen?"

"No, seriously, it's really not something I'd be interested in." I could detect a slight nervous waver in his voice as he replied.

"Don't be shy. Like I said to your colleague, it doesn't have to be long and hard if that's what you're worried about. I would have thought a young man like you would have the balls to give it a try!"

"I don't beg to differ!" he replied indignantly. "I just differ!"

His defiant tone signalled the end of the conversation. Rosemary looked over at me and I shrugged my shoulders and shook my head. Further embarrassment for my colleague was avoided by the timely arrival of the funeral directors knocking at the front door. Andy seized the opportunity to escape by excusing himself to let them in.

"Well, I know some people don't agree with alternative therapies, but your colleague seemed rather appalled by the thought of someone getting inside his head." She seemed genuinely perplexed at his vehement resistance to her offer. "It's not a healthy attitude. If you bury the pain deep inside, that's where nightmares make their homes."

"Maybe he was worried about getting the sack," I replied. "But I really think he needs help." I quickly turned away, my shoulders rising and falling as I tried to stifle my giggles.

"Oh, you poor dear," she cooed. "You're crying, aren't you? Let it out. I was wrong about you: you are in touch with your emotions. Is it the thought of my dead father or that your friend won't seek the help he needs?"

Unable to turn and face her, I mumbled that it was the latter, and that I needed a minute alone. When she went to fetch me a glass of water I used the opportunity to compose myself before going in search of the others. As I entered the lounge, the two undertakers were in the midst of assessing how they could safely remove the body from the house. Andy, meanwhile, was stood back against the far wall, still shaking his head in disbelief.

"Can you believe that?" he asked me, as I stood next to him. "And her father is still warm… well, figuratively speaking, anyway!"

"People grieve in different ways," I reminded him. He sighed and told me that I was probably right.

Rosemary reappeared with my glass of water. "Treasure this man," she told Andy, as she gently patted me on the arm. "You could learn a lot about compassion from him. And he really cares about you!"

The confused expression on Andy's face was priceless.

"See!" I told him as soon as she had left the room again. "Different ways!"

Before Andy could ask if she was seriously referring to me as compassionate and caring, one of the undertakers interrupted, requesting our assistance. "We're going to need you two to help us carry him to the hearse." He then quickly outlined the difficulties in getting such a large man out of the property. "It's the tight turns in the flat… and he's a big man."

The deceased was carefully moved from the sofa and laid on the stretcher; however, due to his size, and the fact that he was so bloated, we were unable to attach the straps to hold him in place. Eventually and not without considerable difficulty, the body bag was zipped up and finally we were ready to begin the removal process. While Rosemary held the doors open, the rest of us strained beneath her father's weight. We managed to manoeuvre our way out of the lounge, but the tight turn from the hallway to the front door proved problematic. We were like a troupe of removal men trying to negotiate an oversized piece of furniture through an undersized opening. We tried all sorts of strategies but without success. We even attempted to tilt the stretcher at one end but hastily abandoned that idea when the body started sliding to the bottom of the bag in an undignified heap.

Ultimately, the only possibility was to turn the stretcher on its side and pivot our way around the ninety-degree angle, forcing the belly of the deceased into the corner of the door frame in the process. Even so, it was still a struggle. We were almost there when there was a dull 'pop'. The bag then slowly started to deflate as liquid began to pool in the bottom and leak out through the zip.

"That'll be the purge fluid," remarked the undertaker matter-of-factly. I'd heard of similar things happening before: historical documents show that when William the Conqueror was buried his body exploded. It seems that as priests tried to stuff William into a stone coffin that was too small for his bulk, they pushed down hard onto his abdomen causing it to burst. And now, just as then, a putrid stench filled the air. As Andy began retching, for once I was grateful for my poor sense of smell.

"I bet you'll be wanting some CBT after that!" declared Rosemary, a triumphant look on her face.

My colleague maintained a dignified if somewhat embarrassed silence as he continued to carry the body to the vehicle. As soon as it was safely stowed in the hearse and Rosemary had returned to the house, the undertaker spoke up.

"CBT?" he queried, addressing Andy. "If you're interested in going for it, my daughter has just passed her test. She said it was quite hard to start with."

"Really?" My colleague once again appeared shell-shocked. "She actually told you about it?"

"Let's just say that we're very proud parents. To be honest, at the start we didn't want her to. We were scared she'd fall off and hurt herself, but she absolutely nailed it! If she had her way she'd be riding it all day long!"

"Just what is wrong with you people!" exclaimed a shocked Andy, shaking his head yet again. He then swiftly made his excuses and left.

"Just to clarify," I asked, as my colleague disappeared

out of earshot, "I presume you mean the Compulsory Basic Training to ride a moped?"

"That's the one. Why, what did you think I was on about?"

"No, that's what I thought you meant."

After the hearse had pulled away, I went back inside to see Rosemary and to help her clean up the mess. When we had finished, I said my goodbyes but not before apologising for her father's undignified departure. It was then that she sat me down and I finally saw a tear in her eye.

"If only we saw souls instead of bodies, how different our idea of beauty would be," she imparted to me. "And you," she added, clasping my hand, "are a beautiful man." Before I left she made me promise to show my emotions and share my feelings more.

True to my word, back at the station I put my promise into action. In fact, I went one step further by sharing my feelings about Andy's CBT gaffe with the rest of the shift… as well as Sam in the front office, a couple of the guys from CID, Jacqueline from CPS, Nancy in Comms and basically anyone else who would listen.

"Where is he, anyway?" I asked Barry after I had finished telling my story.

"He's helping social services with a job. You know that stripper who lives on the Yellow Estate? They're taking her child into care. It'll be like taking baby from a Candi."

It looked like Andy's day was going from bad to worse. Meanwhile, I was having a great time and I was still chuckling to myself when I got home that evening. Chuckling that is until I opened the front door; for no sooner had I stepped over the threshold than the landline phone began to ring… and it never rings. I only ever use it to find my mobile. A chill went up my spine and suddenly those black thoughts came rushing back: the anonymous bag of poo! Someone was definitely out to get me. How did they know I was home? How did they get my number?

I stared at it, letting it ring out before I finally ventured over and tentatively picked up the receiver.

"Did you get it?" It was a woman's voice. Not what I had expected at all. But perhaps the Taxil brothers had a sister? Or could it be the wife of someone I had put away?

"Get what?" I tried to play it cool, but I could feel my heart thumping. I looked around me as I spoke and then switched the main light on just in case someone was lurking in the shadows.

"The shit." Well that was straight to the point.

"Why are you sending it to me?" I needed to know what I was dealing with.

"It has magical properties." That wasn't the answer I had anticipated.

"Who are you?"

"You don't know who I am?"

"I have no idea who you are or why you're doing this to me."

There was a pause at the other end of the line. Then she was back again, but this time her tone was lower, more ominous. She seemed to relish the fact that I didn't know who my tormentor was.

"And I expect you believe that the dead birds you've found outside the door over the last few weeks have been left by the cat next door?"

I felt like someone had just walked over my grave as the hairs on the back of my neck stood on end. There *had* been dead birds left outside; several over the last month. I had assumed it was Colonel Mustard – next door's cat – that had been responsible, but now my world had been turned upside down. Was this anonymous woman killing creatures and leaving them for me as some kind of macabre message? With my mind racing at a million miles an hour I was lost for words, as I began weaving into this web of conspiracy against me every bad or unpleasant thing that had happened to me over the past year.

"Well, did you?" she prompted.

"Yes."

"Yay! That was a lucky guess! Did you think it was the sweet-potato-coloured moggy? The one that teases Barney?" She now sounded suspiciously upbeat, almost gleeful.

"Who is this?" I demanded. How did she even know my dog's name?

"It's me, Liz!" came the reply. "You're so easy to wind up, you loon!"

"But... but what about the turd in the bag?" I stuttered, still confused by the anonymous offerings posted through the letter box.

"It's Alfie's poo!" she exclaimed, as if that would clarify everything. My silence indicated that more information was required. "Alfie, my ferret! You said you had problems with mice in the loft... remember now?"

It all came flooding back to me. Of course: ferret poo! One of the drawbacks of living in the countryside is the rodents. In summer, they happily run about the fields as nature intended, but when the weather turns cold they seek warmer accommodation. For a small number of mice, my attic seems to be the des res of choice. In the spirit of live and let live, I hadn't wanted to kill the poor little creatures, just encourage them to make their home elsewhere. According to Liz, rats are scared of ferrets and, as an extension of her logic, mice must also be scared of them. Therefore, if a mouse thinks there's a ferret about, he'll keep away. And how do you make a mouse think there's a ferret about? Leave one of Alfie's turds casually lying around.

I'm not sure whether Liz is a genius or the best salesperson who ever lived or if I'm an idiot. Judging by what she was telling me now, one and three were both applicable.

"Put one up in the attic and it'll scare off the mice…
and, by the way, you're an idiot."

I might well be an idiot, but I was a relieved idiot. No
one was out to get me after all. I allowed myself a little
giggle of relief.

"It's good to know that you can laugh at yourself,"
she informed me, "as it was getting kind of awkward for
the rest of us!"

# CHAPTER 16

# The Fisher King

"I imagine you're wondering why you're sat here in this chilly canteen at four in the morning on Christmas Eve." Inspector Soaper looked at us expectantly.

If he was intending to work us all into a state of frenzied delirium with his skilful oratory, he was failing dismally. We were cold and tired. When no one took his bait and answered, he continued undeterred.

"My aim," he announced dramatically, "is to spoil someone's day!"

I think he was being far too modest: looking around at the faces of my colleagues, I think he had already spoilt it for at least ten people. This was supposed to be our day off and tomorrow we would be starting our run of day shifts. I didn't think I was alone in finding it hard to drum up enthusiasm. Still, we were here so we might as well get on with it. I shifted uncomfortably on the hard plastic chair as he continued with the briefing.

"This morning we'll be giving one of our newest heroin dealers an early morning call!"

A drug's raid? Things were looking up: police officers love big busts! There's nothing better than putting away a pusher as they are at the heart of the criminality spiral. Thieves only get a fraction of the value of the goods that they steal when they sell it on to their handler, which means that each addict virtually needs to be on a constant crime wave to fund their habit. A user with a £20k habit would need to steal between £80-£100k worth of goods to fund it. It stands to reason that the more customers a pusher gets, the more thefts and burglaries go up.

"Brown, smack, skag – call it what you will," he continued, "that's what we're looking for today." With that he handed over to Barry, who was standing in the corner holding a child's fishing net on a stick.

"Are we off to the beach, Sarge?" I asked. "It's just I assumed that with the net…"

"You know what assuming does?" Barry replied confidently. "It makes a fool out of you and…"

"Ming?" suggested Gwen with a wink, finishing off his badly thought out put-down.

"Dammit!" he muttered, as he tapped the rod on the flip chart to get our attention. On display was a photograph of the suspect.

"This is Gary Leadbetter," began our sergeant, "and to his neighbours, he's just your average bald man in his thirties who shares his rented accommodation with a couple of dangerous dogs. Of course, he denies this; however, if you have to suit your pets up like Hannibal Lecter being transferred to a new prison each time you take them out, I'm hesitant to believe his claims of their gentler nature."

We all made a mental note – there are few things more frightening than a rabid dog trying to rip your insides out as you try and cuff their struggling owner.

"Jessica – you're the exhibits officer."

Well, apart from being the exhibits officer! As the rest of the team are having fun turning the place upside down, the exhibits officer has to bag up and make detailed notes of everything that's found: where, when, and what it was. The exhibits officer is also the person responsible for booking it all into the property store, ensuring the continuity of the evidence and producing it at court. And if there is one thing that can get an officer into trouble, it's property. I breathed a sigh of relief.

We were handed a couple of small fire extinguishers to help frighten the dogs if they decided to attack. The sudden blast scares them and would hopefully make them back off. If I had known, I would have brought my vacuum cleaner: my own dog acts as if his whole family were murdered by a hoover and runs away at the very sight of it!

We were then shown maps detailing the location of his house, along with aerial views and covert photographs of the front door. The rest of us were then divided up into the entry, search and arrest teams. These operations tend to follow a fairly formulaic approach: after enough intelligence has been received, a warrant is signed out and the actual raid can be planned. In theory, it's all pretty simple: we'll force entry to the property, detain the occupier, search the premises and seize any drugs we find.

Time is our biggest enemy: the time between the suspect realising you're at his door to finally arresting him. With every second that passes, the suspect has an opportunity to arm himself and/or dispose of his drugs stash. Some even have booby traps set; and although they sound like the best sort of trap, some can be pretty horrific. I've known dealers turn their houses into a set from *Indiana Jones and the Temple of Doom*, with barrels rigged to roll down the stairs or knives positioned to skewer some unsuspecting police officer entering the property.

The element of surprise is key. On this operation, Ron and Geezer would be wielding the enforcer to knock through the door. It's an effective battering ram: sixty centimetres of tubular steel weighing sixteen kilograms and topped with hardened steel, it can apply more than three tonnes of impact force.

My colleagues carefully studied the structure of the door from the photographs: what it was made of, where the locks were, where the weak points might be – there would be no time for such deliberations when we rolled up on scene. From the images, it appeared as if the house was bristling with CCTV cameras and Leadbetter would be aware of our presence straight away and the clock would start ticking down.

"Oh, and this is for you, Andy." Barry presented our probationer with the net. "You're the Fisher King."

Andy looked slightly perplexed whilst a few of us patted him on the back. We knew what was coming. At one time we'd each been the newest member of the shift, therefore we'd all done it and been on the receiving end of Barry's history lesson in the process.

"Arthurian legend?" prompted our sergeant. "Charged with keeping the Holy Grail?"

With no hint of a glimmer of recognition on Andy's face, Barry gave an overly dramatic sigh of exasperation and was forced to explain.

"Take your net on a stick, find where the main drain is for the house, lift the cover and if you hear a flush, insert said net. You'll either be rewarded with a fresh turd or a bag of smack – that's the Holy Grail I'm referring to. *Comprende*?"

As Andy nodded and went to take hold of his apparatus, Barry maintained his grip on the stick and looked him directly in the eye. "You've got to ask yourself one question," he rasped quietly. "Do you feel lucky, punk? Well, do ya?"

Andy responded with an unconvincing and uncomfortable laugh.

Half an hour later and we were all in our van on the way to the target's address.

"Intelligence shows that he checks the external CCTV cameras religiously," Barry informed us. "And before you say anything, Donoghue, that doesn't mean he only does it on a Sunday." Everyone laughed, but the reality of the situation was that we had to stay out of view until the last possible moment.

"He's got warning markers for violence, too. He's

alleged to keep a knife and baseball bat by his bed, so be careful when you get in there."

Ten minutes more and we were at the end of the street. It was cold, dark and silent. Nothing stirred, not even a mouse.

As soon as we were parked, the Fisher King set off on his noble quest; a shadowy figure disappearing into the night. When he found the sewer cover, he quietly lifted the lid and signalled he was ready by raising the net above his head. Chad was on the move next, making his way around the back of the property in case anything was thrown out of the windows to the rear.

"The eagle has landed," he whispered into the radio when he was in position. In complete silence, the rest of us then made our way to the rendezvous point just out of view of the cameras. Ron and Geezer were at the front of the line, dressed in their protective gear; helmets on, visors down. Gwen and Jess both had shields, while Lloyd and I had a fire extinguisher each. Ben and George stood at the rear, ready to sprint through and arrest Leadbetter as soon as we were in.

Barry looked at his watch, counting down the time to the strike. "On my signal, unleash hell!"

After such a dramatic build-up, a double thumbs-up and a wink wasn't quite what I was expecting, but it did the trick. We all jogged in tandem to the address and a second later the whole street reverberated to the sound of the impact of the enforcer smashing against the door.

Three more bangs and the only thing that was moving were the dogs inside, barking wildly. It quickly became evident that the door was reinforced. If it was designed to buy Leadbetter as much time as possible, it was certainly doing its job.

Two more hits and the door was still holding solid. The thought quickly flashed through my head that maybe we should abandon the door and smash a window instead. Leadbetter would be awake now, checking his

CCTV and seeing us arrayed outside ready to rush in.

Lights were already going on in the other houses in the street. Some peered out of curtains, whilst others turned their lights off again to enable them to see out into the dark; all engrossed in the show unfolding before them. This would be the hot topic over Christmas dinner in most of the houses for sure.

Another series of resounding impacts and the door finally came off its hinges. As the entry team stood back, we quickly rushed in to find ourselves in some sort of contained porch – another solid door directly to our left: we had breached the portcullis only to be trapped before an inner gate. I half imagined arrow slits in the walls and murder holes in the roof, boiling oil and rocks raining down.

We were losing vital seconds. Leadbetter would be arming himself, setting his traps, getting rid of his stash, working his dogs into a frenzy. We had to be in quick.

We unceremoniously squeezed out of the killing zone as Ron and Geezer entered. It was more constrained here: less room to manoeuvre. Within a second, Geezer had the enforcer raised awkwardly above his head to bring it smashing down into the top lock; next, underarm to pound the lower bolt. Another hard smash and the whole centre panel of the door was out. But, the dogs were there waiting: two angry animals barking loudly; jaws gaping; teeth bared. Like Roman legionaries, the two large shields instantly locked together closing the breach once more. Lloyd and I readied ourselves, waiting to discharge the extinguishers to frighten the dogs. We counted ourselves down: two, one... and with that the shields parted, and with a roar we rammed the extinguishers through the opening and pulled the triggers. As soon as the canisters violently exhaled, the dogs turned tail and disappeared, running whimpering, through the front room towards the back of the property. Lloyd and I ran after them and quickly shut the kitchen door, trapping the rabid dogs inside. He looked over at me and we breathed a sigh of relief.

With the dogs no longer barking, the house was now eerily silent: something wasn't right, but there was no time to dwell on it. Racking our batons, Lloyd and I sprinted upstairs along with Ben and George, closely followed by Gwen and Jess; flashing our torches before us and yelling loudly and aggressively to announce our presence. Our adrenalin was pumping; blood pulsating through our bodies and reverberating in our ears.

As we reached the landing I half expected a baseball bat to come swinging around the corner – but nothing. Doors were kicked in as we stormed into each room in turn, bracing ourselves for a counter-attack. There was no time for niceties: wardrobe doors were flung open, almost pulling them off their hinges in the process; we kicked at bundles of dirty washing on the floor in case he was hiding amongst them; down on our hands and knees we went, checking under beds. This man was highly dangerous and was known to be extremely violent towards the police: we weren't taking any chances.

"He's here!" yelled Gwen. She was stood in the doorway of the last bedroom, clearly hesitant to enter.

"Has he got a weapon?" shouted Barry.

"Well, I wouldn't want him coming at me with what he's got in his hand," came her cryptic reply.

With batons raised and pepper sprays levelled, we all dropped what we were doing and quickly went to join Gwen at the entrance to the room only to see why she was reticent to proceed: Leadbetter lay sleeping; stark naked apart from a pair of dirty white socks; his wilted member grasped firmly in his right fist. It was just as well he had dozed off with his headset on as, usually, people who are masturbating have super-enhanced hearing: one little creak on the stairs and they are up like a shot.

A TV was in the corner, the static snowstorm on the screen lending a warm glow to proceedings. Judging by the cover of the DVD case lying beside the bed, he appeared to have been watching some 80's porn – the type that gives you unrealistic expectations of how quickly a pizza can be delivered.

"I think he's been spanking the dragon," Gwen whispered softly, looking a tad embarrassed but also slightly pleased with her witticism.

"Someone go and wake him up," instructed Barry. "NOT YOU, PC EVANS!" he quickly added as Jessica stepped forward. "Your keenness is noted, but it's not really appropriate in this case."

The pair decided instead to fetch the search kit from the van and as they wandered off down the stairs I could hear Gwen explaining her joke to Jess. "Spanking the dragon – you know, he's a heroin dealer – as opposed to chasing the…"

"Chasing the monkey?"

Back outside the bedroom, Barry was giving out his orders again. "Let's get him handcuffed and downstairs. Ben and George, in you go and give him a shake."

As soon as the puerile giggles started he sighed and rolled his eyes heavenwards. I think this was our way of relieving the tension after being tightly wound up, ready for a violent struggle. I'm not sure if Barry agreed though. I decided it was best not to add to the film quotes with '*Say hello to my little friend*'.

Ben and George approached the bed and, being careful not to make contact with Leadbetter's offending appendage, quietly applied the cuffs as he slept.

"Wake up," whispered George, lifting up the headphones from Sleeping Beauty's ears. "Santa's been."

Leadbetter slowly came to; waking from a deep slumber to suddenly sitting bolt upright when he saw Ben and George towering over him.

"Only joking," George clarified. "We've checked the list and apparently you've been a bad boy this year, so we've not come bearing gifts: we've come to take stuff away."

"Happy Christmas!" added Ben, before informing him of his rights.

While the suspect made himself presentable, the rest of us got on with the search. It wasn't long before we discovered some dubious substances.

"Sarge, I think I've found some brown!"

Barry came into the bathroom to find me pointing at a dirty toilet bowl with dried faeces encrusted around the rim. It didn't even warrant a reply – he just shook his head and walked out. I chuckled to myself and continued the search.

The house was one of the worst I'd seen since we had taken the neglected toddlers and their brother into police custody. Filth and grime were everywhere and nearly every room was filled with the usual discarded cans of lager, fast-food boxes, dirty clothes, plates cultivating some sort of penicillin, overflowing ashtrays and used needles. Leadbetter's dogs' health could also be charted from their deposits on the carpet – and clearly one of them now had diarrhoea. As I searched under the bed, I was sure that I could feel fleas on me. I quickly withdrew my arm and brushed myself down. Massive spiders lurked inside the cupboards, looking as if they would stand their ground if I ventured further. I moved stuff about with my asp before closing the doors. And of course, there were the grubby yellow capsules about the place: you know that you're a police officer when you look at *Kinder Eggs* differently from everyone else. Elsewhere, my colleagues were reporting tales of similarly disgusting rooms.

The bathroom was a particular lowlight: mould everywhere; damp patches on the walls. Normally, I'd look to see if the toothpaste had been squeezed from the middle – a sure sign of a psychopath; but there was no toothpaste... and no toothbrush. In fact, there was no shower gel, no soap, not even any toilet paper. I hate it when you've done your business and then discover there's no loo roll and you have to waddle away to get some with your pants around your ankles. The staff at McDonalds hate it when I do that, too.

If drug dealing is such a lucrative pastime, I often wonder why the people we arrest live in such squalor. I suppose the answer is that we generally deal with the pushers low down on the chain: the addicts who sell on to other addicts; all their profits are shot up their arm. The big players drive around in fancy cars, whilst our dealers in Sandford ride around on pushbikes.

Hopefully, each arrest would net us information on who was supplying the local supplier and, soon enough, we'd be raiding their homes – it was only a matter of time. At least I wouldn't get so filthy when I visited their mansions.

We made our way downstairs to continue the search. By now Leadbetter was sitting in the lounge with a cup of tea. He appeared quite affable, but, then again, I don't expect you get to recruit new customers by being surly. Mind you, I still think the cleverest salesman ever was the guy who convinced blind people that they needed to wear sunglasses.

Leadbetter was being friendly enough to us now, but I presumed that was only because he realised the game was up. Looking at him, I was certain he could change in an instant. His record of violence certainly suggested he wasn't the most understanding of people when one of his customers fell behind with their payments.

"Sorry for the mess upstairs," Leadbetter apologised, glancing up as we entered the room. "It's the maid's day off."

"She's had the day off for the last six months by the look of it," replied Lloyd.

"You just can't get the staff nowadays," Leadbetter added with a wink.

In contrast to upstairs, the downstairs looked positively immaculate, but then again a glitter ball tends to brighten up any room. The space was notionally split into two – a previous resident having taken out a dividing wall. The lounge area was bare, save for the faux leather sofa Leadbetter was sitting on, a low table resplendent with ashtray and empty beer cans and, of course, the massive flat-screen TV, PlayStation and Xbox ensemble. The floor was covered with linoleum and muddy paw prints, as well as a long, thin line of runny dog mess left by one of his animals as they had retreated to the kitchen.

At the back of the room – the once separate dining area – Jess was seated at a Formica-topped table, the search record and evidence bags arrayed around her. We handed her what we had found: four mobile phones, numerous SIM cards and a book full of coded names and amounts. It was the usual paraphernalia of a dealer, but so far we had failed to come up with any drugs. As we went back into the lounge to continue the search, I noticed a lone Christmas card perched on the mantelpiece.

"It's from your boss," Leadbetter commented when he saw me looking. I picked it up and checked it over. It was indeed from the Chief Constable.

It seems that all the criminals on our patch had been sent cards from the constabulary with warnings that we were watching them and if they didn't want to spend the festive period behind bars, then they had better stop whatever villainy they were up to. For the ne'er-do-wells, I suppose when that dropped through their letter box it was the equivalent of seeing that poster with the eyes looking out at you. The front of the card actually showed Father Christmas staring out through the bars of a prison cell.

"I bet Santa was shitting himself when he went for a shower," joked Leadbetter. Well, I suppose that's one way to deter your fellow inmates.

"Over here!" My musings were disturbed by Chad, shouting through to Barry as he waved a thick wad of ten and twenty-pound notes that he had found tucked inside the fireplace.

"It's for buying presents for my mates," explained Leadbetter. "You've got to hide your cash – there are criminals about, you know!"

We continued searching the room, leaving no stone unturned, moving our host off the sofa, checking under the cushions and behind the seats. We found his TV remote, fifty-eight pence in change, various mouldy food items and a dead mouse; but no drugs.

It was quite important that we found what we were looking for, for a number of reasons: Firstly, I didn't want my cancelled rest day to be for nothing. Secondly, if we smash down someone's door and we don't find anything to arrest them for, the police pick up the tab for the repair – if we do arrest them, they foot the bill. So far, we had circumstantial evidence, but I knew Barry wanted something concrete.

Just then I saw a figure walk in through the entrance and bend down and knock twice on the inner front door which was now lying broken in two on the floor.

"You're tardy," scowled Barry as he recognised the dog handler.

"Actually, I don't think you're supposed to call people that anymore," came the reply.

"Well, get him in and see what he can find," added Barry gruffly.

With that, the dog handler disappeared again. A minute later and a shiny wet nose came through the door, closely followed by the furry body of an enthusiastic springer spaniel, shaking with excitement and straining on his lead. He was wearing a set of little leather bootees on his paws to guard against any needles that were lying about. He started upstairs, and we listened intently as we heard him jumping up and down off the furniture, searching for anything we might have missed. Ten minutes later and he was back, empty pawed. Barry's face dropped.

"There's other dogs in the house, Jeff," Gwen warned the handler, although I think he had already suspected as much by the abundant turds on the bedroom carpet.

"I'll move 'em," volunteered Leadbetter. "They can get a bit nasty with other dogs. I'll take 'em into the yard."

Accompanied by Ben and George, he then went to usher the animals outside. Meanwhile, Police Dog Bouncer sniffed his way through the lounge and kitchen, his little tail wagging ten to the dozen as he jumped up on the sofa, dived into cupboards and zigzagged along the work surfaces. Alas, however, he found no drugs.

"He's detecting something," Jeff told us. "It looks like there's been something here, but it's gone now."

Next to be searched was the backyard and so the dogs were swapped over – Leadbetter's dogs being taken back into the kitchen, leaving Bouncer the full run of the outside area. His actions seemed to indicate that illegal substances had been there but, again, he didn't find anything. Maybe people had bought their drugs early for Christmas: stocking up for that strange limbo period between Christmas and New Year in the same way that we panic-buy dozens of loaves of bread and gallons of milk when the shops are only closed for one day. Perhaps we had arrived a day too late and his regulars had stripped his heroin shelves bare.

A despondent Barry watched Jeff lead Bouncer out of the house and drive away. He stood for a few seconds thinking deeply and then rallied the troops.

"Jeff said the best reactions from his dog were in the kitchen and yard. We're going to turn over every inch of the place again: something *must* be here. I want everyone out there searching."

It's not unknown for dealers to hide their drugs outside as it gives them a potential defence that a wry lawyer can work on if any substances are found: "*Outside my client's property? My client knew nothing about the*

*package found. Anyone can get into the backyard.
Someone else must have gained access and just left twenty
thousand pounds worth of illegal narcotics there."*

We also searched for any stamped addressed
envelopes as we rifled through Leadbetter's belongings.
A rumour had gone around the criminal fraternity that
police couldn't open mail addressed to a third party and,
as a result, they were now advising their friends to slip
their drugs in one if we happened to knock on the door.

The backyard was a total dump: junk, rubbish, broken
furniture, bicycle parts and dog turds covered every inch
of the ground. Lloyd, Gwen and I quickly started looking
through the kitchen cupboards, ensuring we stayed in the
warm, whilst the rest of the team, including the Fisher
King, braved the elements outside.

It being unlikely that Leadbetter would tell us if we
were getting 'warmer' or 'colder' as we searched for our
prize, Ben kept a careful eye on him to see if his body
language gave away any telltale signs as the search
progressed. However, he sat on the backyard step, as cool
as a cucumber, stroking his dogs and smoking a cigarette.
We were five minutes into a fruitless quest when someone
stumbled into the house calling Leadbetter's name.

"Get rid of him, John," Barry instructed and I poked
my head around the door, shielding myself so he couldn't
see my uniform. As I did so, I heard the sound of a phone
ringing.

"Hold on, hold on." The dishevelled male motioned
for me to stay quiet as he picked up his mobile and
slumped down onto the sofa.

"Wassup!" He was now engaged in conversation
whilst I looked on like a spare part. "Yeah, I'm still half
bladdered from last night... what? You never! You're an
animal! What? I'm here now ... yeah... yeah... I'll pick
you up and we'll get shit-faced in town later..."

I coughed to get his attention. He responded by
looking over and pointing to the phone. He then rolled

his eyes before performing an exaggerated wanker sign at whoever he was talking to.

"Yeah, yeah… anyway, look, Mum, gotta go… there's some bloke wants to speak to me."

"Look, fella," I told him, "we're a bit busy. Can you come back a bit later?"

"What's happened to the door?"

"It was a persistent Jehovah's Witness," I said solemnly.

"Ha! You're mint! Have the cops been 'round? You know there's a cop van parked at the end of the street, do you? They've been 'ere 'aven't they! The bastards! Anyway, where's Bedwetter?"

The questions were coming thick and fast. I told him 'Bedwetter' was out the back and that he was also a bit busy right now.

"The bastards didn't get his stash, did they? I told him they'd never find it there!" Motormouth winked as he babbled away.

By now Barry and Gwen were pressed close behind me, listening intently. In fact, they were so close I could feel breath on the back of my neck. I hoped it wasn't Barry's. Lloyd, meanwhile, had used his initiative and had led Leadbetter to the top of the yard out of earshot.

"Those mugs never found it," I reassured him. "Those lot couldn't find their bloody arse with both hands!" As I did my own particular version of a condescending laugh, I felt someone dig me in the ribs. I was getting into role – method acting!

"I told him where to hide it. That was my idea. I'm a feckin' genius!" Our visitor was becoming more animated by the minute.

"So where was it, then?" I asked. I'm not sure how ethical it was – not letting on that I was a cop – but it wasn't like I was a member of the House of Commons, asking cash for questions in Parliament. It was a pretty direct question and I just hoped it wouldn't put him on his guard; although the way he had laughed at my door-knocking gag, I think he was now a friend for life.

"Like I said to him: who in their right mind is going to look in a pit bull's harness for gear?"

"We are," I replied, walking into the room accompanied by Barry and Gwen.

"Oh, shit!"

Despite all the swearing on the telephone, it was a bit of a turnaround to find out that he was pretty feckless after all. Evidently, he was the sort of person they put instructions on shampoo bottles for; although by the look of him, he preferred to go with the *au naturel* look. After a little chat, our unwitting whistle-blower decided it was time to meet his mum in town, and we saw him on his way with a cheery wave before going through to the yard and calling the dogs over.

"They don't like strangers," Leadbetter told us, his voice rising by a few octaves as he did so. Lloyd grabbed the leads off him and led the animals over. Gwen and Barry crouched down in the yard and started to pet them. It seemed these dogs were just like my dog, Barney: he barks like mad if someone's at the door because he thinks that's what he's supposed to do, but when they come in he's their new best friend. The dogs were harmless enough – the muzzles were just part of a smokescreen and to big up Leadbetter's hard-man persona.

It turned out that the dogs were used to being handled by anyone and everyone as apparently that was the way that Leadbetter conducted his business. Nothing changed hands between the dealer and his customers; instead, under the pretext of patting the dog, the buyer slipped payment into his customised harness before turning his attention to the other dog in whose harness the wraps of drugs were kept hidden.

"Bob's your Monkhouse!" Barry announced as he produced a handful of heroin wraps from one of the harnesses. "You're coming with us, Mr Leadbetter!"

Two and a half hours later, and with everybody pitching in to help, the job was finished: Leadbetter was in the cells, statements were done, the evidence had been booked in and the dogs had been rehoused in the council kennels. It seemed unlikely that our dealer would be celebrating Christmas on the outside and besides, when his suppliers found out that he had lost so much stock, I think he might actually prefer to be safely tucked away from them!

Anyone who tells you that the happiest moment of their life was the birth of their first child has obviously never been told that they can go home early on Christmas Eve. When Barry came in to inform us that we'd achieved our objective and were free to salvage the remains of the day, we decided to do what any other decent, civilised group would do: we decided to go down the pub for a lunchtime drink.

Putting my coat on I went back into the parade room to collect Gwen; she was holding court, telling the day shift how she had stumbled on Leadbetter in his compromising position.

"I just came... and saw!" she informed them innocently.

As coincidence would have it and judging by the pornographic DVDs lying around on his bedroom floor, it was the exact same thing that Leadbetter had done only a few hours earlier... except perhaps in the reverse order.

# CHAPTER 17

# Schrödinger's Cat

Denial, anger, bargaining, depression, acceptance: the five stages I went through while getting ready for my early shift on Christmas Day. Unfortunately, added to this, I tend to suffer from an acute form of *procaffeinating* in the morning: the tendency not to start anything until I've had at least two cups of coffee. As I sat on my couch in a trance-like state, cup in hand, I came to the conclusion that the seven dwarfs were either on medication or taking hard drugs: who in their right mind sings '*Hi ho, hi ho, it's off to work we go*', especially when it's cold, dark and miserable outside? At least getting up at 05:30 this morning had seemed like a lie-in compared to the early start to yesterday's drugs raid.

Meanwhile, Barney, my dog, seemed to be going through the same dilemma that he goes through most days: wondering if I was just going to work or abandoning him for ever. After finishing getting ready, I patted him on the head, told him he was a good dog, gave him an apple, and then set off. I'm sure he thinks I've been out hunting all day when I return and give him his dinner. This evening he'd think I was a crack shot as I was planning to swing by Miss Jones' house on the way home to collect some leftover turkey for him.

After saying my goodbyes, I then sat for a further ten minutes in my freezing car waiting for the ice to melt on the outside of the windscreen and the condensation to

271

disappear from the inside. It would be too awkward to go back inside after all the fuss I'd made of him – a bit like when you chat to someone in the street, bid them farewell, and then find they're walking in the same direction as you. It's just embarrassing!

I was shivering by the time I eventually set off but, despite the freezing temperature, I still tried to garner some enthusiasm for the day ahead; after all, today was the anniversary of the birth of Christ, when someone had grandly announced that: *'from this day forward, we shall count the years'* … and everyone had agreed… but then thought they'd give it a week first.

I arrived at the police station along with Gwen, Lloyd, Jessica and Andy; early enough to give the night shift a flyer so that they could at least make the most of the day with their families before returning again that evening. Merry Christmases were quietly exchanged as they sleepily slipped out and we sleepily slipped in: I say 'quietly exchanged', but with one notable exception:

"Greetings, gentlefolk! How the very goodness are we? Tidings of great joy to you on this auspicious day. You'll observe that it's been a not so 'Silent Night', and that there are currently two young ruffians languishing in our boutique hotel. A minor brouhaha outside one of the town's splendid watering holes has resulted in them accompanying Her Majesty's constables back to this fine establishment."

It was jarring to hear someone so rambunctious at this hour, but we were used to it by now.

"Sandford and its environs are now in the capable hands of the glorious men and women of E shift," he continued, theatrically. "Compliments of the season to you all, but, alas, I must depart!"

The ACK-TOR informed us that his carriage now awaited and, as he bid us all adieu, he tossed his cape over his shoulder and disappeared into the swirling fog. Well, he went and got his anorak on, climbed into his Ford

Fiesta and drove off onto the by-pass. I genuinely think he was born a hundred years or so too late as he would have fitted perfectly into 1880s' Whitechapel. Personally, I liked The ACK-TOR; he added a bit of colour to proceedings, but he wasn't to everyone's taste, especially at this time in the morning.

"Has Lord Olivier gone yet?" asked Barry, poking his head round the corner. When he saw that the coast was clear he came through, clutching the file for the suspects in the cells. On public holidays staffing is pared down to a minimum, which meant that today there were only five of us on duty in total, and none of us particularly relished the prospect of spending half the day down in the cells interviewing suspects. Reading our faces, Barry decided that the fairest way to determine who would be dealing with the prisoners would be to put names in a hat.

He carefully tore a piece of paper into five strips and handed one to each of us, waiting patiently while we all scribbled down our names and then crumpled up the scraps and threw them into his cap. We sat quietly as Barry made a big show of mixing them up; ostentatiously swirling the names around. We waited with baited breath as, with a flourish, he produced one of the scrunched up pieces of paper and opened it.

"And the loser is…" Lloyd and Jess improvised a drum roll as our sergeant kept us all in exaggerated suspense. "And the loser is… Andy!" Ba dum tssss!

We all made conciliatory noises, feigning disappointment that it wasn't our name that had been plucked from the cap. We then commiserated with our colleague, patting him on the back as he grabbed the paperwork and despondently slunk off down to the cells. Meanwhile, the rest of us went to top up our caffeine levels before helping ourselves to the cakes that Gwen had kindly brought in to share. As we made our way back to the parade room, we debated whether or not Father Christmas had shared our views on which of the townsfolk had been naughty or nice this past year.

"Do you like Kipling?" asked Barry as we all sat down.

"I'm not sure, I've never been kippled," I answered, wondering where this was leading.

"Rudyard Kipling – the author," clarified our leader. He appeared to be in a very reflective mood today. "Maybe we should take a leaf out of his book – literally. He said: *I always prefer to believe the best of everybody, it saves so much trouble.*"

"Well, I guess it would for Santa," I conceded, although he was always welcome to check our intelligence briefings if he was in any doubt who'd been bad. The others laughed, but not our sergeant. We were only having a bit of fun in deciding who in the town should be awarded a gold star and who deserved a black mark against their name.

Our leader solemnly looked down; toying with the crumpled strips of paper. He appeared deep in thought and we glanced at each other questioningly as we ate our Danish pastries. This wasn't like the Barry we knew. He had a disappointed look on his face, as if his son had just told him that he wanted to ride unicycles professionally for a living. We wondered what could be wrong. Eventually, he glanced up. The room fell silent: the stage was his.

"An old Cherokee Indian once told a story to his grandson," he began, "about the battle between two wolves that rage inside us all."

We all leant in, our curiosity piqued.

"One is Evil: it is anger, jealousy, greed, resentment, inferiority, lying, laziness and ego," he continued. "The other is Good: it is joy, peace, love, hope, humility, kindness, hard work, empathy and truth."

We shuffled our chairs closer, not wanting to miss a word.

"The boy thought about what his grandfather had said. He spent seven days and seven nights dwelling on it." Barry left a pause for dramatic effect. It worked: we were hooked. "Eventually, he approached his grandfather and asked him which wolf wins this battle."

A longer pause followed as Barry looked down, again shuffling the papers. At long last he stopped and looked each one of us directly in the eye. We all stared back, every one of us keen to know the answer: which wolf triumphs?

"The old man then sat him down," he continued, "and told him that in the battle between Good and Evil, the wolf who wins is the one that you choose to feed."

We sat back in our chairs, slightly disappointed. I think we had all thought that there would be more to the tale. Moreover, I don't think any of us could work out why our sergeant had decided to enlighten us with this pearl of wisdom on today of all days.

"And by the look of things," added Barry sarcastically and just when we had thought it was all over, "it appears that all your evil wolves are partial to cakes."

"Ah," we all repeated quietly. The purpose of his anecdote now dawned on us – we'd been rumbled.

Barry laid out all the pieces of paper in front of him to reveal our deception: Andy's name was written on each and every one of them. It was the old joke on the probationer. I'm sure Andy would eventually see the funny side of it... when he wasn't a probationer anymore... and there was a new probationer on E shift.

Quickly, we each took a set of panda keys from the board and hurried out of the room before he could call us back to admonish us further. I drove all the way to the deserted town centre before pulling over and allowing myself a little giggle over our failed prank. My mind then wandered to how today's shift would pan out. It was Christmas Day: the most unpredictable day of the year, in my policing experience. Who knew what the day might hold, but I had brought a banana with me just in case.

In Belgium, it's legal for children to throw bananas at police cars on Christmas Eve, but, on Christmas Day, the police are allowed to get their own back and it's legal for police officers to throw bananas at children. Goodness knows how that all started, but we are part of the European Union now and so we might as well get some benefit from it.

However, even if we were to ever leave the EU, we still have some peculiar laws of our own: to this day, in our own capital city, it remains illegal on *any* day of the year for someone who knows that they have the plague to wilfully flag down a taxi or ride a bus. That'll be a long walk to the hospital, then... and as for the rest of the country, you still can't order your servant to stand on a windowsill to clean the window, you can't operate a cow when intoxicated, it's forbidden to handle a salmon in suspicious circumstances and, finally, woe betide you if you die in the Houses of Parliament – it's against the law!

Nevertheless, I still think the Europeans beat us hands down when it comes to eccentric legislation. We often get called to noisy parties, but in Switzerland they seem to take things one step further: not only is flushing a toilet in a Swiss apartment after ten o'clock at night illegal, it's also against the law for a man to relieve himself standing up, although I'm not sure how they find out – unless they check the toilet mat.

Still, not all the bizarre and idiosyncratic laws are stupid. Maybe we could learn from police in Helsinki who sometimes save on parking tickets by letting down the offending car's tyres instead.

I was still daydreaming about which criminal's tyres I'd let down first when the radio sprung into life, making me jump. It was a call to the old part of the town where a squirrel was going crazy. A squirrel at this time of the year! Shouldn't they be hibernating? So, it was going to be one of those sorts of days!

Usually, it wouldn't be deemed a police matter, but the creature was running around in circles in the street and one of the residents was afraid that it might attack a child; as is the want of crazed rodents. I drove over post-haste and pulled into the cul-de-sac, but couldn't see any sign of the little furry maniac anywhere. I rang Comms to ask if the caller was still on the line and whether they could tell me exactly where the animal was, only to be informed that I could now cancel the job as, according to the informant, I had just run over it.

Before I had a chance to get out of the vehicle, a large, rugged-looking man appeared at the side of the car, holding a spade menacingly in his hands. I reached for my pepper spray but, instead of caving in the windscreen, he gently tapped on the window. I lowered it and he told me his name was Gordon Bennett. I responded and told him I was PC Donoghue.

"I know," he replied. I found his admission slightly unnerving. I hadn't fully recovered from my encounter with the Taxil brothers and was still on edge.

"You don't remember me, do you?" he questioned, bending down so that his face was level with the window.

He was right – I didn't.

"The man who was slightly upset at the insurance office on Gladstone Street?" he prompted. "The one you wrestled to the ground? That was me."

I vaguely remembered it now. Hadn't he been in some sort of disciplinary meeting at work that hadn't gone well...? Yes! That was it! When he had been told that his appeal had failed, Gordon, in the words of the caller, had gone 'bat-shit crazy'. Of all the shits, I'm not sure why bat shit is the craziest, but, based on seeing this gentleman in flagrante, clearly it was. He had already thrown a bin through the glass wall of the manager's office, and when we arrived he had been in the process of clearing every single desk in the room with his feet before kicking over every workstation, sending papers and telephones flying. I remembered Gordon all too well. The name didn't really suit the stocky man who was now standing in front of me – and it certainly didn't suit the madman that we had fought on that day. In the end, it had taken three of us to overpower him, and even then it had been a case of dragging him out of the office still kicking and screaming.

"I know it probably doesn't matter to you, but what I had actually said was: 'glorious tits' – not 'Gloria's tits'," he added reflectively, "but either way, in the end I don't think that really mattered to HR."

As he stood up to his full height, still clutching the shovel in his big hands, I quietly slipped off the handbrake ready to accelerate away if he made any sudden moves.

"What's the spade for, Gordon?" I asked tentatively. I decided to confront him here and now as the last thing I wanted was for him to go on a violent rampage around the streets of Sandford on Christmas morning.

"To clean up the squirrel you ran over," he replied buoyantly. "Can't leave that thing in the road for the kiddies to see!"

"Ah, yes, of course! Very public-spirited of you!" I breathed a sigh of relief.

"Well, Happy Christmas, Officer. I hope it's a quiet one!"

I thanked him, returned his seasonal greetings and then slowly drove away. I was relieved that my head wasn't going to be cleaved in two – at least not today, anyway – and not by Gordon. He'd said the Q word too, but, after being spared my life, that didn't really bother me. It's one of those old police myths: if someone says it's going to be a quiet shift usually all hell breaks loose. I've never really believed in it myself, and was confident that the criminals of the town would give their illegal activities a rest for the remainder of the day. However, I had barely pulled out of the cul-de-sac when Comms were on the radio to say that they had an urgent job for me. Maybe there really was a Q-word curse!

A hysterical woman had rung in to report that something had been thrown through her window as part of a revenge attack. She had refused to say what the object was, but would show it to an officer on attendance. How bizarre! My mind raced as I thought of what it could possibly be: a brick, a paving slab, a tree branch, a toaster?

Five minutes later and I was looking at a small pool of diarrhoea on an upstairs windowsill.

"You mean to tell me that you think some unknown person has let himself into your back garden and, for want of a better word, thrown a sloppy poo all the way up to your bedroom; in through the small opening at the top of the window and it's now landed on the inside sill?"

"Exactly that!"

Mrs Schrödinger, the householder, told me she had discovered this heinous act when opening the curtains this morning. I checked the inside of the curtain material and on the window itself but there were no signs of any other dubious 'matter' on either; or anywhere else in the pristine bedroom.

"This may be a long shot, Mrs Schrödinger, but do you have a cat?"

She nodded.

"Can I suggest that this may not be the evil doings of a madman intent on revenge, but rather the evil doings of a feline with a bad belly?"

"I know what you're intimating, Officer, but you're wrong. My cat would not debase himself! No, this is a revenge attack because of Samuel's thieving."

From the flush that had slowly crept up her neck and had now reached her lined cheeks, it was clear that the elderly lady was genuinely alarmed by the morning's events.

"Look, I think I'd better talk to Samuel to try and get to the bottom of this."

I was then led downstairs and into the conservatory where a large ginger tomcat was reclining on a rattan chair. He surveyed me nonchalantly through slitted green eyes, as though I was some kind of trained helper monkey there to attend his every whim.

"There you go!" declared the woman with a flourish.

After such an introduction, I felt I had to make some sort of effort to look interested in her pet. As I approached the animal our eyes locked, and I sensed this cat was setting me a challenge: 'stroke my belly, but only I know the exact number I want – anymore and I'll cut you!'. I thought better of it and resumed my position.

"Lovely cat, Mrs Schrödinger, but it's Samuel I need to see."

"That, dear boy, *IS* Samuel."

"The thief?"

"The very same!" she confirmed, drawing my attention to a large pile of items which overflowed from several boxes in the corner. I knelt down and began pulling some of them out. I had soon amassed quite a collection: a gardening glove, a pair of pink silk knickers, a single slipper, a face flannel, a baby's small cloth dinosaur, running shorts and a cuddly toy. Didn't he do well!

The very amiable – if not a little highly strung – Mrs Schrödinger told me how Samuel seemed to take the role of hunter-gatherer that one step further. Whilst some cats leave a gift of a dead mouse or bird on their owner's doorstep, Samuel, she confided, frequently returned home with a variety of items that he had pilfered from houses in the surrounding neighbourhood. In fact, I recognised some of the items as having been reported stolen under mysterious circumstances. I was looking at a box full of unsolved crimes… and it appeared that I had also found the culprit.

Luckily for Samuel, we've come a long way since the Middle Ages: in those dark times all manner of creatures, from pigs to caterpillars, were put on trial for a variety of offences ranging from murder to obscenity. And these were anything but kangaroo courts as the trials were conducted with gravitas, with evidence being heard on both sides and witnesses called. In many cases, the animals were even granted a form of legal aid, with a lawyer being appointed at the taxpayer's expense. Records show a pig hanged for murder, sparrows prosecuted for chirruping in church, a cockerel burnt at the stake for laying an egg and rats charged with criminal damage. The rodents, however, failed to attend their trial, which left their embarrassed barrister having to make his apologies to the judge. A donkey was even charged with being complicit in acts of bestiality, but, fortunately, the local priest was willing to be a good character witness and stated that it was: 'the best ass he'd ever had'. As a result, Eeyore was let off with a warning.

I thought it best not to go into the detail of these animal trials with Mrs Schrödinger. Instead I informed her that I wouldn't be taking Samuel into custody just yet, but that he shouldn't go anywhere in case I needed to speak to him later. She gave me a look that told me she wasn't entirely sure whether I was being serious or not and I returned that look with one that gave nothing away.

"I try and return things if I can work out where they've come from, but for most of the items I haven't got a clue," she explained in mitigation, her fingers worrying at one of the pleats on her navy tartan skirt as she spoke. "Maybe I should put a little camera on his collar to find out where he's been?"

"I'm not sure that's such a good idea," I countered.

I had heard about a few experiments where a camera had been attached to a cat and, unfortunately, most had ended in disaster. It had revealed how much time cats spend just sitting on window ledges and staring into people's houses... and that's where the problems started.

When one set of footage was reviewed it showed that Mrs X from number 22 was more than a little friendly with Mr Y from number 23, and that Mr Z, who lived in the bungalow around the corner, now had a new girlfriend who was inflatable... After such sordid revelations the project was shut down for good.

They should have learnt from the CIA who had tried to use cats for spying during the Cold War; after all, who would suspect that as you held your discreet meeting in the park with your spymaster, the innocuous cat strolling nearby was actually recording your every word? Over $25 million was spent on project *Acoustic Kitty*; devising and implanting a battery and microphone inside a cat and turning his tail into an antenna. Unfortunately, they couldn't control his road sense, and on his very first mission he was run over by a taxi on his way to the job. The entire programme was then hastily abandoned. Yet the search to harness the power of the cat continues – but to date, no one seems to have had any success. Our feline friends just continue to do exactly what they want, when they want and where they want and usually showing you their asshole in the process.

I informed Mrs Schrödinger that I would be taking Samuel's haul back to the police station where I could go through it in detail and try to identify where it had all come from. In the meantime, I told her, I wouldn't crime the windowsill poop as a revenge attack as I still believed Samuel to be the culprit. I advised her that she was now free to clean the mess up as I wouldn't be taking samples for analysis and DNA testing. These CSI programmes really do have a lot to answer for!

I also told her to have a word with Samuel about drugs. Well, if the owner won't talk to their cat about catnip, who will?

"Give your pussy a little tickle from me," I called back

to her as I got into the car, and then, realising what I had said, quickly shut the door and sped off before she had a chance to answer.

I arrived back at the station with an armful of stolen booty and began reviewing all the unsolved thefts from the last six months to see if I could marry them up with my goods. Gradually, one by one and case by case, I was able to link missing items to the exhibits laid out before me. After three or four hours, the majority of the items were accounted for. It was now my turn to play Santa as I rang each of the victims, apologising for disturbing them on Christmas Day, to give them the glad tidings.

It felt good to be able to finish the year on a high note. I allowed myself to bask in the moment as it's not every day in this job that you get to make lots of people happy – that's usually the job of the oldest profession in the world, although there may be some competition to retain that accolade: it seems that criminals come first – if being a crook can be called a profession, and prostitutes come a close second. Crime has been with us since Adam and Eve, and even God didn't have the solution to it (although perhaps he ought to have put the apple on a higher branch so that it was harder to reach).

Gwen came in to see me just as I was finishing up. I told her that there was one particular used toy whose owner I hadn't been able to find. Before I could elaborate any further, she informed me that she would take it to the church playgroup when it reopened after the holidays, as they were always grateful for toys.

"They call them pre-loved nowadays – not used," she added.

"To be honest, I don't think they'll want this," I began to explain but it was too late as Gwen had already delved into the box and was fishing it out.

"Oh my good God!" she exclaimed, quickly throwing it back in again. "You never told me it was a used adult toy!"

"Pre-loved, Gwen," I corrected her as she quickly ran to the toilet to wash her hands. "It's a pre-loved toy."

I then headed back to see Mrs Schrödinger to update her on the investigation and to tell her that, despite her protestations, I was still convinced that there was a more reasonable explanation to the mystery of the liquid poop than a revenge attack. When I arrived, I informed her that I had reunited most of the stolen belongings with their rightful owners before once again enquiring about her feline's health. Mrs Schrödinger, however, remained insistent that the mess she had found on the bedroom windowsill had been hurled there by some criminal, and wasn't down to her animal. All the while, Mr Schrödinger had stood behind his wife, rolling his eyes in an exaggerated fashion and emphatically shaking his head as she vehemently asserted her claim. There was no more I could say to convince or appease her, so I bid her goodbye. As her husband led me through the kitchen I noticed something on the Aga.

"It looks like those vigilantes have a pretty impressive throw," I remarked to him.

"Margot!" he bellowed through to the lounge, "That bloody cat of yours has done a shit in the frying pan!"

"And a Merry Christmas to you, Mr Schrödinger!" I smiled cheerfully before letting myself out of the back door.